Pro Pinstripe Technique

East Coast Artie
with
The East Coast
Pinstripe Police

Published by:
Wolfgang Publications Inc.
Stillwater, MN 55082
www.wolfpub.com

Legals

First published in 2010 by Wolfgang Publications Inc.,
PO Box 223, Stillwater MN 55082

© Art Schilling, 2010
All rights reserved. With the exception of quoting brief passages for the purposes of review no part of this publication may be reproduced without prior written permission from the publisher.

The information in this book is true and complete to the best of our knowledge. All recommendations are made without any guarantee on the part of the author or publisher, who also disclaim any liability incurred in connection with the use of this data or specific details.

We recognize that some words, model names and designations, for example, mentioned herein are the property of the trademark holder. We use them for identification purposes only. This is not an official publication.

ISBN number: Apple # 978-1-935828-14-3
Printed and bound in U.S.

Table of Contents

Chapter One
    Nub's Guitar 6

Chapter Two
    Nub's Guitar - Part Two 22

Chapter Three
    Mikey's Big Panel 30

Chapter Four
    Metal Flake from Mikey 42

Chapter Five
    Howie's Panel .50

Chapter Six
    Howie's Gold Wing 64

Chapter Seven
    Artie's Brush Case 72

Chapter Eight
    Artie's Victory .90

Chapter Nine
    Artie's Computer 98

Chapter Ten
    Mr. J's Ranchero 102

Chapter Eleven
    Zeke's Panel .122

Sources/Catalog 142

Acknowledgements

This book is dedicated to our wives, who let their boys go out and play.....

In memory of Larry Watson

Thanks to:
Watkins Auto Body for the beautiful painted panels
Coastal Victory Cycles for the project motorcycle
Xcaliber Corporation for the finest striping brushes in the world
Nico's of New York for the best Italian food in Myrtle Beach
Nibil's on the Pier for great breakfasts, exceptional waitresses and good morning Karma
The guys at PPG paint for all their support.

East Coast Artie

From the Publisher

When I approached East Coast Artie about doing this Pro Pinstripe book, his immediate answer was yes, with one condition. "I want my pals, what we call the East Coast Pinstripe Police, involved. If I can bring them into the project, then you've got a deal."

Agreeing to Artie's demand was easy. I mean, why *wouldn't* I want five additional and very talented pinstripers involved in a new pinstriping book. Each could - and did - add their own spin to the art and business of pinstriping.

Mikey added two very unique panels and demonstrated his own way of striping with the mahl stick for support. Nub gave us both a pinstripe and a cartoon sequence, done on a very interesting canvas. Howie contributed two projects, each unique and very different from the other. Mr. J breathed new life into an old Ford in dire need of resuscitation, and did it all in about three hours time. Zeke provided another panel to the book, but it couldn't be any different from Mikey's panels if I told him that was the goal - and of course I did nothing of the kind. Artie, master of ceremonies, and the man who kept everyone working and laughing through a week of long days, showed the full range of his talent by painting first a very elaborate brush case, then a motorcycle, and finally a computer.

I am grateful to each member of the East Coast Pinstripe Police, but have to add special thanks to Artie. Without his energy and organizational skills, this book never would have happened. Thanks to one and all.

Timothy Remus

East Coast Pinstripe Police

The East Coast Pinstripe Police – Mr. J, Mikey, Howie, Zeke, Nub and I - came about on a "field trip" we took to California for the Winfield-Watson Gathering in 2009. We all share a passion for pinstriping and hot rods, but of course each of us brings something unique to the group.

Mikey Frederick is a class act, cool striper and signmaker who tries to keep us under control, but always fails. He made the magnetic signs which went on our rental van, they made for great parking privileges at LAX when I was picking everybody up. He's also a very funny guy.

Mr. J, Julian Braet, is a great talent and a real innovator, creating the Jersey-style of lettering. He is also my best friend and always keeps us laughing.

Howie Nisgor, I've known Howie for so long we don't remember where we met. His striping work is among the best and he's always there to help me out. A true friend.

Zeke Lemanski is a striper with a real unique style. He also a very successful businessman. He turns out more panels in one day than is humanly possible.

Nub is Nub. Airbrush artist, striper and TV personality. He does some killer work AND he lets us hang out with him!

Collectively, we are: The East Coast Pinstripe Police.

East Coast Artie

Here's the official East Coast Pinstripe Police staff surrounding their hero, the late Larry Watson. Left to right: Zeke, Howie, Mr. J, Mikey, Artie, Nub.

Chapter One

Nub's Guitar

Front Panel

The hard part of striping a guitar is to embellish the instrument without overwhelming the original design of the guitar itself. The task of striping this Epiphone fell to Nub, the same Nub often seen on TV as part of the Orange County Chopper building team.

Much of Nub's work, done in three colors with Ronan enamel, follows the natural shape of the body and the f-holes. Like any good striping job, these pinstripes instantly become an integral part of the instrument, as though it came from the factory with the outline along the body edge and the series of arches and speers seen at the bottom of the guitar.

Bright and attractive without overwhelming the original design, Nub's work looks like something that might have been done when the guitar was built.

The guitar's surface is wiped clean with wax and grease remover before any striping or layout is done.

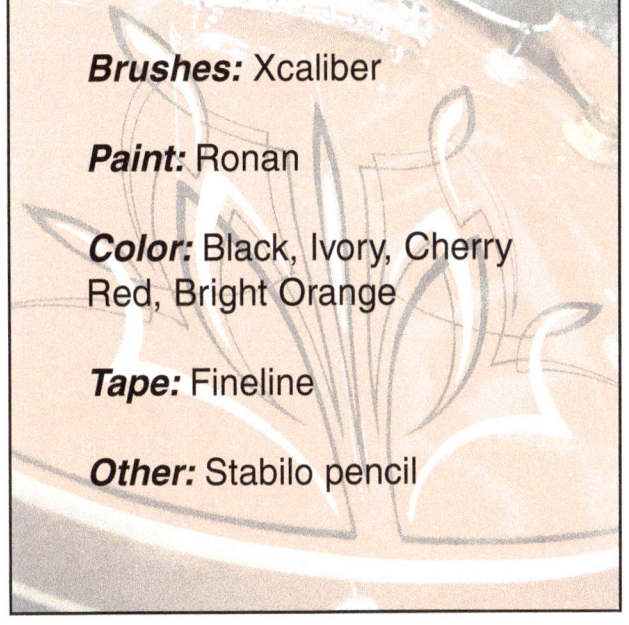

Brushes: Xcaliber

Paint: Ronan

Color: Black, Ivory, Cherry Red, Bright Orange

Tape: Fineline

Other: Stabilo pencil

I'm using Ronan lettering enamels, Xcaliber brushes and a script brush for the project.

I start off by striping the outer edge of the guitar...

...working my way down to the bottom...

...and back up the other side.

The outer edge is done.

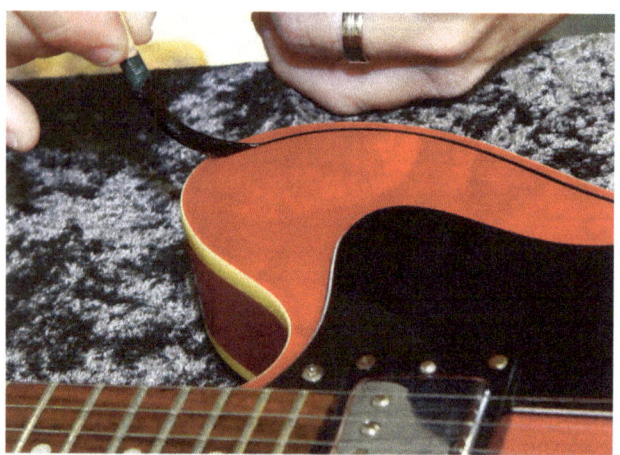

Working at a very odd position, when I get back up to the top portion of the guitar, I end my stripe in this direction...

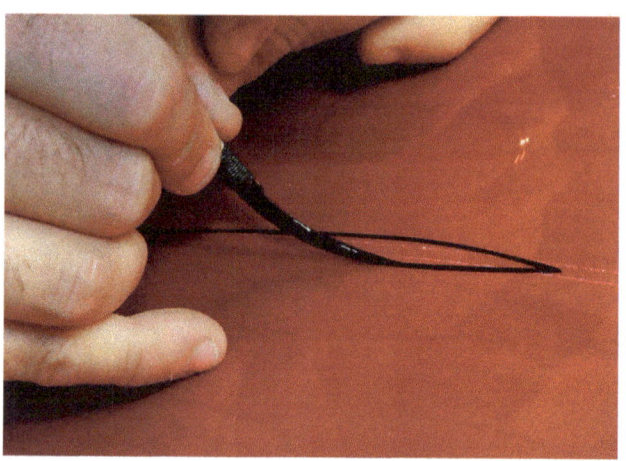

I start my design with two lines down the center...

...turn the brush around and stripe outward from the neck to meet up with where I had to stop.

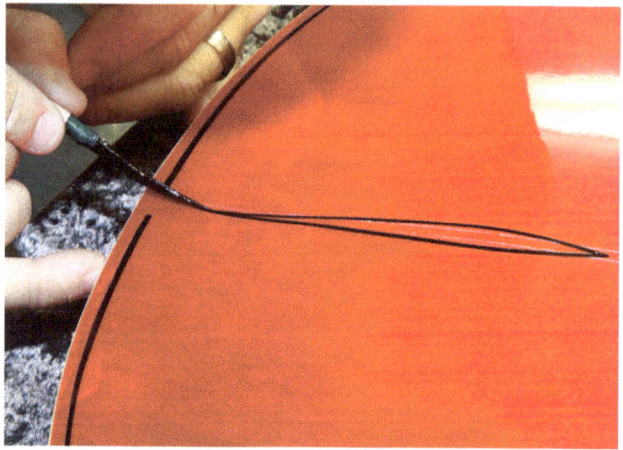

...connected on the top and bottom. Notice how I left my outer guitar edge line broken to give myself a place to tie it into the center design.

I give the center lines a little more weight at the top by adding another set of lines on the inside...

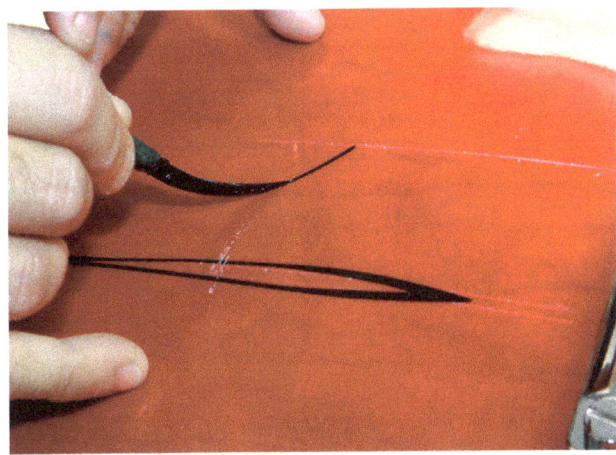

Working downward toward the center...

...then filling in between them.

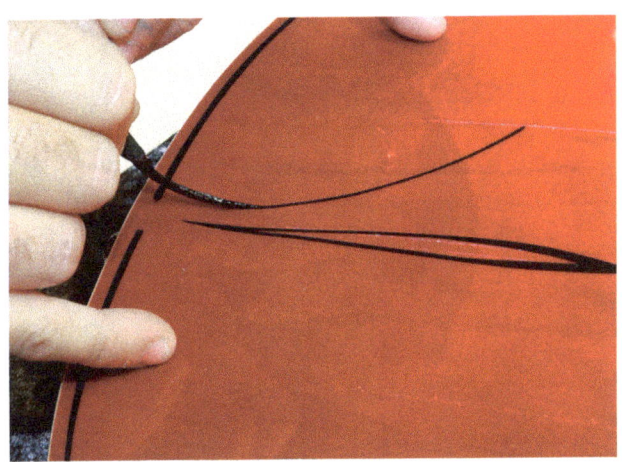

...I connect the line with the outer edge striping.

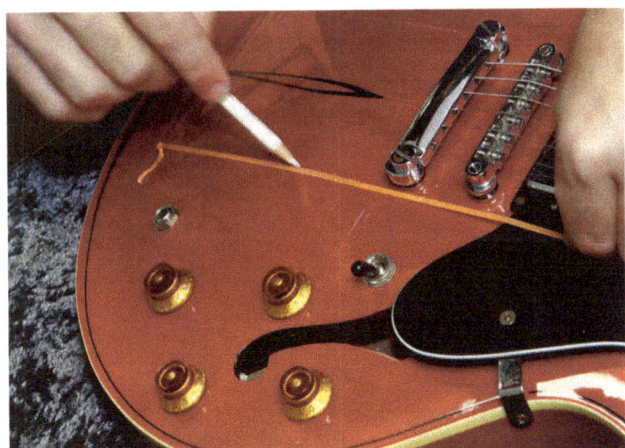

I use my fineline tape and a white stabilo pencil to layout a few reference lines so everything stays even from side to side.

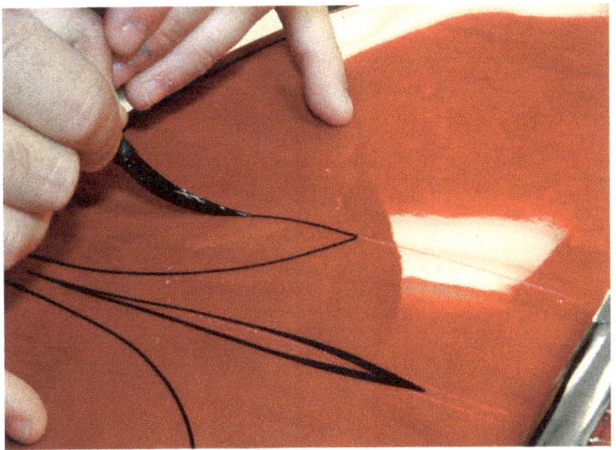

Working from side to side, I continue building up the initial framework for my design.

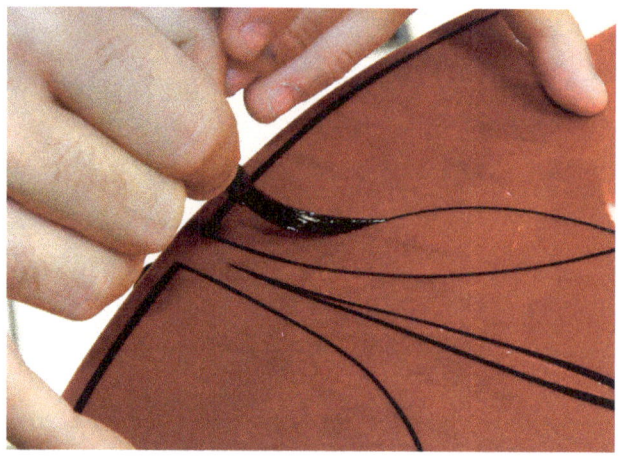

Notice how I use my pinky fingers to steady my hand. I think that's their only purpose.

More weight is added to a few select areas...

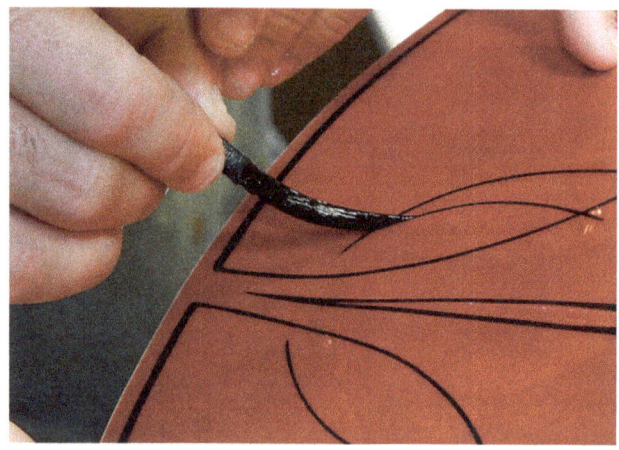

I work another stripe toward the center connecting it with the previous stripe to a point. I'm leaving enough room between the stripes so I can come in later with my second color.

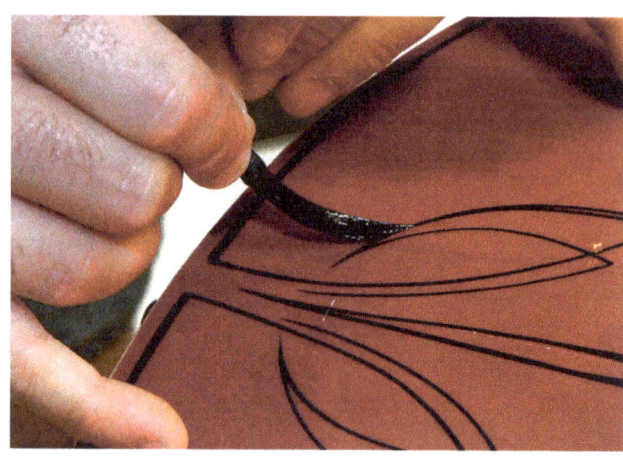

...gives a nice feel to the design.

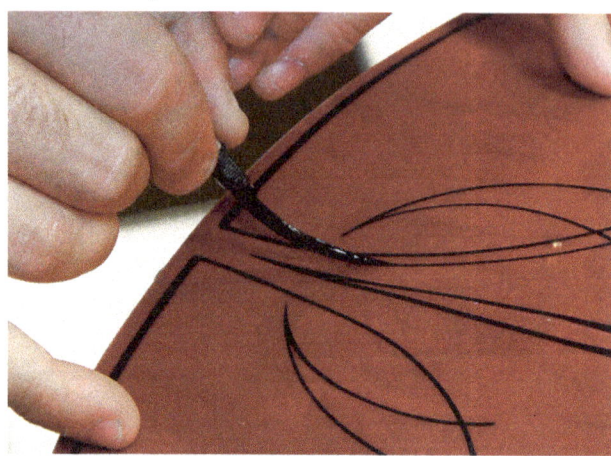

I bring the next two lines down the center and leave them open to start working the design back out.

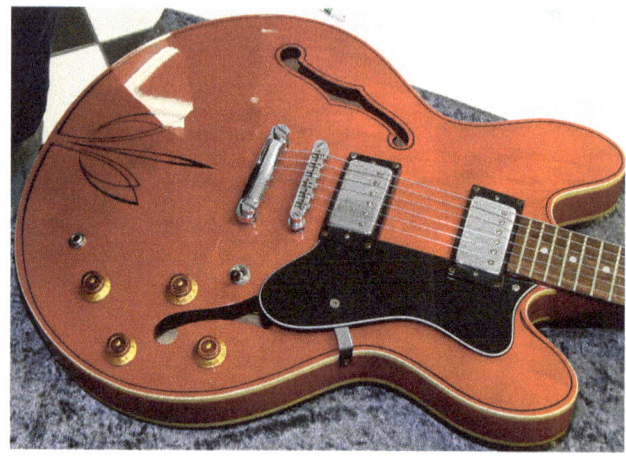

Step back, take a breath and plan your next move.

I add a little more to the inner line to balance it out.

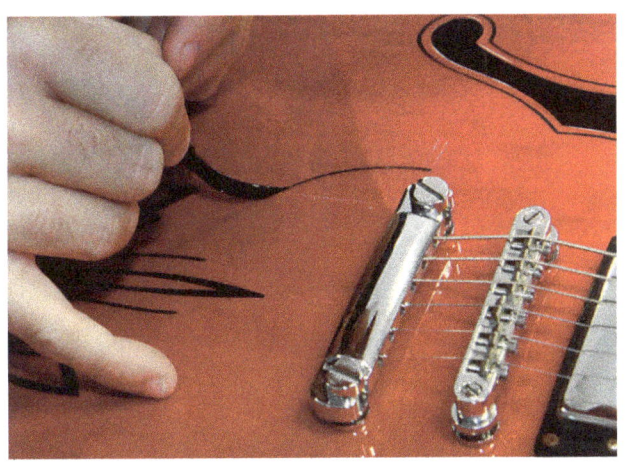

I come out of left field now, sweeping back in.

Now it's time to start focusing on branching the design out.

Notice how the brush is flipped over. In this position, I can use it as a quill to get a nice square corner where the two stripes meet.

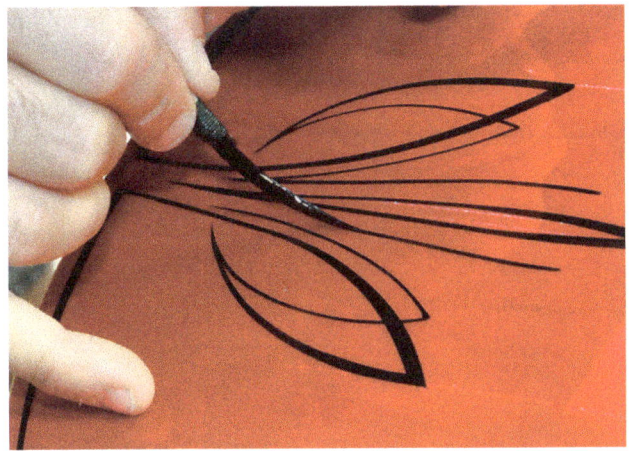

These two lines run down to the previous lines I left open.

I cross back over my line...

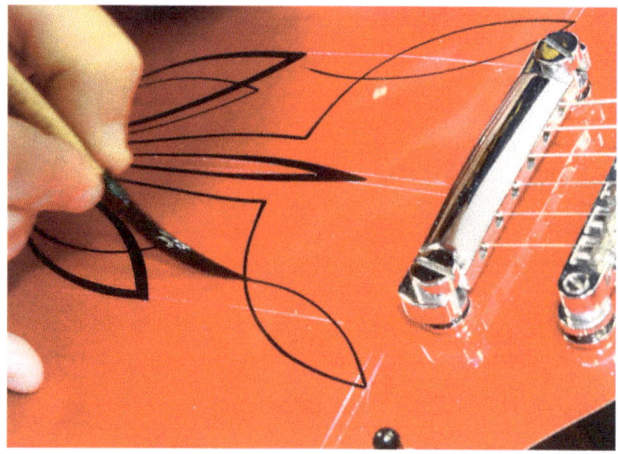

...and follow suit on the other side. Kinda looks like rabbit ears.

Next, I bring a stripe in from the outside. I'm not really crowding anything with this line, I'm just kinda throwing it out there.

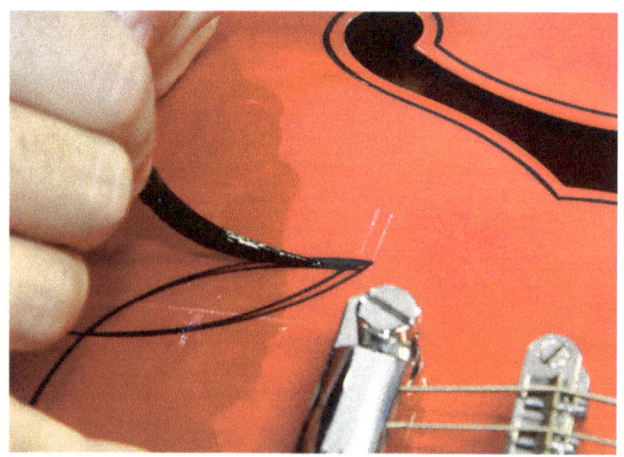

I add a little more weight again.

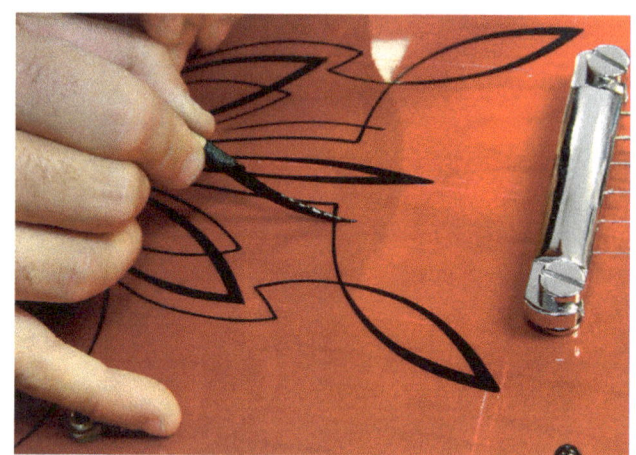

Moving back to the center again...

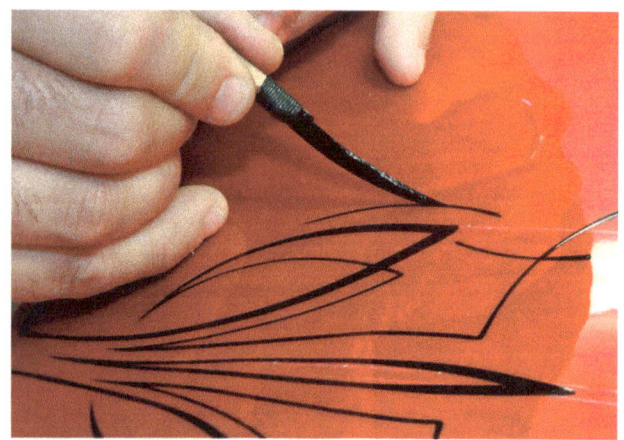

This is where I start to add lines that will enhance the graphic when I add other colors farther down the road. I add a small line that follows the contour of what I have already done in the center.

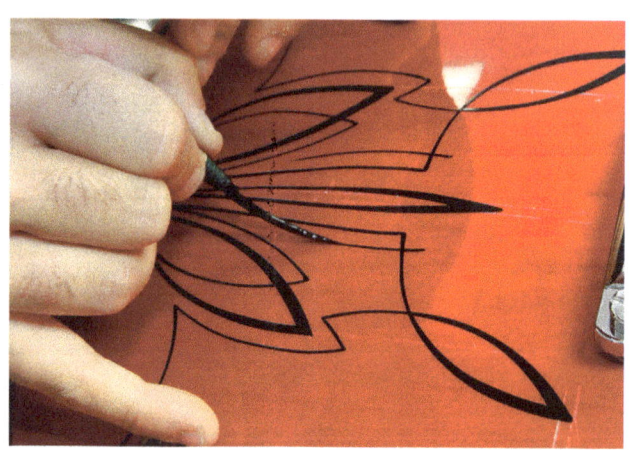

...I add two more lines, leaving both ends open.

I bring the top out into the rabbit ear.

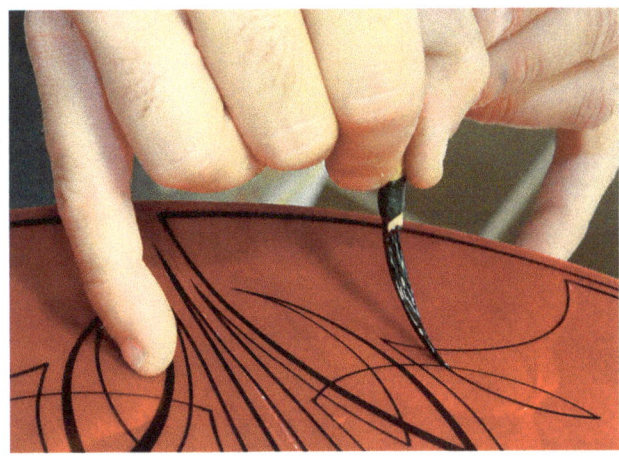

I cross back over my lines...

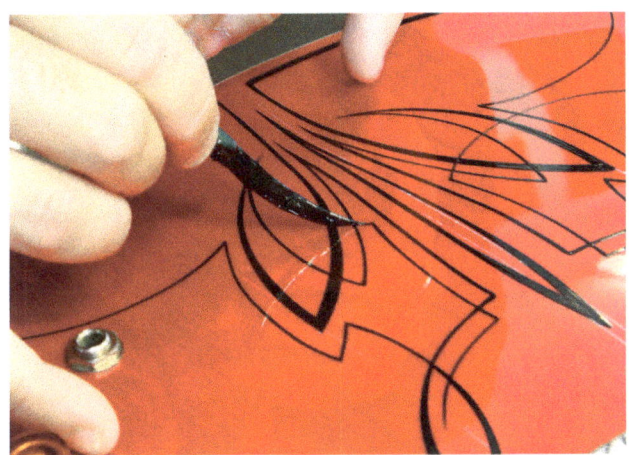

The bottom sweeps outward...

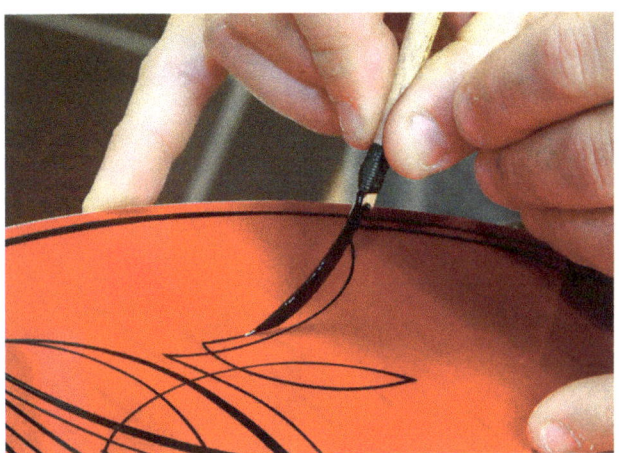

...then make a turn and follow an earlier line...

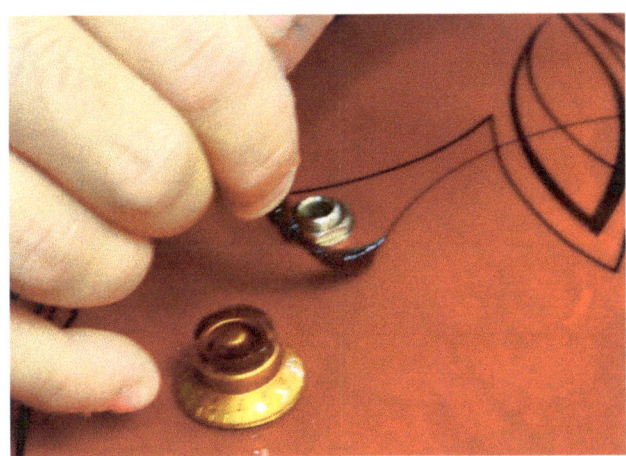

...just missing the knobs and jack.

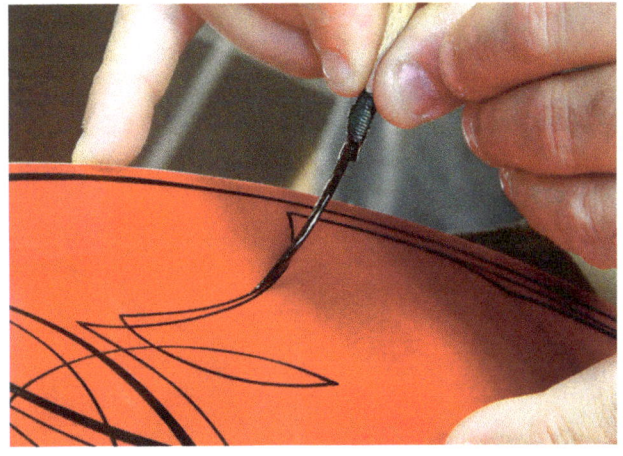

...gradually bringing the stripe back into the existing line...

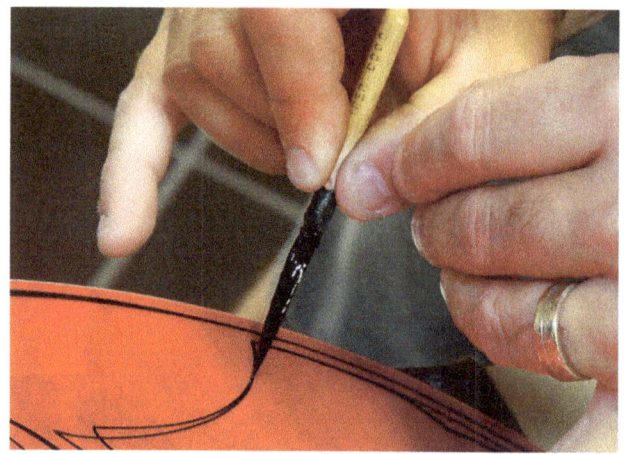

...finishing it off at the edge.

...to right about there.

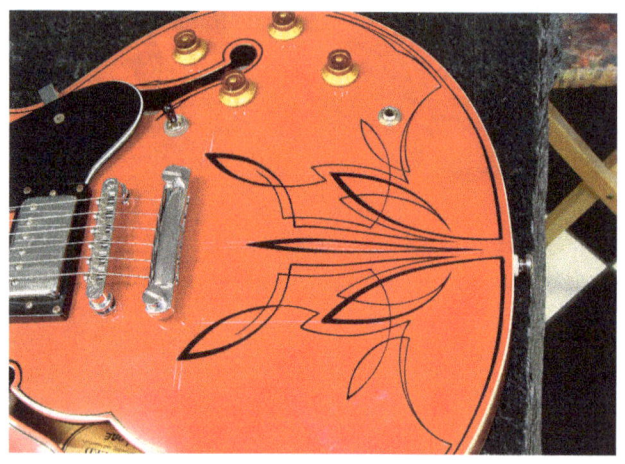

OK, almost done with the black. I just need to tie up the two loose ends at the top.

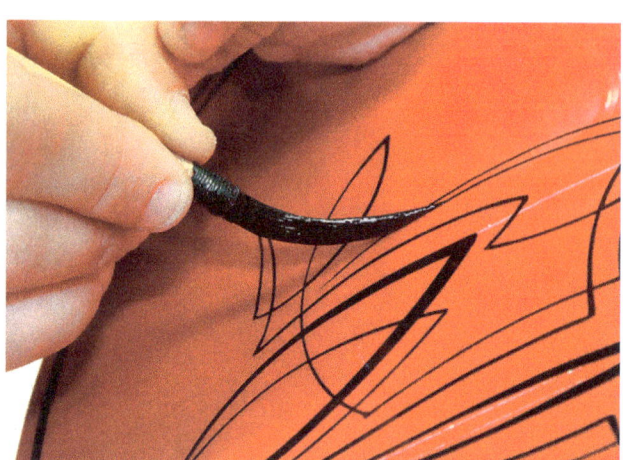

Then another one down to the same point.

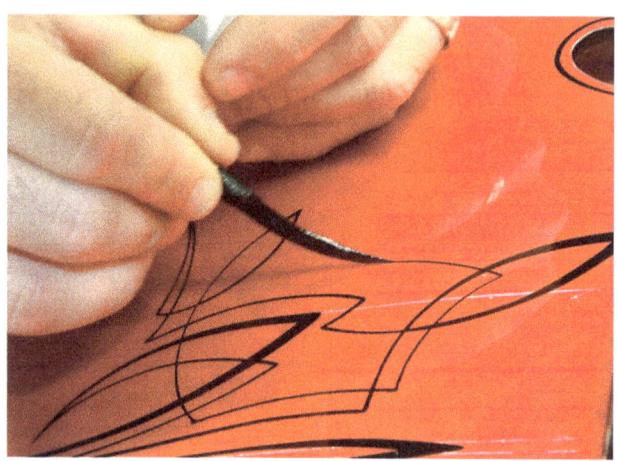

I decide to make a nice dagger type end by bringing one line down...

Now that the black is complete, it's time to clean the brush.

For the second color, I choose ivory, with a few drops of orange, to tie the striping into the binding around the edge of the guitar.

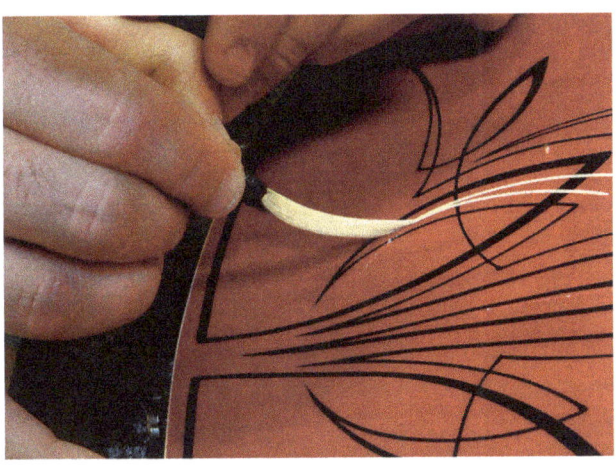

...and convince myself that I'll be able to tie everything together with the next color. (I'm very convincing when I talk to myself).

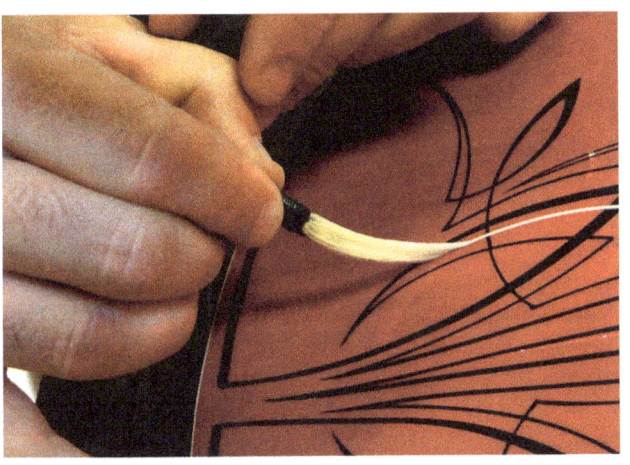

I want to use the ivory as a graphic element in this design...

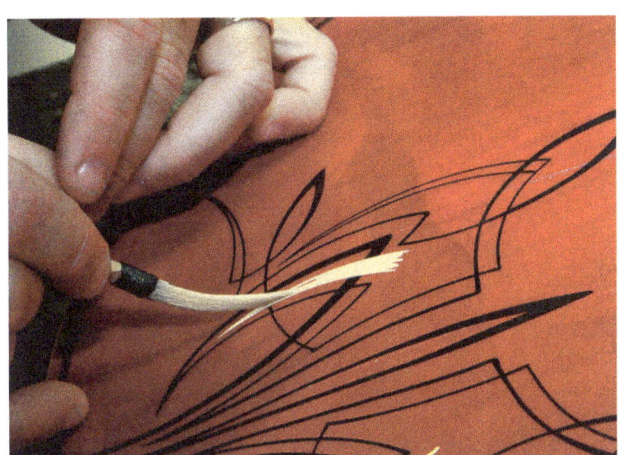

My only plan here is to fill in some of the areas that I had originally left open for another color...

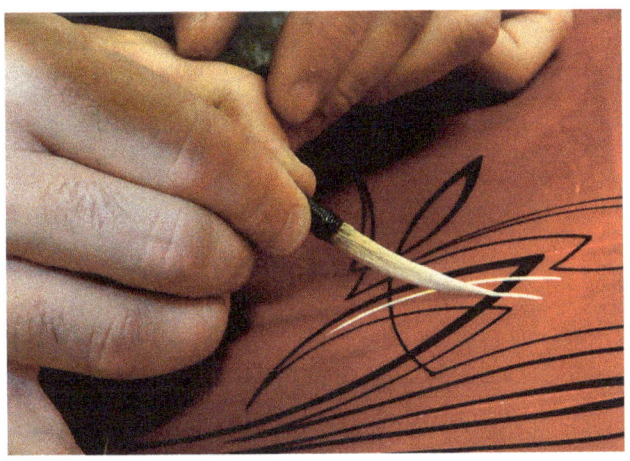

...so I decide to put bold fill lines in various places...

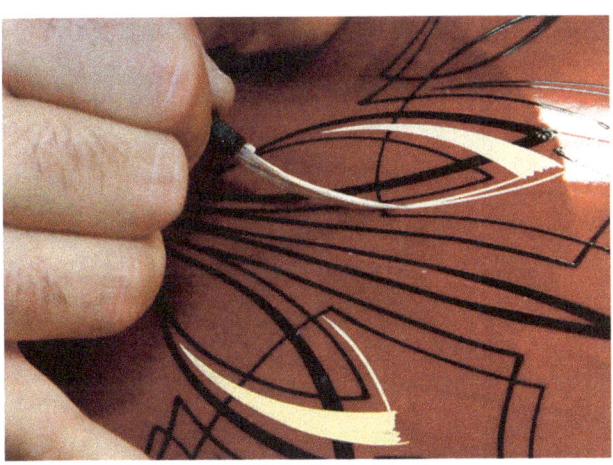

...so I continue to randomly add fill lines.

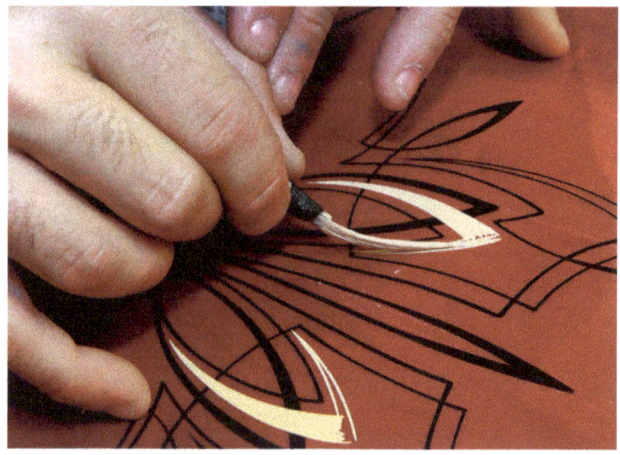

Paying close attention to the points and corners of the fills, I make sure they aren't too different from each other.

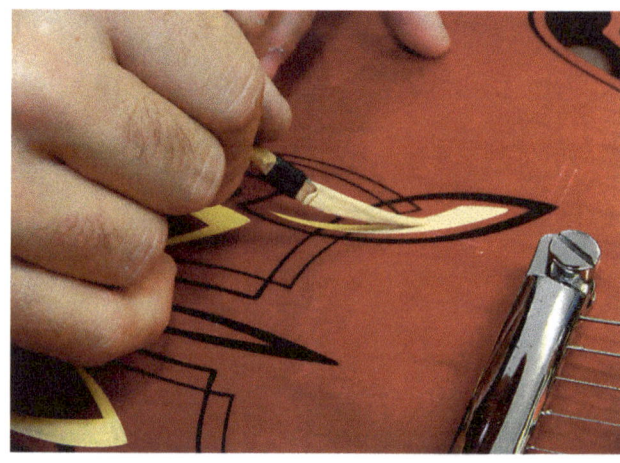

The purpose of the fill lines isn't to crowd the design, so I try to add just enough, but not too much.

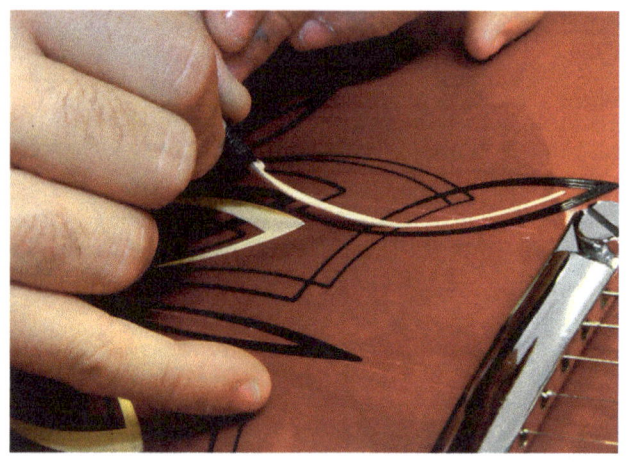

After each fill, I step back to look at the design as a whole, finding the areas that look the most empty to me...

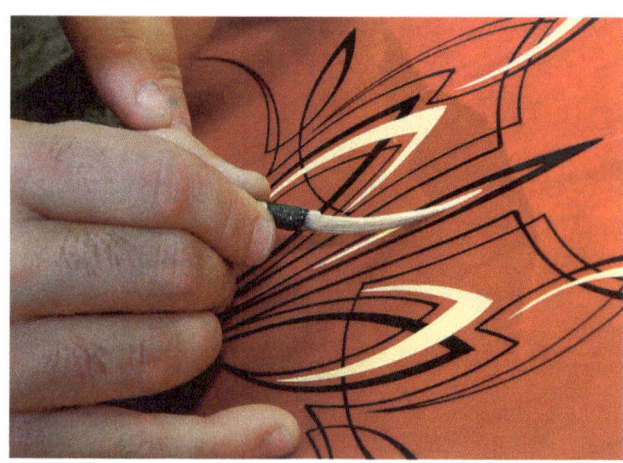

The center gets a simple teardrop.

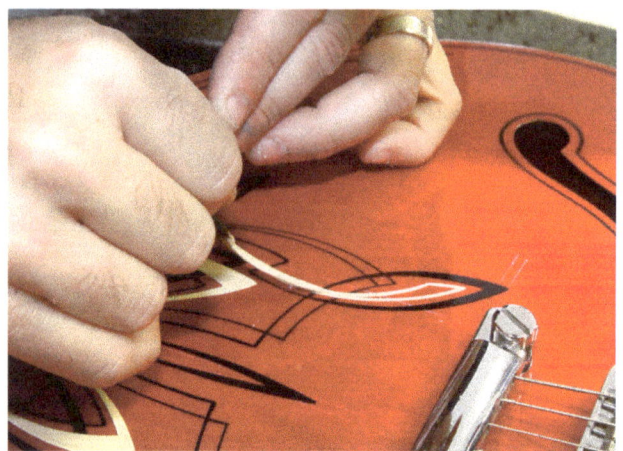

...then I fill those as well, starting here with an outline, and then a fill line.

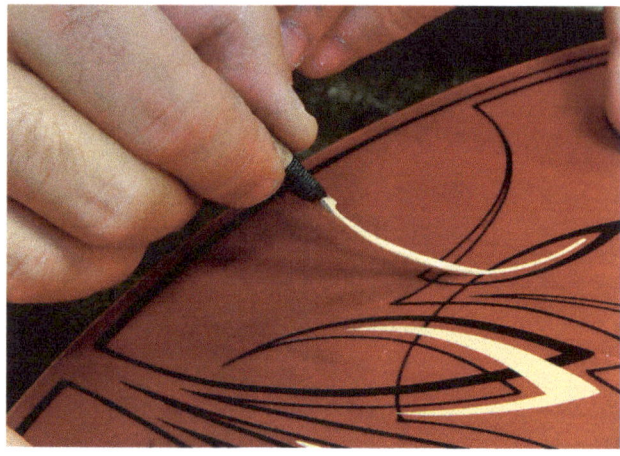

Now I move to the final fill.

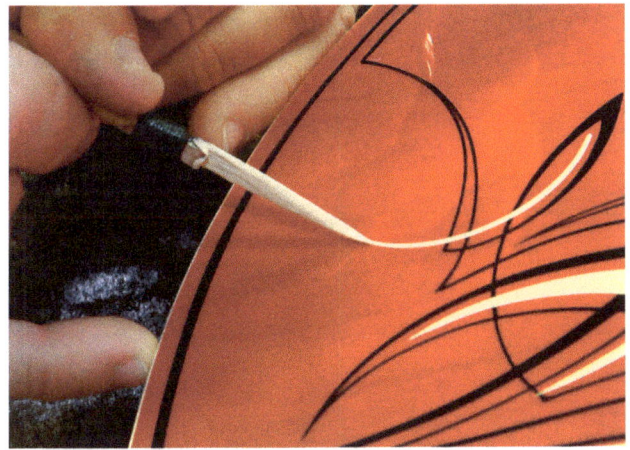

This one sweeps outward...

...fill it in...

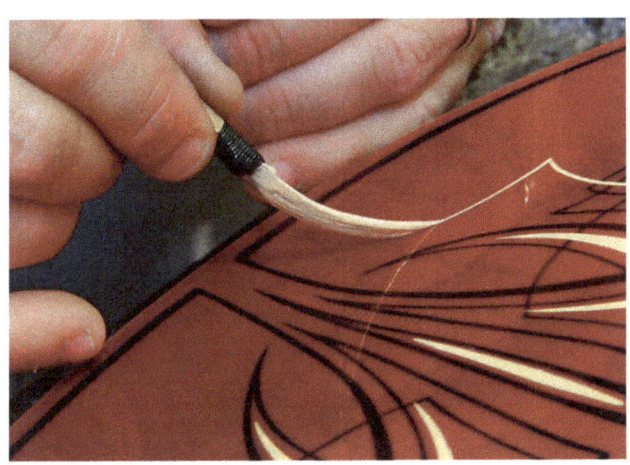

...then back toward the center.

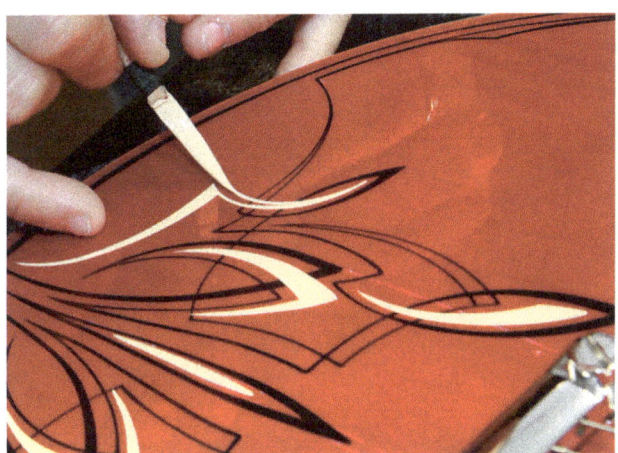

...and the last of the ivory is done.

Another line down to a point...

Two colors down...one to go.

A nice mix of orange and red works perfect on the red base color of the guitar.

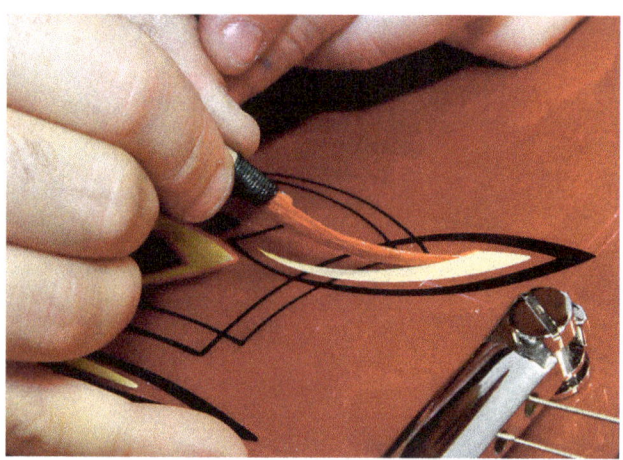

I start by outlining the fills...

The orange alone was too bright...the red alone, not bright enough.

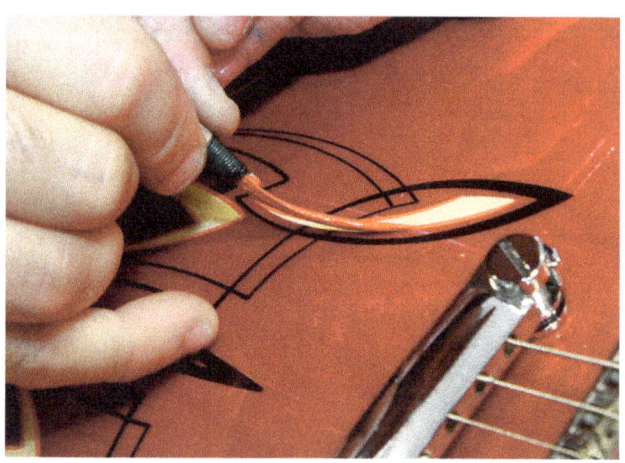

...trying to keep an even distance away from the other striping.

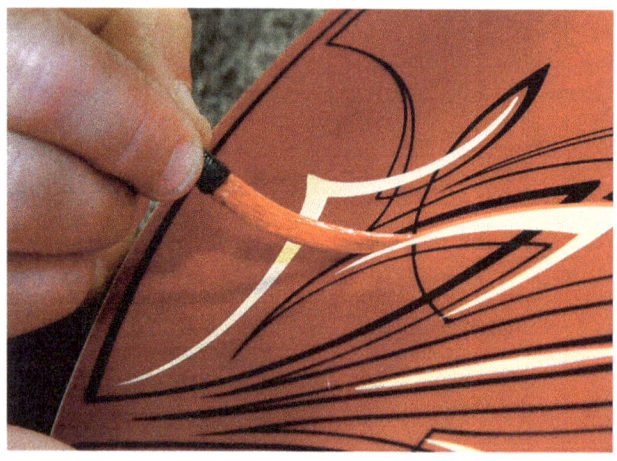

Now it's time to blend all the ivory into the design.

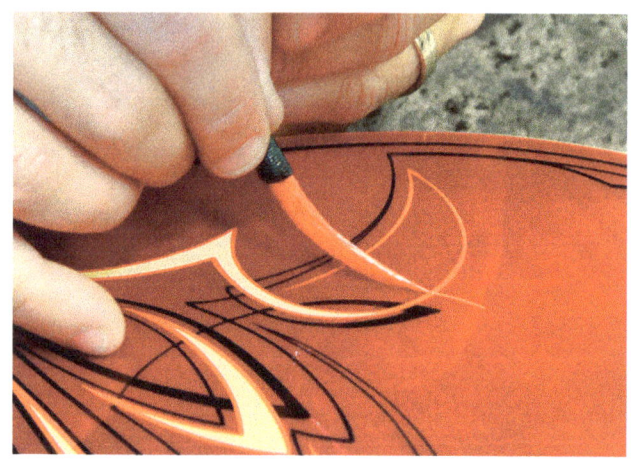

It's time to start branching out.

My thought process at this point is to partially mimic what I have already done in black, and partially add another dimension to the design with a new set of swoops that do their own thing.

...no worries...just steer around it...

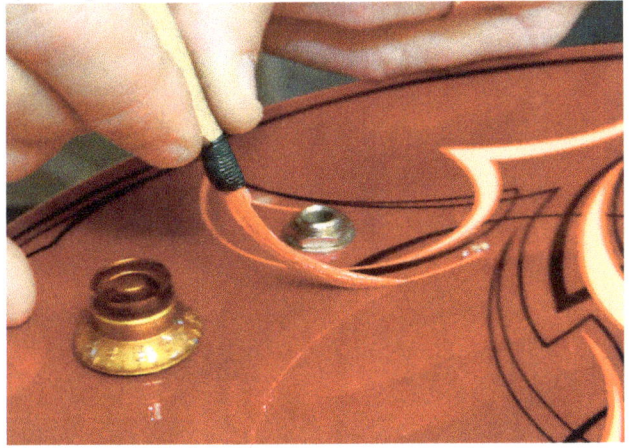

This area differs slightly from the opposite side because of the output jack.

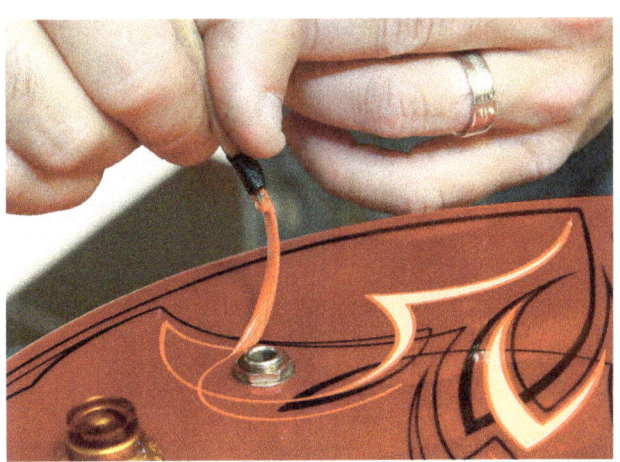

...no problem.

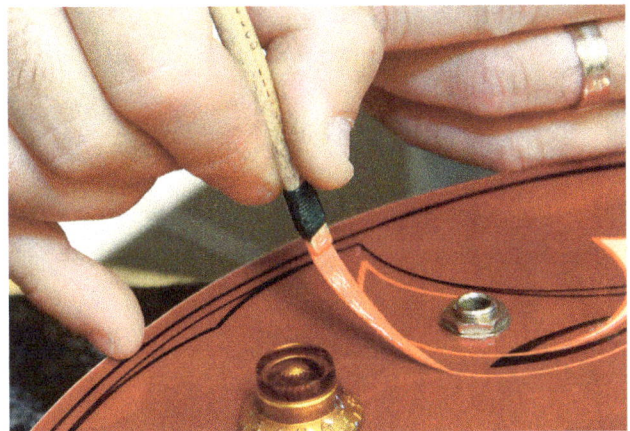

When something gets in your way...

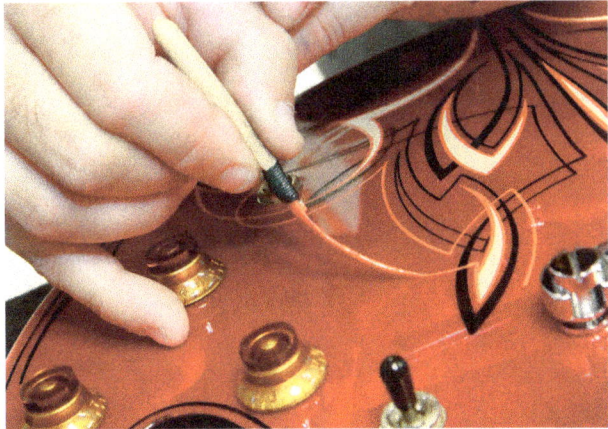

This line starts from the upper fill and curves back into the design. Note how the brush position changes in the next 4 photos. The line is only about 4 inches long and the brush spins a complete 180 degrees.

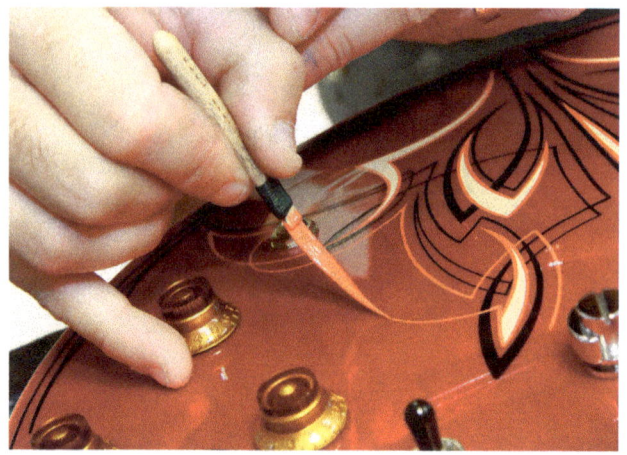

45 degrees from the starting position....

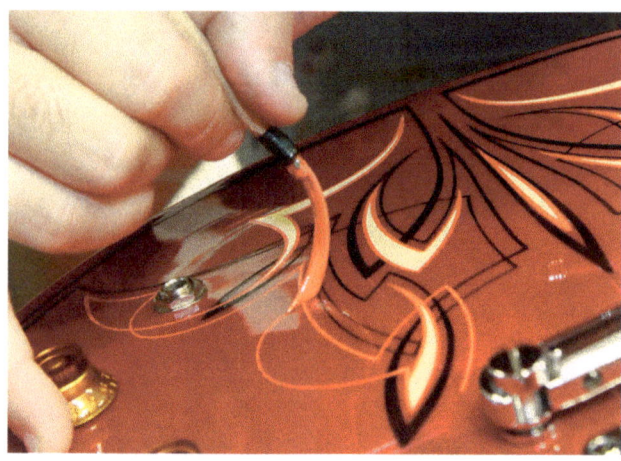

...and a complete 180 degrees.

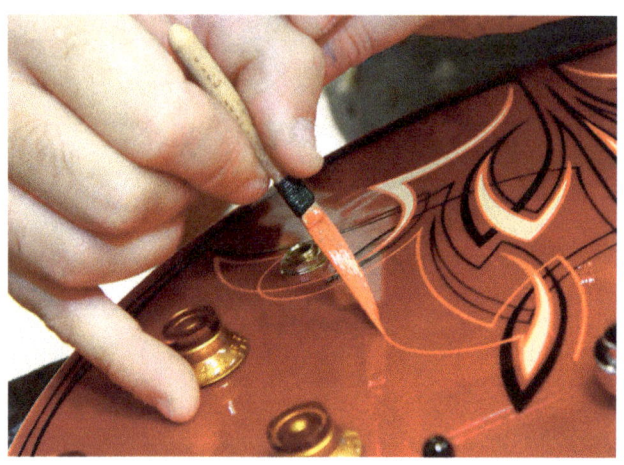

...90 degrees...

Here I pull a line in from the side...

...ummm...45 plus 90....135 degrees...

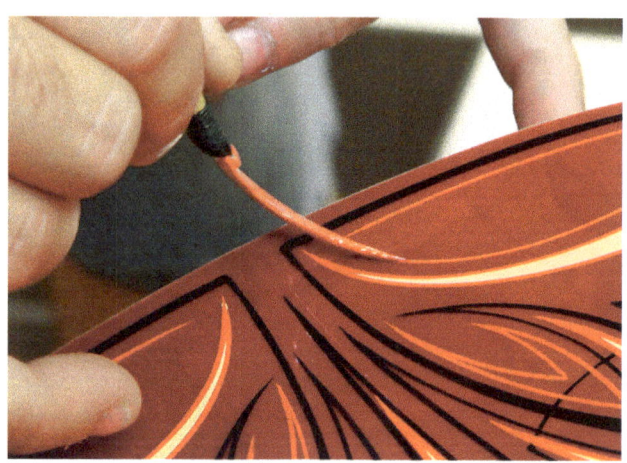

...and another to meet up with it.

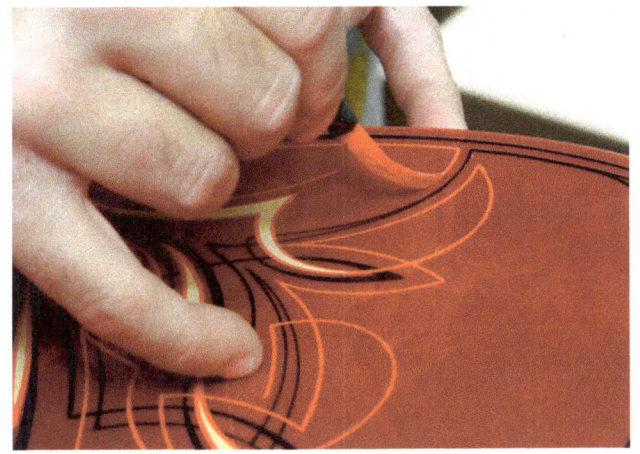

Knowing when to say when is key.

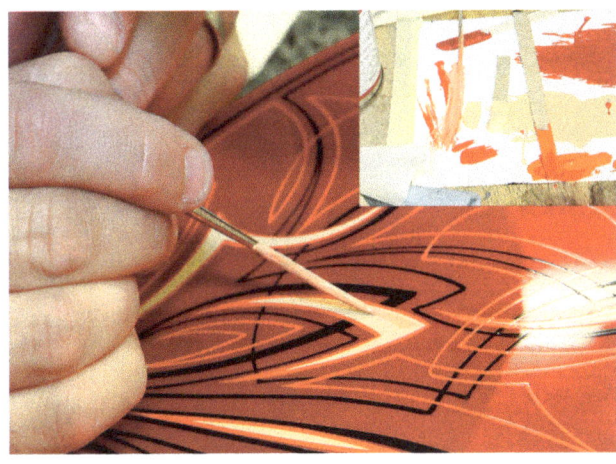

A few drops of the red/orange mix in the ivory is perfect to add a shadow to the fills.

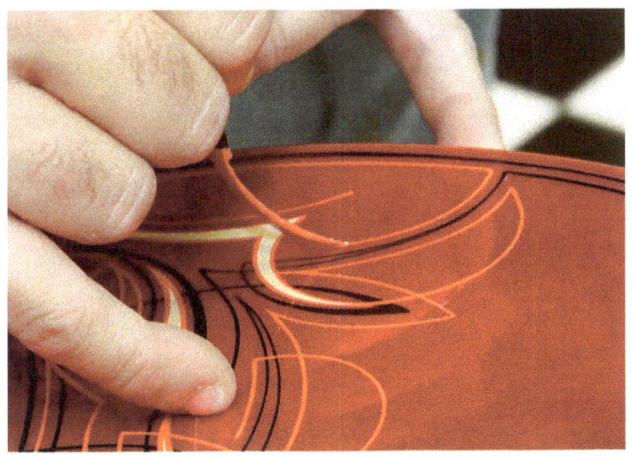

Keeping this in mind...I'll just pull a few more lines before the design gets too cluttered.

It gives them a beveled look....and it's very easy to do with the script brush.

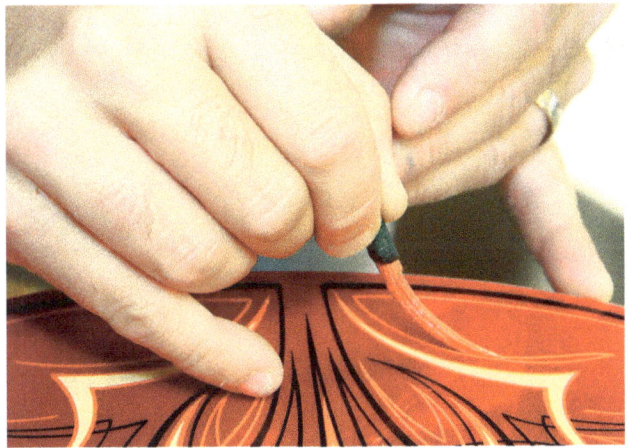

I finish off the orange line with a teardrop end instead of bringing it back into the design. Now it's time to clean the brush.

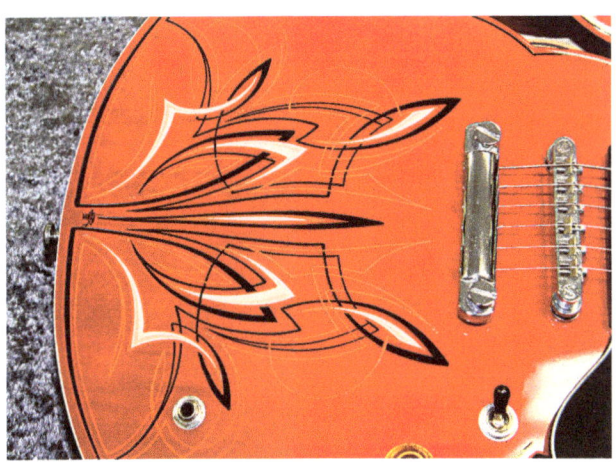

Finally done!!!

Chapter Two

Nub's Guitar - Part Two

Rockin' Cartoon

If you ask Nub, whose real name is Robert Collard, he will tell you that one of his favorite things to do, on his own time, is to mix cartoons with pinstriping. For the back panel of this guitar, Nub started with a caricature that's someplace between Elvis and the owner of the guitar (who's a bit of an Elvis look-alike himself).

Surrounding Elvis is a complete pinstripe design. Because this pinstripe work is similar to that already seen in Chapter 1, we elected to use these pages to show off Nub's abilities to paint cartoons - or in this case, the caricature Nub refers to as, Mr. Rock-a-Billy.

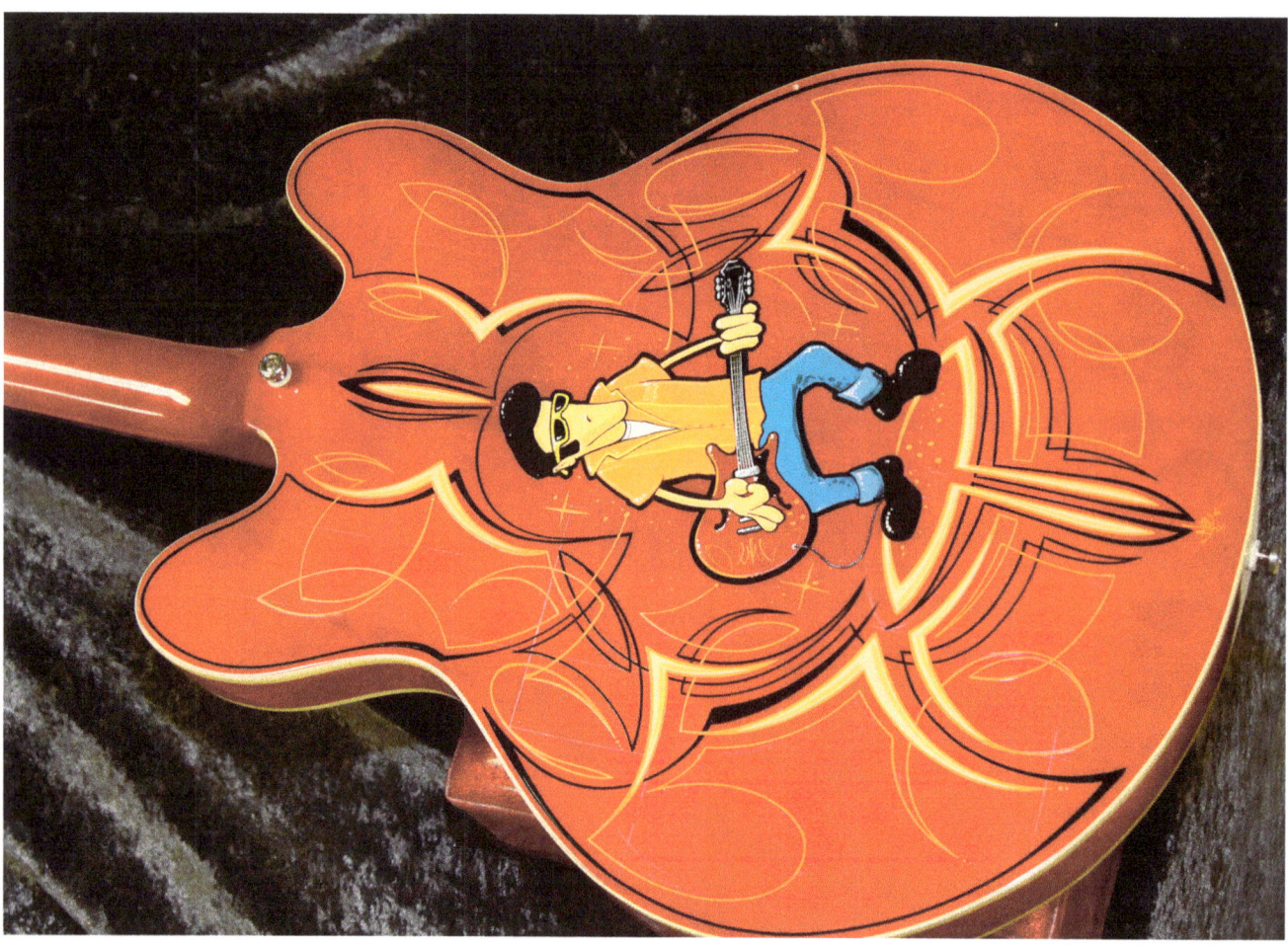

The design on the guitar's back panel is a combination of the pinstripe design on the front panel, and a cartoon character that Nub calls, Mr. Rock-a-Billy. Note the detail on Rock-a-Billy's guitar.

I start out with a quick sketch of "Mr. Rock-a-Billy" to give myself an idea of where to start with the design.

Brushes: Xcaliber

Paint: Ronan

Colors: White, Ivory, Orange, Process blue, Black

Tape: Fineline

Other: Stabilo pencil

Using 1/8 inch fineline tape, I lay out a grid and make reference lines with a white stabilo pencil before removing the tape. A ruler would have been great......couldn't find one.

Now I lightly sketch the character and get ready to paint.

Just making sure it matches......not sure why I spent the time sketching it on the paper first. I think Artie was making me nervous.

I start off with an ivory/white/orange mix for the skin color.

Orange always seems like a good color for a shirt.

When I'm doing cartoons and small characters, I always jump back and forth between my quill...

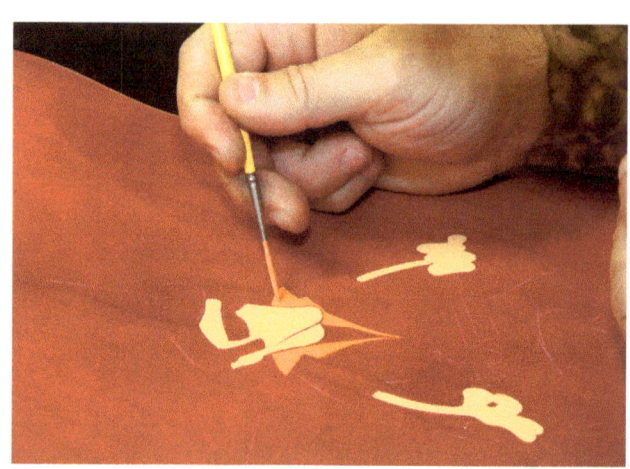

Continuing on his collar with the script brush...

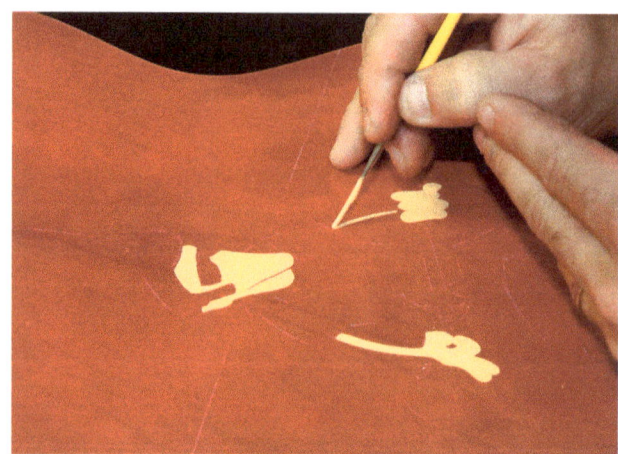

...and my script brush.

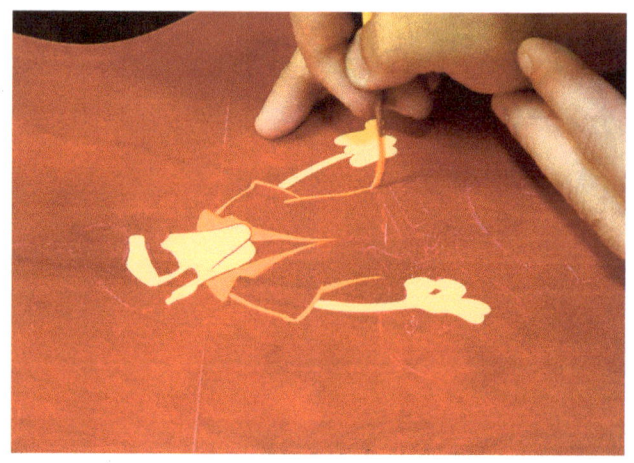

...and outlining the remainder of the shirt.

I fill in the lower portion of the shirt...

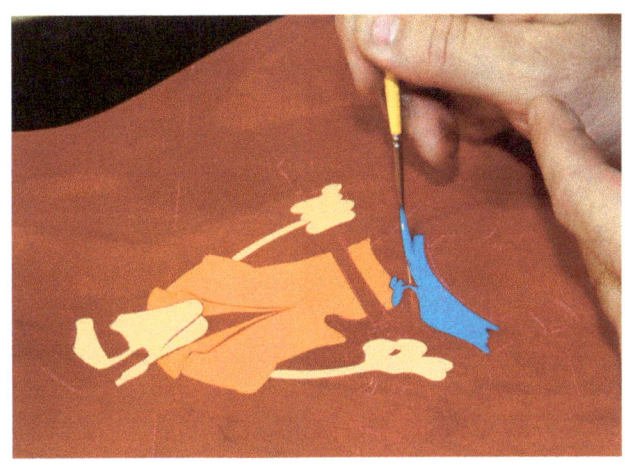

Now to get some pants on the little fella.

...then grab the quill...

Light blue is the color I choose...

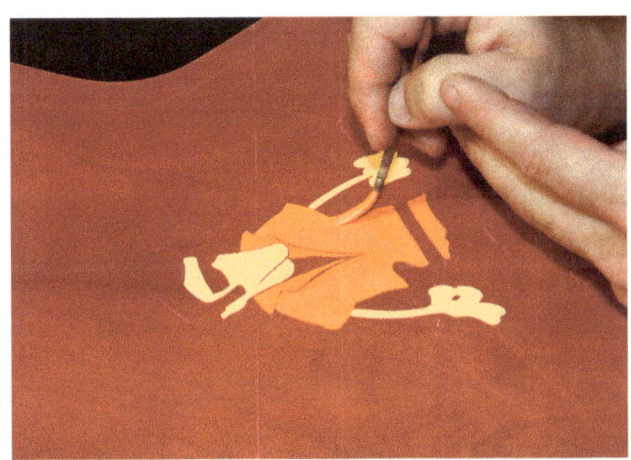

...and finish blocking the rest of the area in with orange.

...and my trusty script brush.

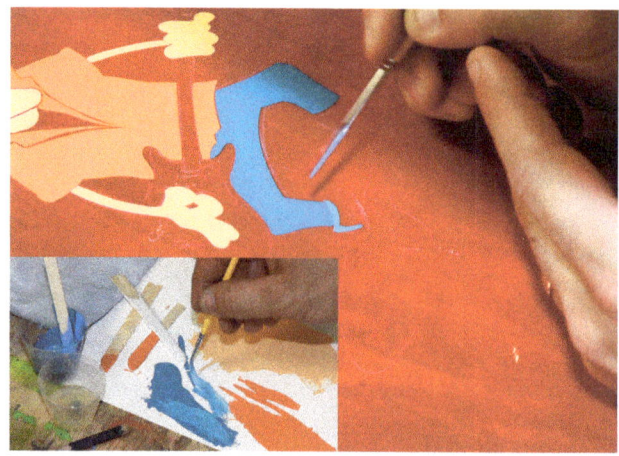

I mix in a few drops of white to lighten up the blue for his cuffs.

...and black shoes to match.

A nice white shirt...

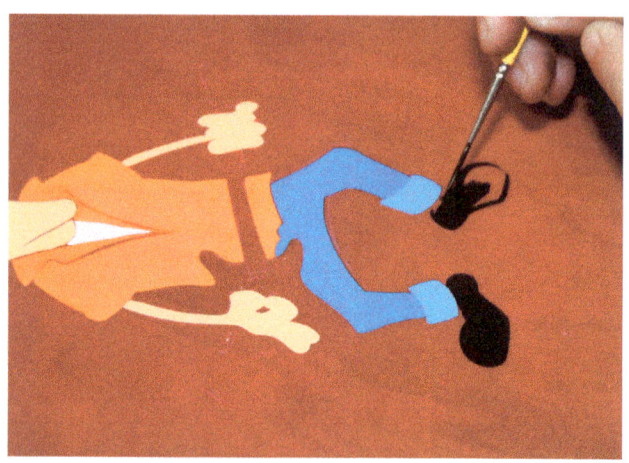

I use the script brush for 90% of the cartoons I do.

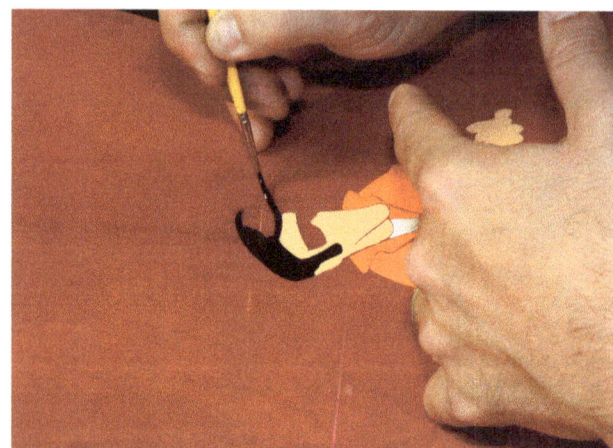

...black hairdo...

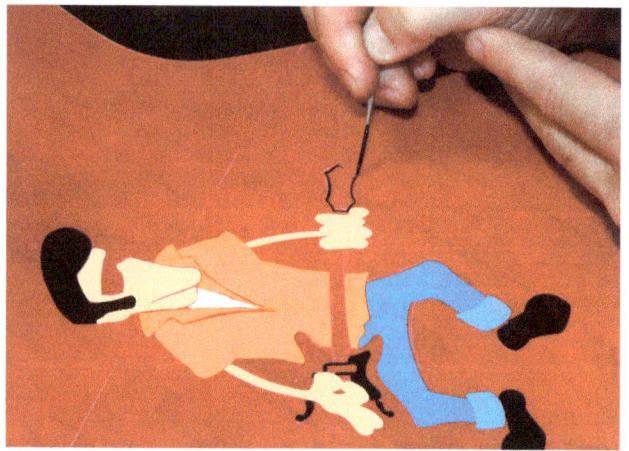

Now I start working in the details of the guitar, starting with black.

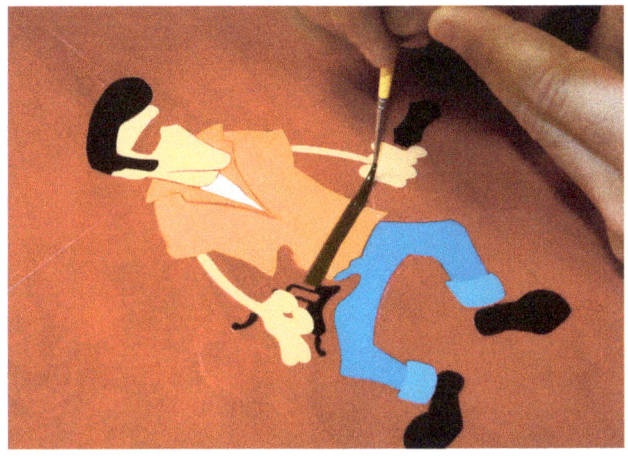

I mix some orange and black to get a nice brown color for the fingerboard.

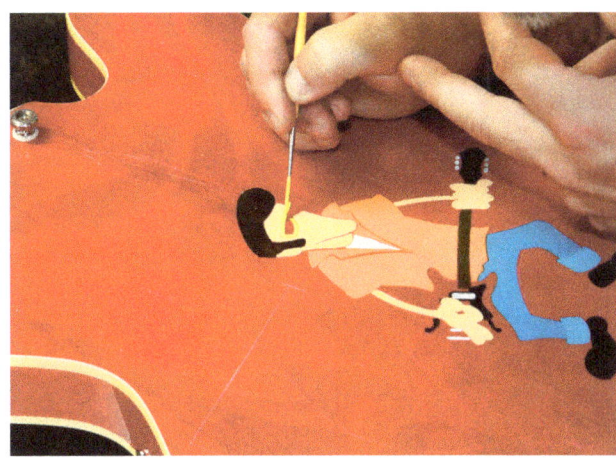

I jump to yellow for his shades...

I knock down the pureness of the white with a little bit of blue for the chrome parts of the guitar body...

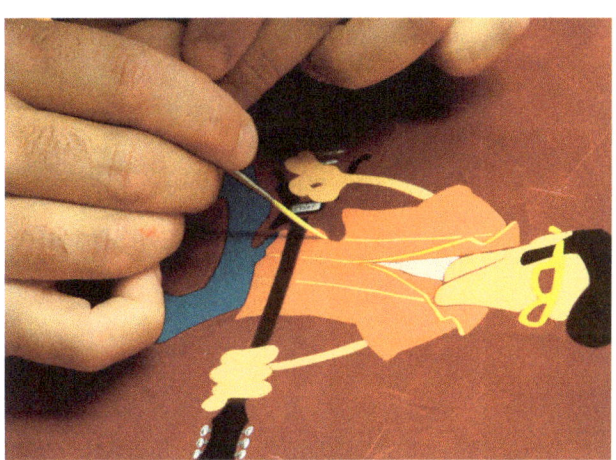

...and accents on his shirt.

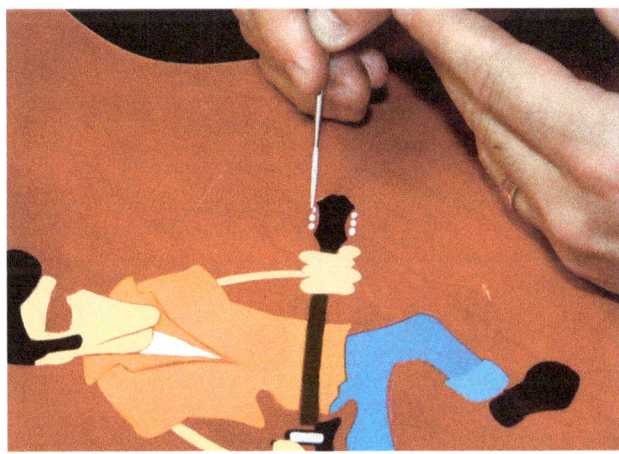

...and the headstock.

I let everything sit for a half hour or so before I start the pinstriping and outlining around the little guy.

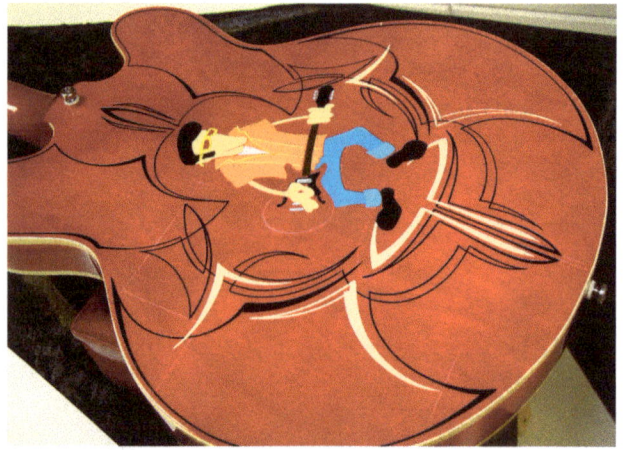

I start the pinstriping portion of the design in the same fashion as the front of the guitar. First, with the black...and then with my ivory/orange mix.

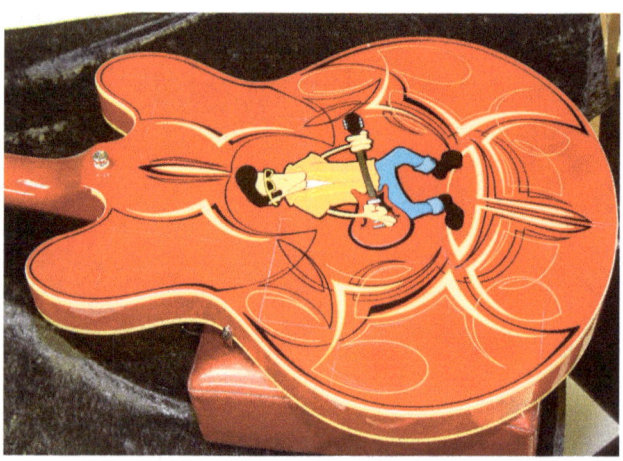

Following with the same striping colors as the front of the guitar, I continue with the red/orange mix to bring the whole thing together.

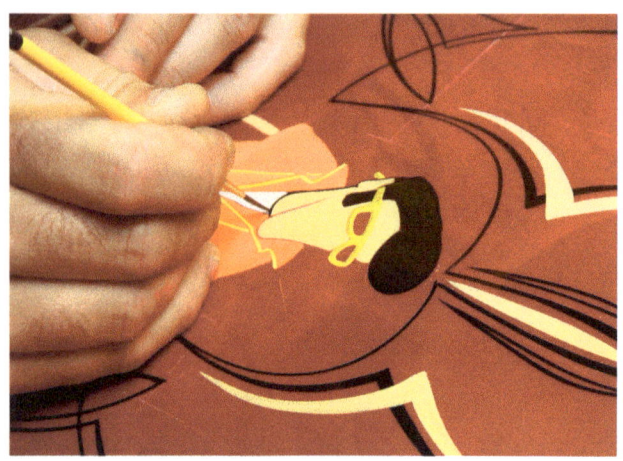

I break out the script brush once again and start outlining the character with black. I like to give the cartoon a nice thin outline...

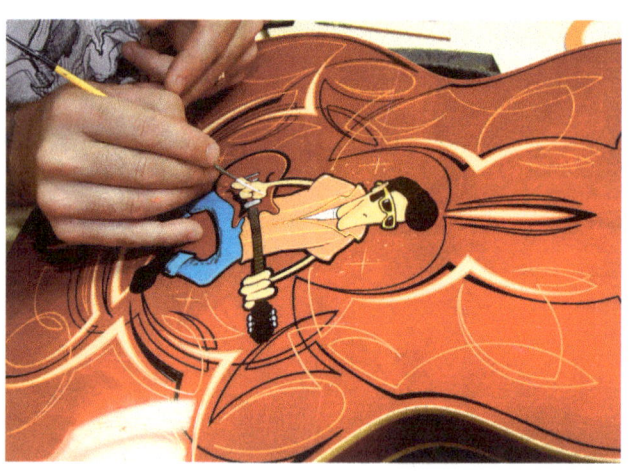

A few final details to the center...

...but give the entire outer edge a bolder outline to help pull it away from the background color.

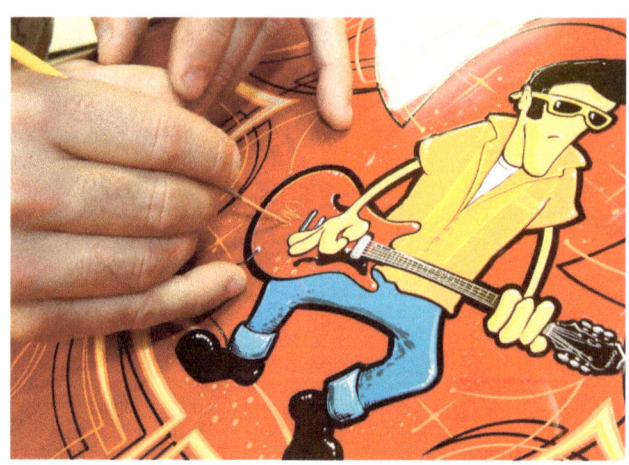

...and a little micro-striping to finish it off.

Q&A: Nub, aka: Robert Collard

Tell us a little about yourself, and how you became a striper?

I got into the whole thing through the sign business. I worked for a sign shop and the job gave me my basic knowledge. That morphed into custom painting. I started to take all the stuff I learned from signs and put that into the paint jobs. I look at my early work and I can see when I started using what was in my head, design wise, and that's when everything got better. That's when the pinstriping started.

What do you like to use for brushes?

Xcaliber, and the Mack Bobbo.

What do you like for paint?

If I'm clearing over the stripes, then I use House of Kolor urethane. If it's going to stay on top I use One-Shot or Ronan. It's getting overwhelming now because there are so many different striping paints coming out these days.

When you're doing something like a panel, do you plan it out ahead of time or just work on the fly?

Usually on the fly, but there are times I lay something out. Even when I do a layout though, I still veer off the chosen path.

Are there absolutes in terms of design, in terms of placement and how many times a line can cross another line?

There are things you learn striping. When I look at my early stuff, there are too many crossovers in the same spots, like a pizza being cut. If I know I am using lots of colors I leave open spaces so I'm not putting four lines in a one inch space. These are things you learn with experience.

Who inspires you, where do you get your ideas?

Everything inspires me, other artists' work, my surroundings, my mood, music. Really, hanging out with guys like Artie, Mr. J, and Zeke has been a huge inspiration to my work. Good company makes good work.

How do you pick colors, and how did you learn to mix colors to match a certain color?

I kind of learned along the way. You learn what looks good with what, and what looks bad. A lot of times I look at my early stuff, and ask myself, "why did I pick that color?"

As far as mixing, I was taught the whole autobody-shop thing early, in a collision shop. That's where I learned the basics of color theory. Now, sometimes when the customer wants some gawdawful color and I just tell them, "I won't do it." With striping, the simpler the combos the better it is. The color theory is in the back of my mind, but I pretty much work from experience. It becomes second nature. Sometimes you take a chance; it may work, it may not.

Final words of advice?

Practice, practice, practice. I wouldn't recommend striping on someone else's stuff until you are extremely comfortable with the whole process.

As comfortable with a pinstripe brush as he is with a spray gun, Nub likes the creative outlet that pinstriping affords.

Chapter Three

Mikey's Big Panel

Stripes and Fades

Though some painters start with nothing more than an idea, or maybe a rough sketch, Mike Frederick likes to make a pretty complete drawing of the design ahead of time, and then transfer that drawing to the panel or door skin. As Mikey likes to say, "I think this method works well. I'm sure anyone who tries this will notice that their striping seems effortless. The preparation in the beginning helps maintain the quality of the work, and the work takes a lot less time."

In terms of the design itself, Mikey prefers colors that jump off the panel, which is especially important when the paint is being applied to a super bright panel like this one. Rather than use pure pinstripes, this particular panel includes spears of color that run through the design from one end to the other, complete with color fades within the spear itself.

With his careful preparation, mahlstick for support, and the use of super bright colors, Mikey is in a class all his own.

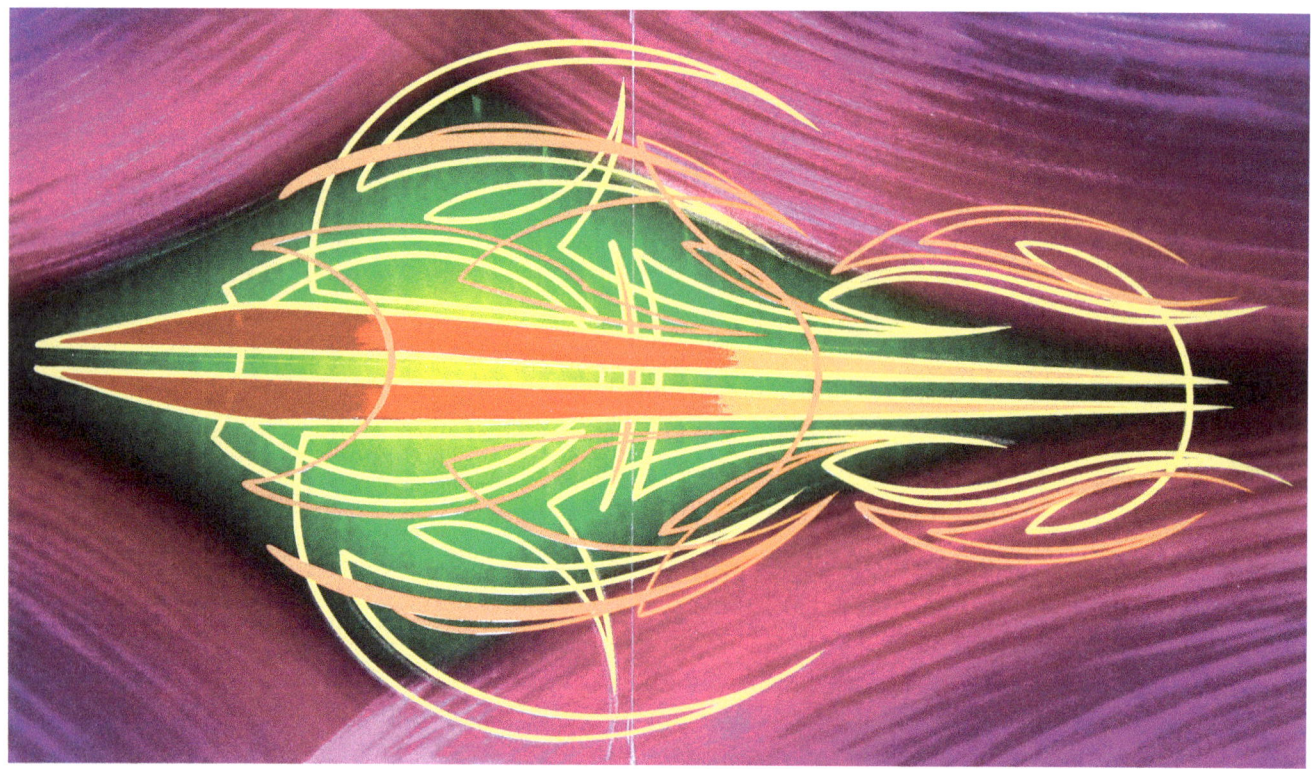

We're going to do a three part striping design on this purple and green kandy panel. It will have a main striping part, an accent stage, and then a fill-in stage at the end.

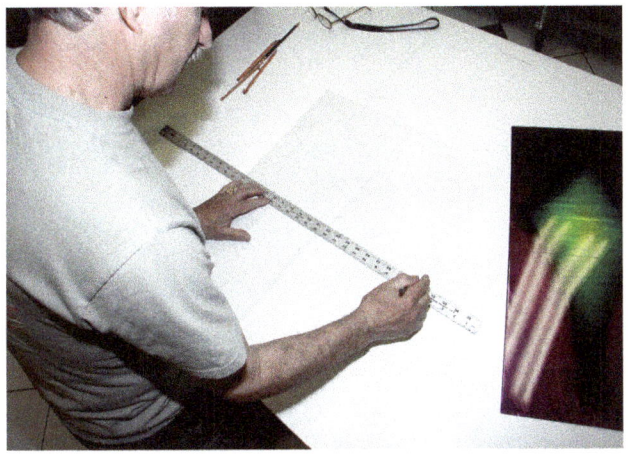

On occasion, I'll use sign painting techniques to help me with pinstriping projects. I think I work more efficiently this way. I begin by folding a piece of tracing paper vertically and horizontally.

Brushes: #000 Xcaliber Striping brush

Paint: Ronan lettering enamel. Cherry Red, Bright Orange, Maroon, Ivory, Lemon yellow

Wax & Grease Remover: Dupont 901

Other: Charcoal pencils, both white and black. Mahlstick, Stabilo pencil

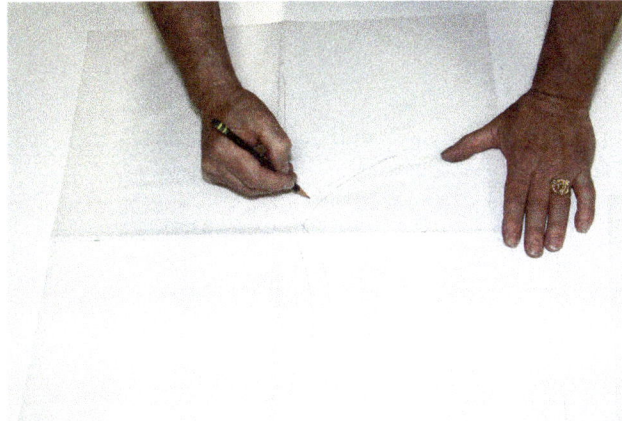

Draw a design on one side of the tracing paper. Refold the paper and trace the design onto the other half...

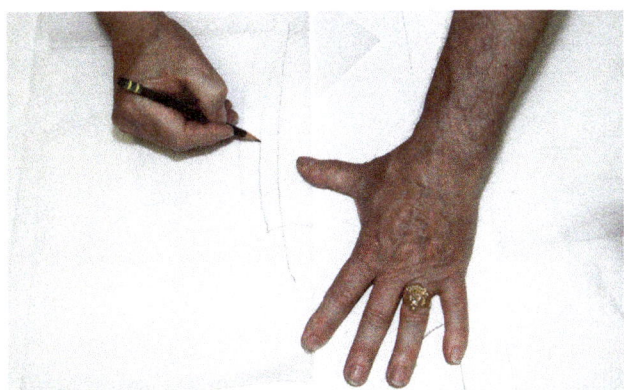

...this will give you a completed design, one that's even right to left and top to bottom. Turn the unfolded tracing paper over and with a charcoal pencil retrace the design onto the backside of the paper. In this case we use white charcoal due to the dark panel.

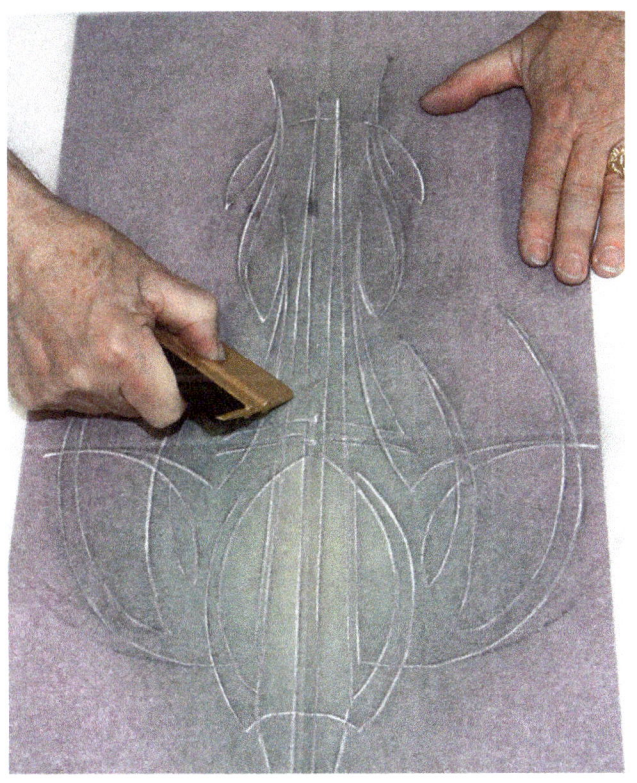

Mark center lines on your panel with a stabilo, up and down and across. Evenly place the paper onto panel, line up the folds with stabilo lines and tape down. Now, go over your lines again with a pencil, or just rub the paper with your hand or a squeegee...

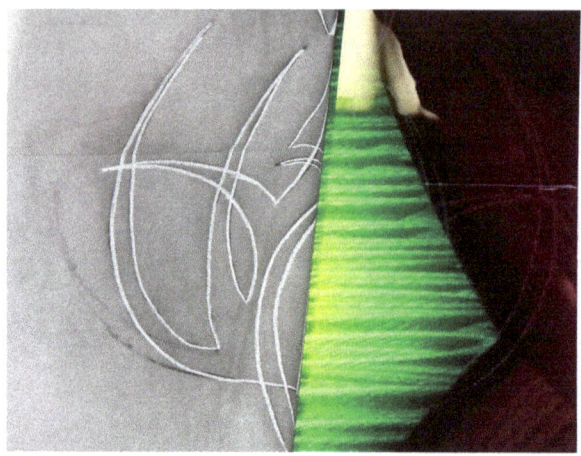

1. ...and then lift one side of the tracing paper to make sure your design has transferred.

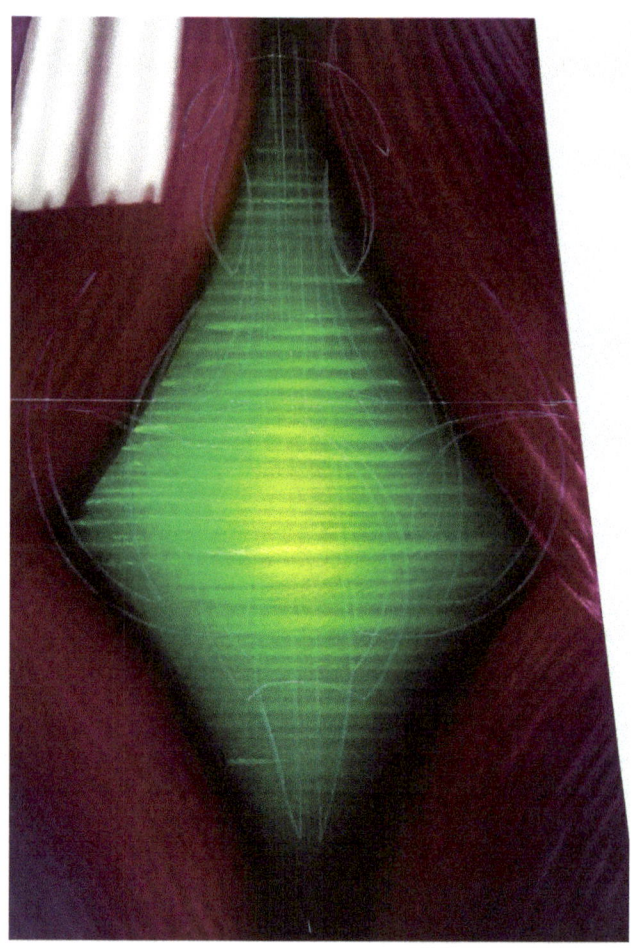

2. It's easy to see why we used a white charcoal pencil. This panel is pretty dark. Look closely, you can easily see the pattern.

3. I mix ivory with a little lemon yellow, to give a butter-cream color. This gives me eye-popping contrast, and helps with coverage on this dark panel. I'll do this panel with a #000 Xcaliber striping brush.

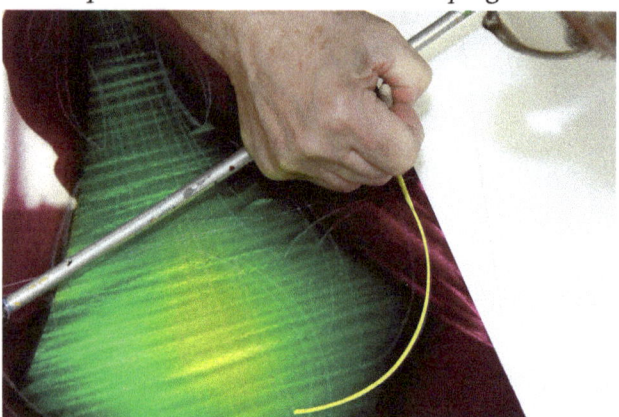

4. Here's where this method pays off. With the pattern in place, I can begin to paint, and concentrate on painting. I will not have to figure out where to stripe as I go. Instead of typically going back and forth...

5. ...left to right, right to left, I'm going to paint this entire panel going completely left to right. Sounds weird for striping, but this way I won't have to stop and study so it will go quickly. Start with the farthest outside line.

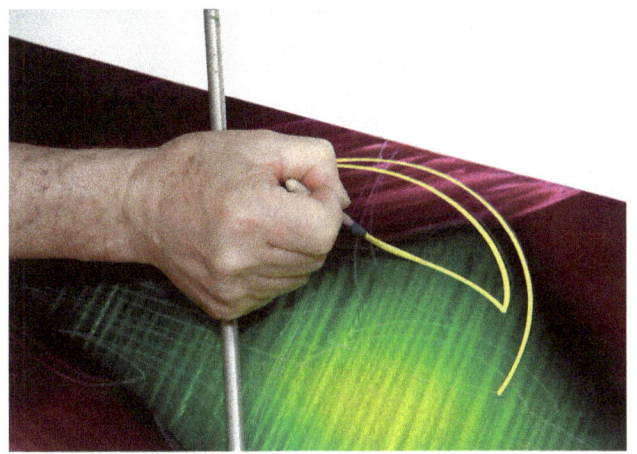

Follow the pattern, one line after the other.

The mahlstick acts as a bridge. It helps to suspend my hand over the work area and also helps me pinpoint the placement of the brush for accurate starting and stopping.

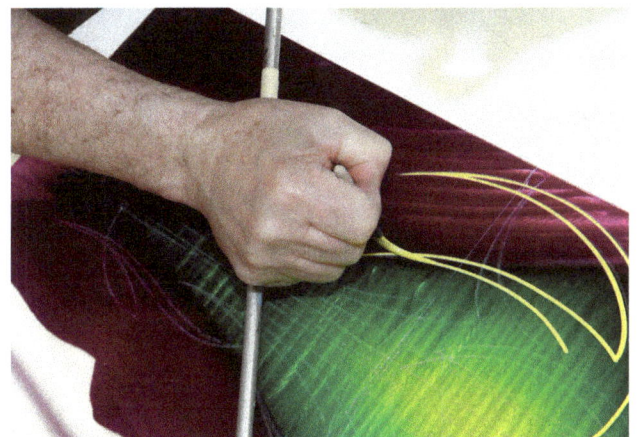

Start and stop on the pattern line.

Work your way down the panel, keep going from left to right.

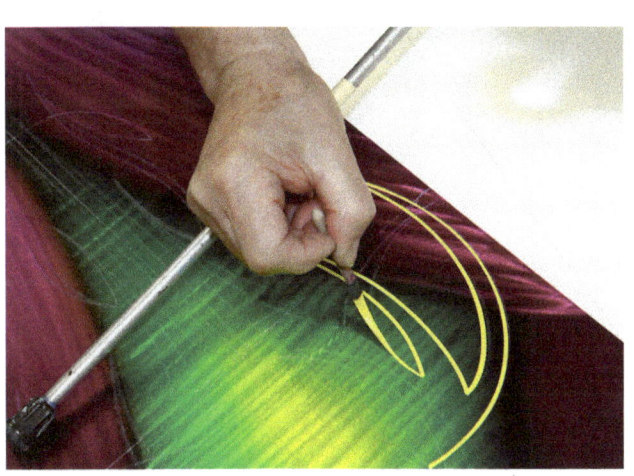

Notice, I'm also using my mahlstick. This keeps my hand off the panel and out of the wet paint.

The last line at the bottom of the panel is going to cross over the center, onto the right side of the design.

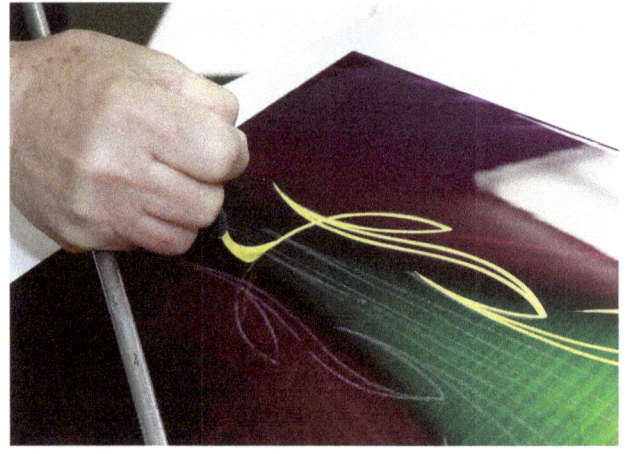

I'll stop this line in the center and finish it later.

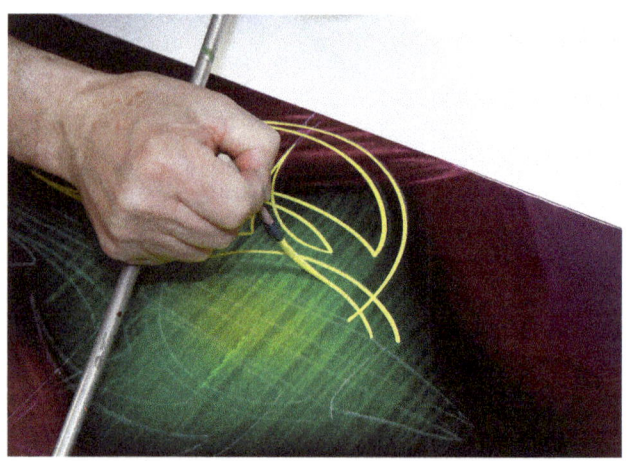

The next line gets pulled, and it finishes at the center.

Back up near the top, I'll do the next line. Again, the one that's farthest to the left.

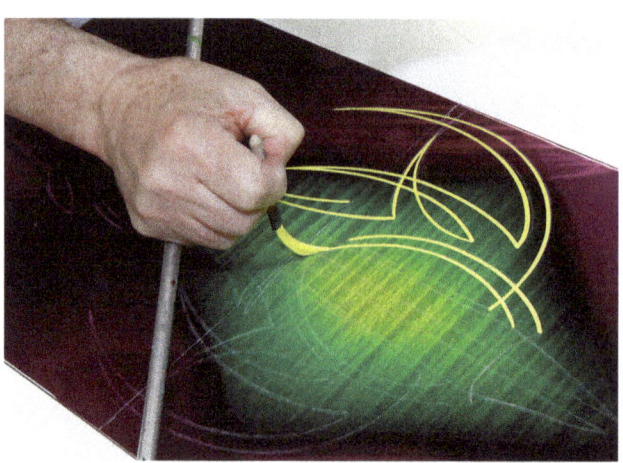

Notice the beginning of this stroke in the previous picture, and how the brush is rolled at the end of the stroke in this picture.

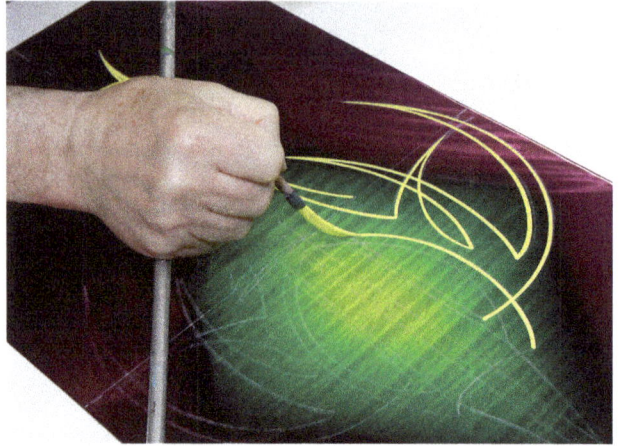

This line stops just short of center.

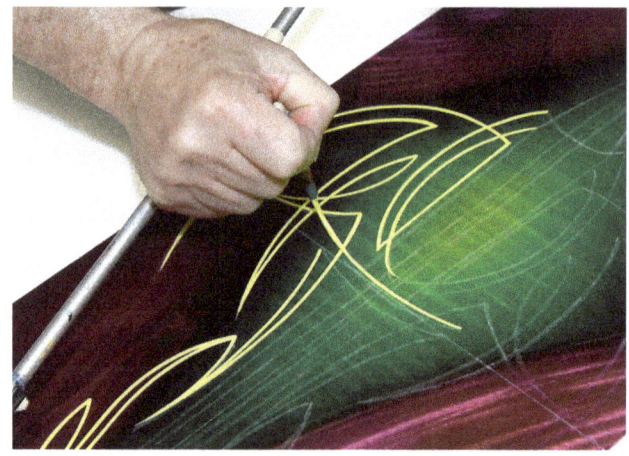

Some of the lines crossing over the center can be done now. Here is an exception to completely going left to right. There's an exception to every rule.

The pattern is easy to see here. I do all the lines that cross over the center.

The next line runs straight down the middle, coming to a point with the previous line.

There are four main lines to this design. These lines will form two large open areas in the center which will eventually be filled in with another color. This area will become the focal point of the entire design.

Finish up the first of these near the bottom of the panel.

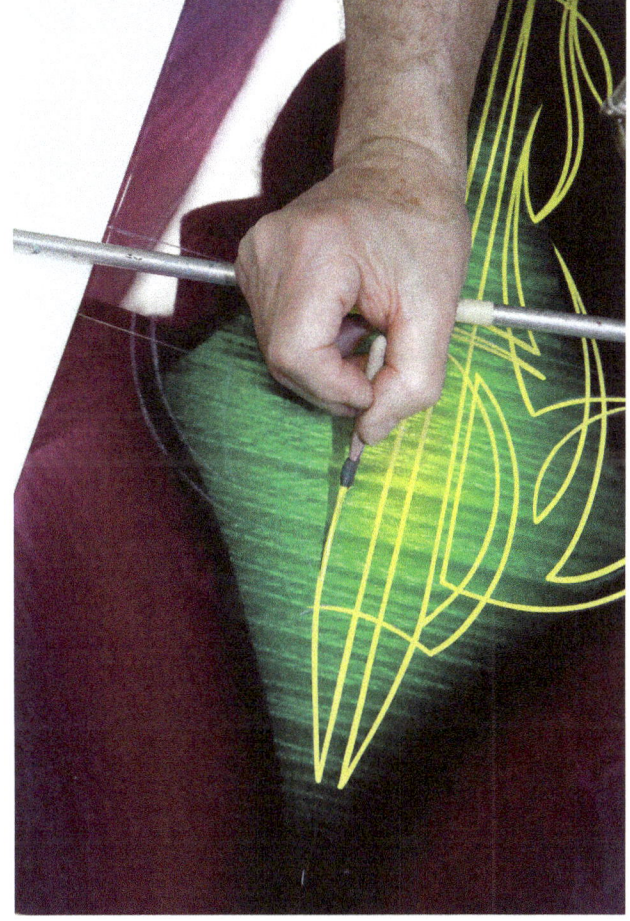

Now we've reached the center of the panel. From here everything will be a mirror image of what we've already done.

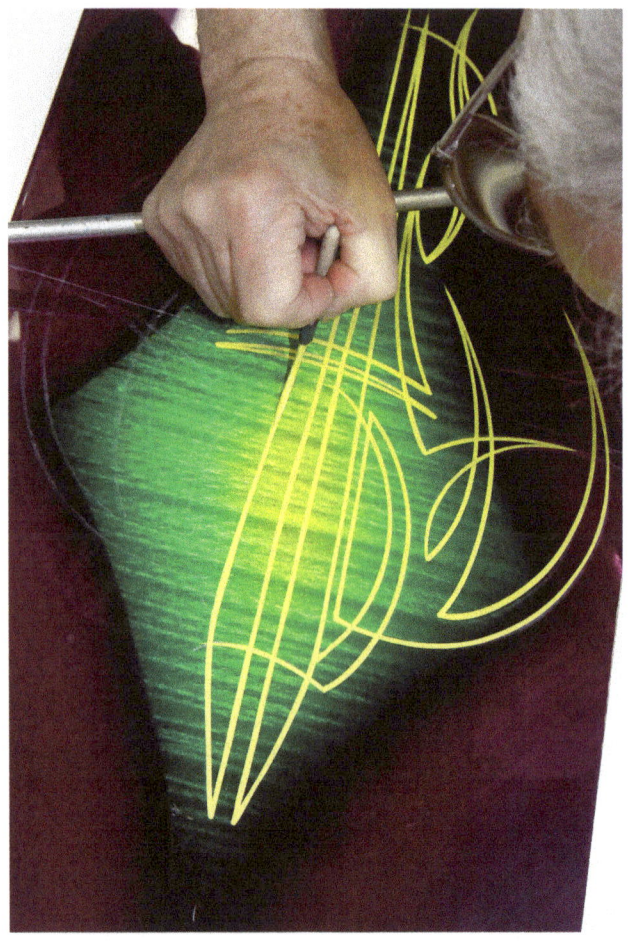

1. Pull this line down to a point.

3. Finish this line to a point as well.

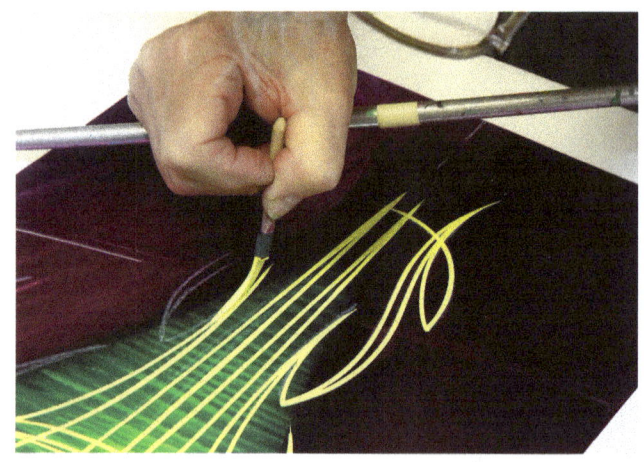

4. This picture shows the lowest portion of the panel. You can easily see the charcoal pattern for the next line.

2. While near the bottom I pick up the next line, still going from left to right.

5. After painting a small connector line, I'll do the double feather-type lines.

Another small connector line gives me the starting point for the lowest line. I place the brush at the top of the connector and roll it slightly down.

Look closely, you can see the end of this stroke. Pick up the brush right here.

Check out how I lean on the brush in order to make this line bend.

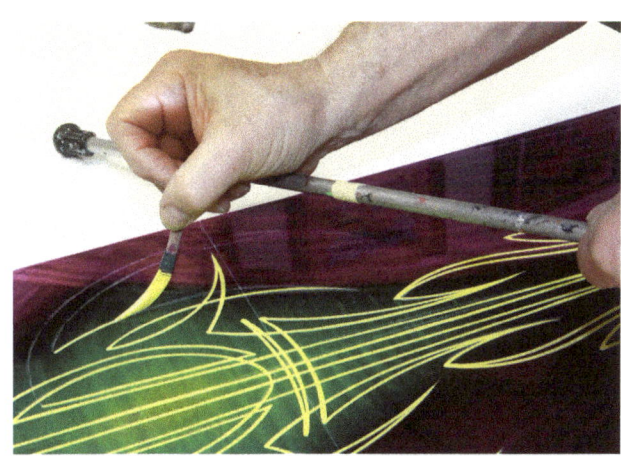

After finishing a connector line that curves outward and down to a point, I move slightly up and start a new line downward.

Back up near the top of the panel, I continue working left-to-right. Using our pattern, the striping will mirror the completed side easily. You don't even have to look at the other side, just keep painting.

I bring the line down to a point.

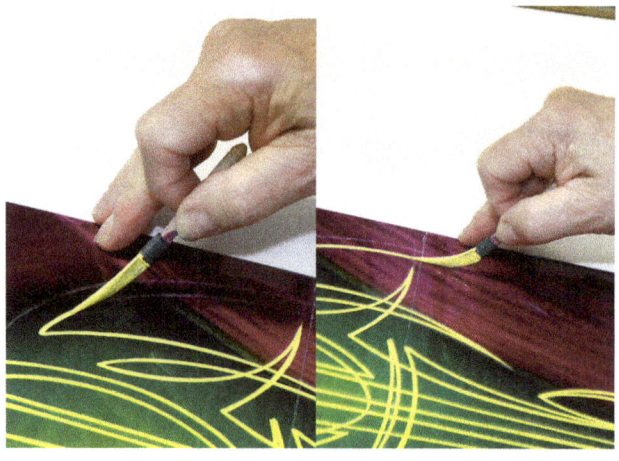

I connect at the top of the previous line and pull down, curving outward, then move back in towards the center, stopping at about the middle of the panel.

Here I continue the design, working my way down the panel...

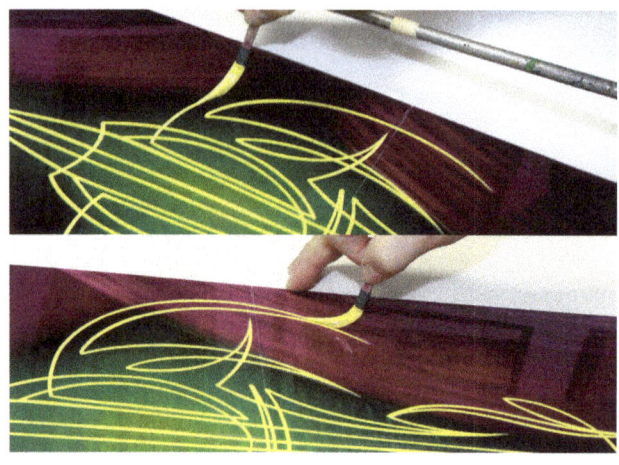

Here I bring the last line around and down to a point. We are now done with the base color.

...with two more small connectors that come to a point.

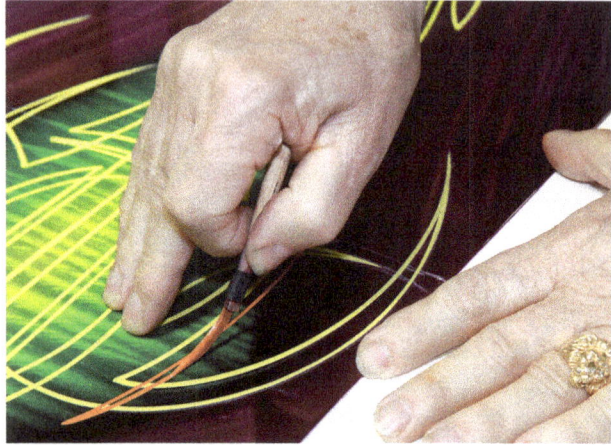

Using a second color, vermillion, I start at the top again and pull a second line. I'll fill these two lines in later to give a small burst of color near the outside.

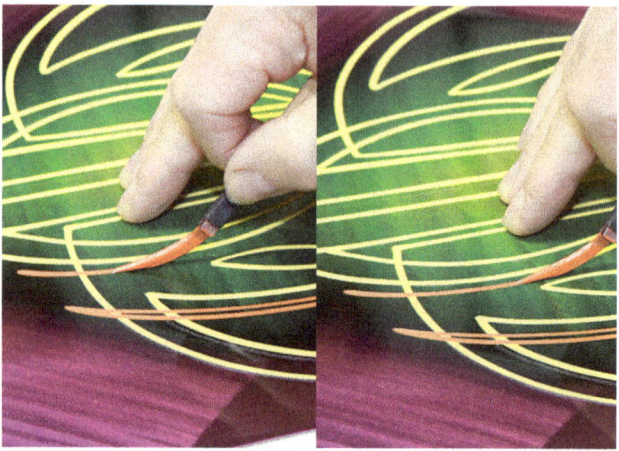

The pinstripes done with the second color follow the basic shape I painted earlier.

This crossover line ties the two sides together.

Again, these two lines merge to a point.

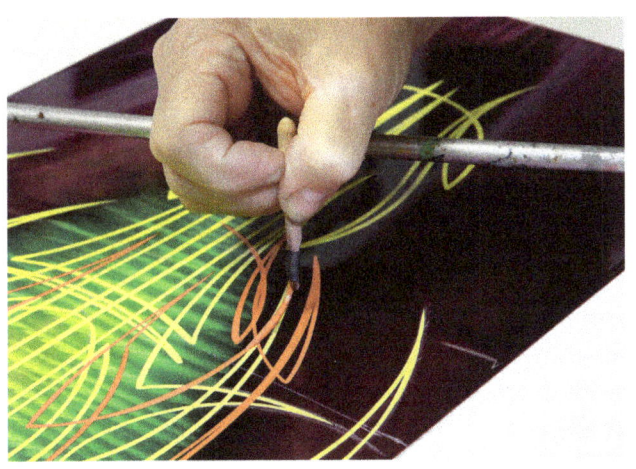

Now I come up about mid panel and pull a couple of lines down inward and then outward, down to a point.

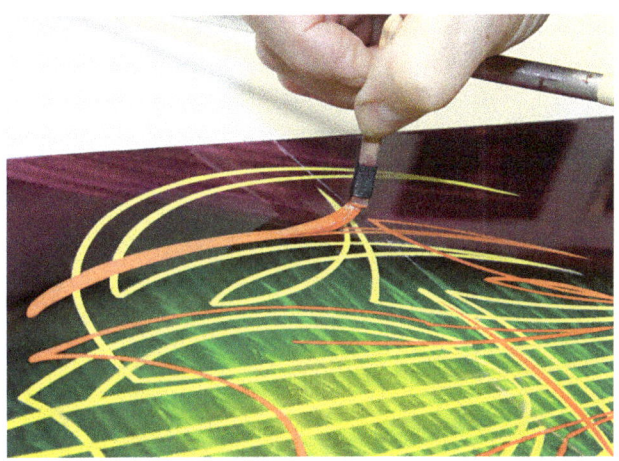

Another big splash of color on the outside.

I run a horizontal line on top of my first color, then I continue the design down the right side.

Here is the design so far, and some of the paints I used to get here.

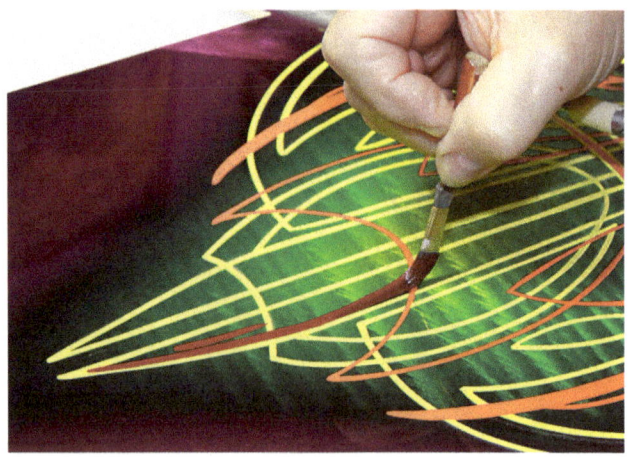

Here's my third color; maroon...

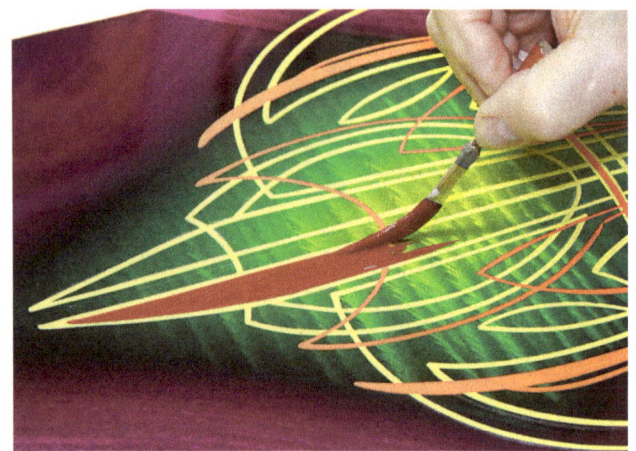

...which I use to fill in the top of the two big spears.

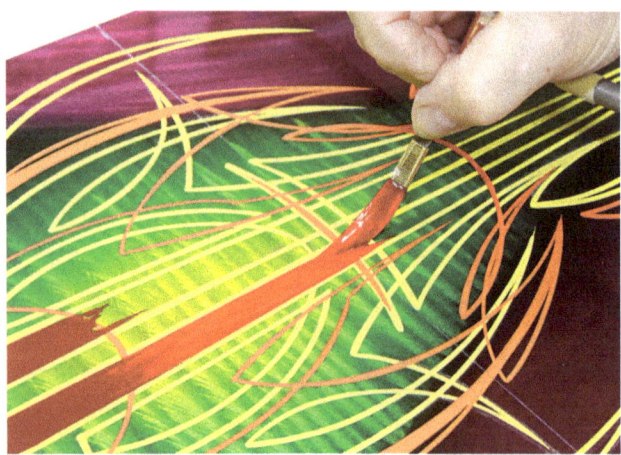

Part of the way down the spear I fade to another color, red...

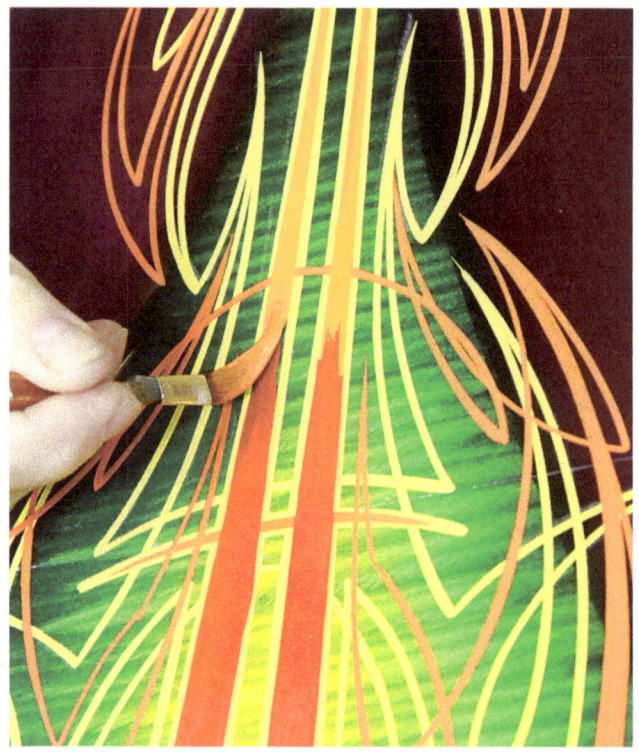

...and at the end I do one more fade using orange so I have two, three-color spears.

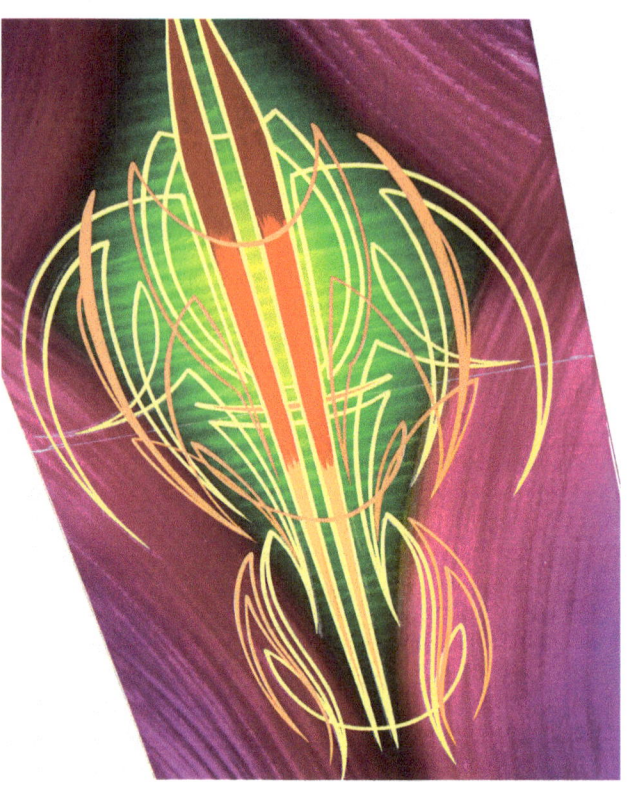

The finished panel. It all came together fairly fast because I did the preparation on the front end.
Captions by Mikey

Q&A: Mikey

Tell us a little about yourself, and how you became a striper?

I always wanted to do striping way back when. As a kid I used to steal a quarter from Mom to buy one of the little custom car magazines. They had stories about guys like Larry Watson and Dean Jeffries. I remember an article about Dean Jeffries striping a set of wheel covers, and I thought, "I can do that."

I got started as a teenager, sitting in the street lettering trucks and striping dashboards. I don't know if it was great work at the time, but I was just doing it and doing it again.

What do you like to do when you don't have a customer looking over your shoulder?

I stripe a lot of panels, and I like to do test panels for flame jobs.

What do you like to use for brushes?

For scroll work I use Xcaliber, and for straight-line work I use one of my old Grumbachers, or a new Mack with a similar style.

What do you like for paint?

I've used Ronan for the last couple of years, it's made right here in the Bronx. I do use House of Kolor and Kustom Shop when we have to clear over the stripes, but otherwise it's Ronan.

When you're doing something like a panel, do you plan it out ahead of time or just work on the fly?

I do both, if I have a company truck, I just wing it. When I want to do a really neat piece, I plan it out. I draw out the design on tracing paper so I have a pattern. That way I get better looking designs overall, nice and even, and crisp. It's easy to use the tracing paper technique, it's quick and comes from my sign painting techniques, so when I do striping it's natural to use the same technique.

Are there absolutes in terms of design, in terms of line placement and how many times a line can cross another line?

I don't have a formula, I just do a nice basic design with a main color, then come back with one or two accent colors. It depends how big it is and how elaborate I want to make the design.

Who inspires you, where do you get ideas?

Larry Watson was the best for me, we were good friends. I have a whole list of guys, Mr. J, Hightower, Tom Kelly, Mike Lambertson. I try to draw from all of them. I look at what they do and think, "I'd like to try something like that," I try to expand on what they do in my own way.

How do you pick colors, and how did you learn to mix colors to match a certain color?

I like big contrast, the first color is big contrast. The second color is an accent, it's complementary. I don't often use neutral colors, black, white or gray, I like bright colors. I'm all about scallops, and big color combinations

Any final words of wisdom?

It's also important to have support; for me it's my wife, Diana. This is a tough business, you have to live it as well as love it. Get involved, go to pinstriping and lettering meets, and car shows. Broaden your horizons, don't become stagnant. Develop friendships with other stripers, such as I have with the stripers in this book. I admire and love these guys and I cherish their friendship. It's been a great ride!

Mikey Frederick uses some old sign-painting tricks to make his pinstriping projects go quickly and smoothly.

Chapter Four

Metal Flake from Mikey

Back to Basics in Two Colors

There are all kinds of pinstripe designs. In this particular example Mikey shows us that it doesn't take a lot of paint, or a lot of lines, to make a bold statement or an intriguing design. The metalflake panel, devoid of any color, is a perfect canvas for this simple statement in black and red.

As is often the case, Mikey starts with a design that is drawn out ahead of time on tracing paper and then transferred to the panel. The method ensures accuracy, and allows Mikey to "just paint" as he likes to say. The paint is enamel from Ronan, the colors: black and cherry red. If the colors are traditional, does that make this an old-skool panel?

This is my nearly finished design before adding the border.

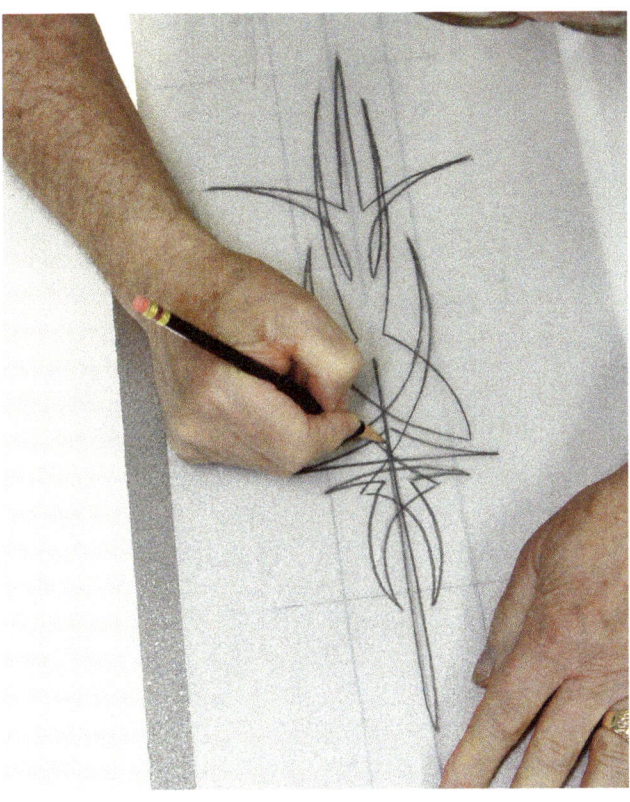

I start by making a pattern on tracing paper with a pencil.

Brushes:
Xcaliber & Mack Striping Brushes

Paint:
Ronan Black & Ronan Cherry Red Lettering Enamel

Other:
Blue Stabilo, Black Charcoal Pencil (soft), Tracing Paper

Using a charcoal pencil to trace over the pencil lines, I can place the pattern onto the panel and rub the design, transferring it to the panel.

Choosing black for the main part of the design gives great contrast to the silver metallic panel. Starting at the top I pull a long straight line down the center using an Xcaliber brush.

A second line - placed right next to the first - creates a teardrop shape that will be a focal point on the completed panel.

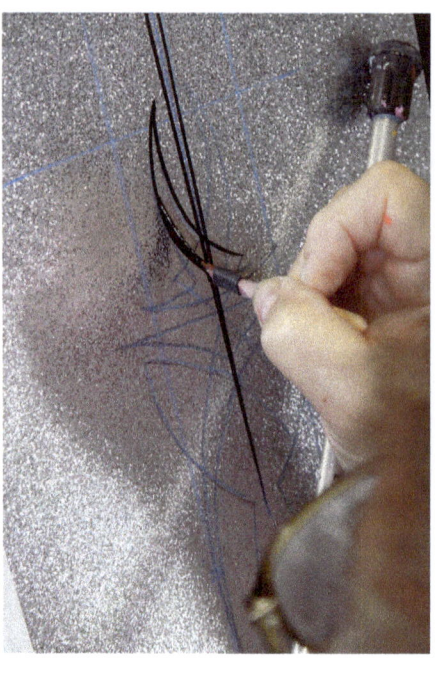

I begin at the upper part of the design, stroking the brush first on the left side, one or two strokes at a time.

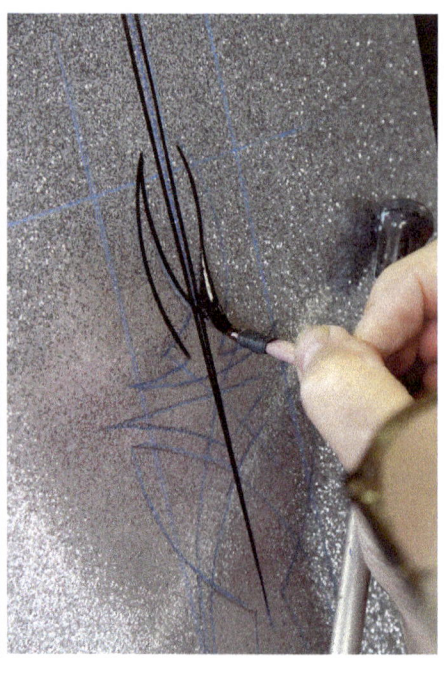

Moving to the right side I mirror the lines we just made.

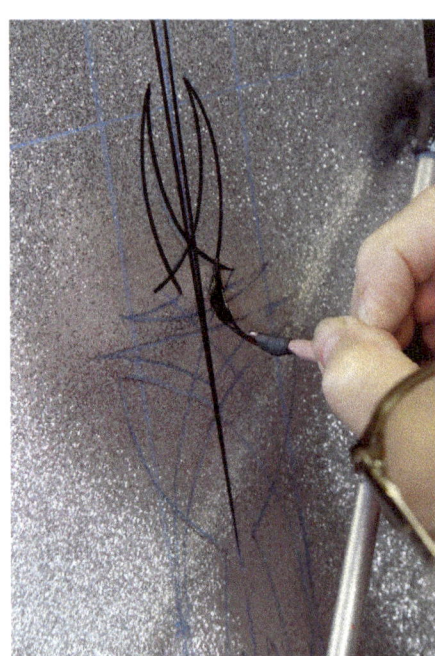

Here the top of the design starts to take shape.

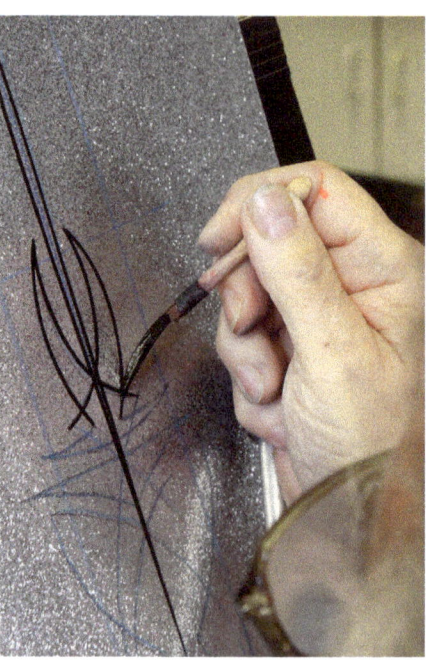

This is how I even up the end of the stroke.

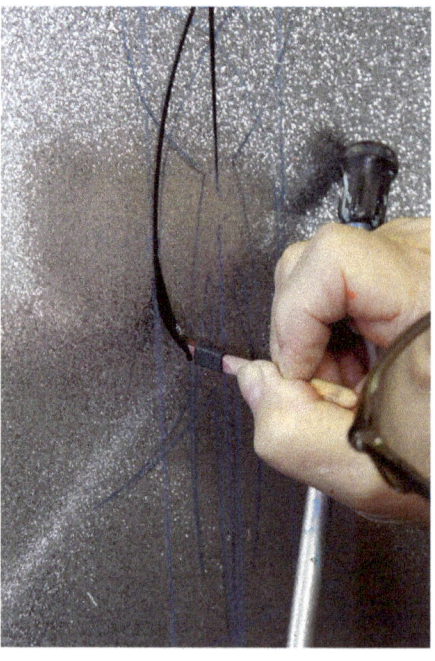

I make the next line pulling downward and to the outside, then curving back towards the center.

Now cross to the right side.

Notice how the brush is rolled slightly in order to make this stroke.

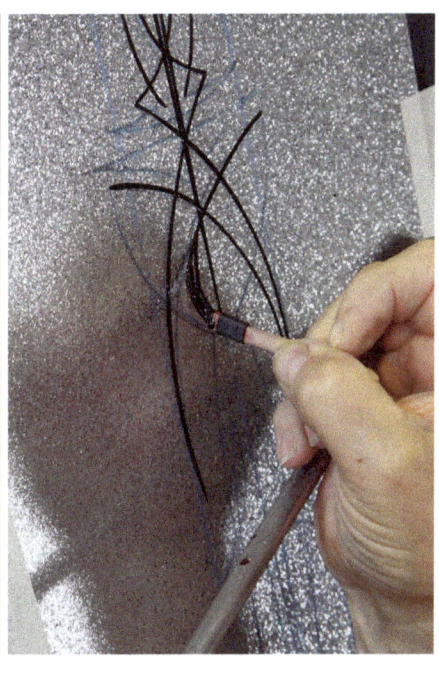
Dropping down, the next two lines go left to right, then right to left.

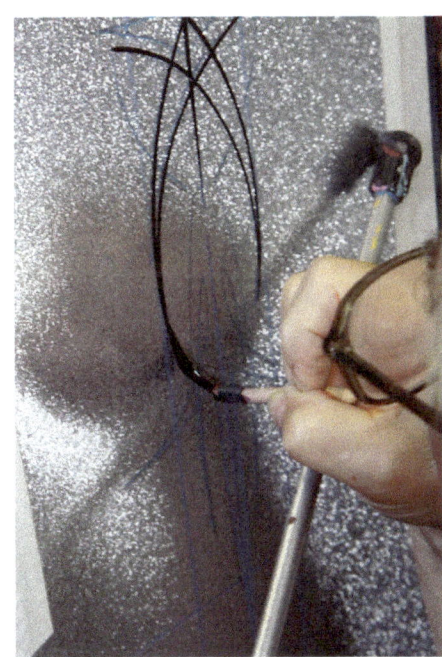
I bring these lines down and connect them with a point at the end of the stroke.

Following the pattern, the next line needs to be pulled down and inward.

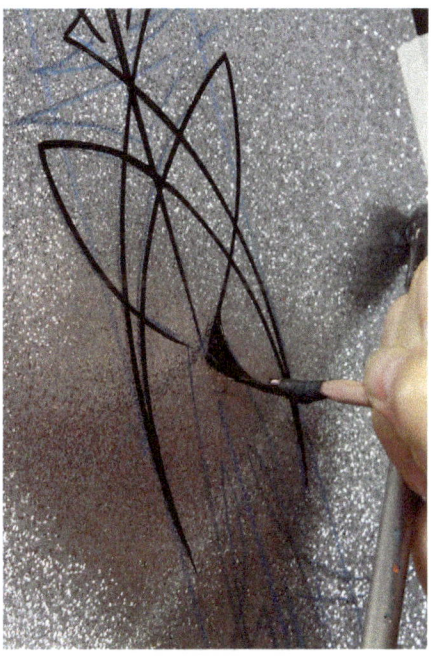
Now the right side. Down towards the center, stopping just short of the teardrop.

It seems the right time to go back up near the top and do the two short cross pieces going outward from the center.

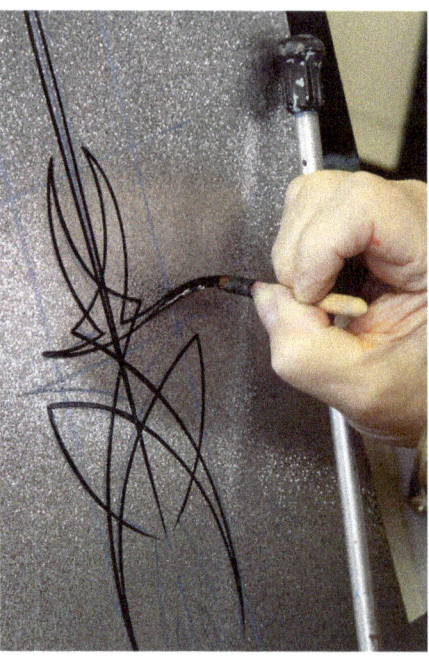

Connect the two center pieces to a point. Then it's back to where we left off.

I connect to the last line and pull another line down toward the bottom to a point. I also connect the inside line and pull a short curve in toward the center across the previous line, and then outward.

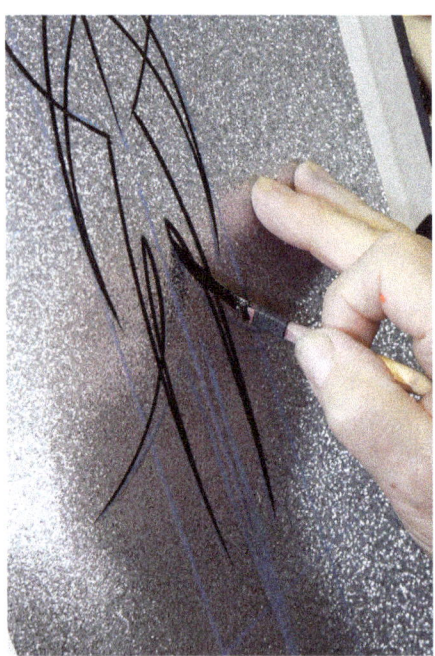

This picture shows the beginning of the short curved motion and the cross-over of the previous line.

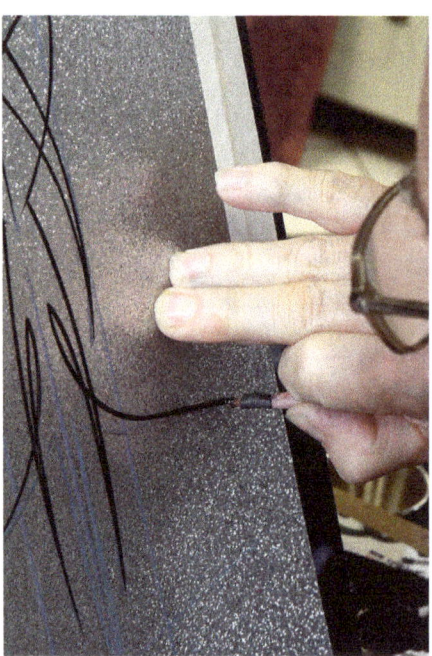

Now I finish the outward curve on the right side.

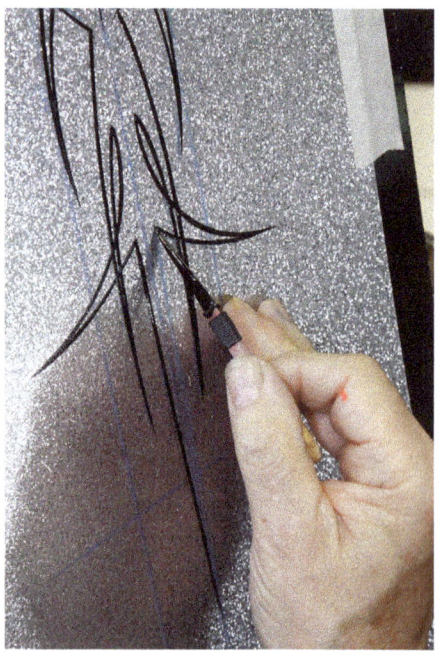

Then I come back inside with a line under the short curved line we just made. From where you see the end of the brush, I pull down about four to five inches...

...and connect the lines near the bottom of the design.

I like to finish the line to a sharp point.

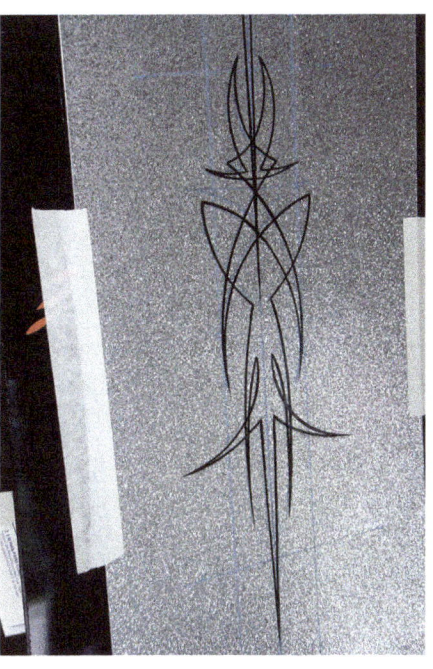

Okay now, all the black is done. Here's the completed design waiting for some red accents.

This triangular piece was part of the design scheduled for black, but while we were painting I skipped it, I thought it might be better in red.

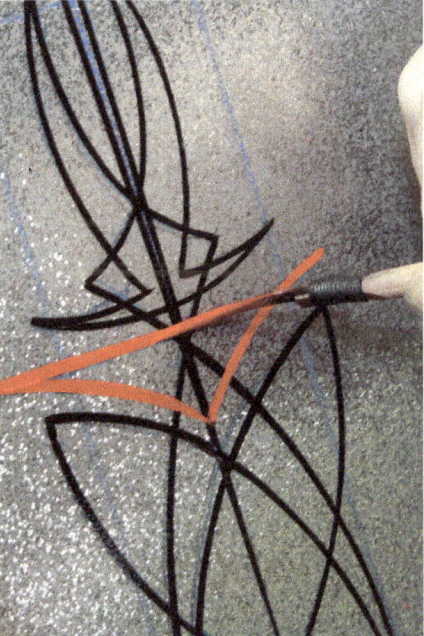

After the two curved pieces are done I add the horizontal line.

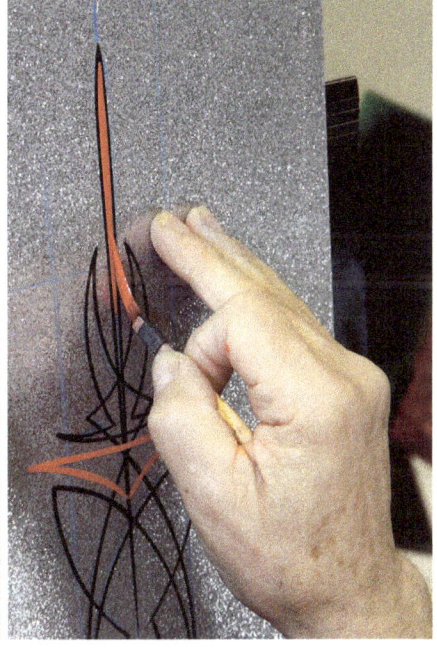

I add red to the large teardrop shape. Now it looks like it's outlined in black. To me this is the focal point of the design.

I add a solid red teardrop shape in the center lower portion of the design, smaller and shorter than the one at the top.

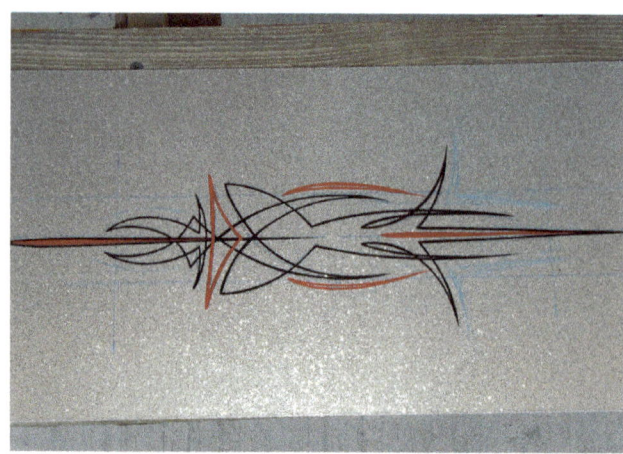

So far the design looks good, but it needs a little tweaking.

I notice that I need to make some adjustments. I do this now before going any further, so I don't forget about it.

I decide to add two double lines at the bottom on the outside of the design to help with the overall balance. I sketch them in first with a stabilo pencil.

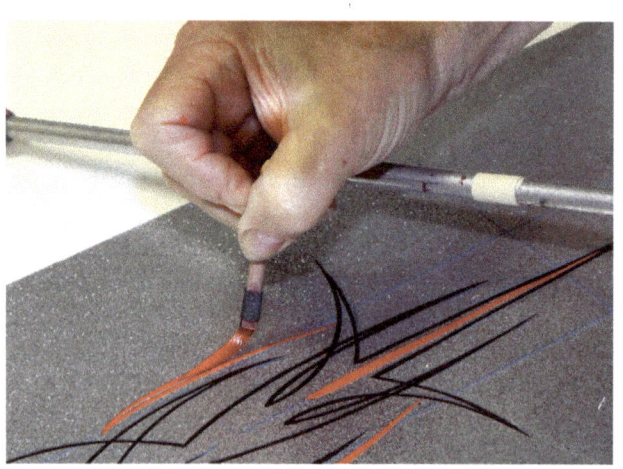

I'm back to red. I put a feather type shape on the outside, near the middle.

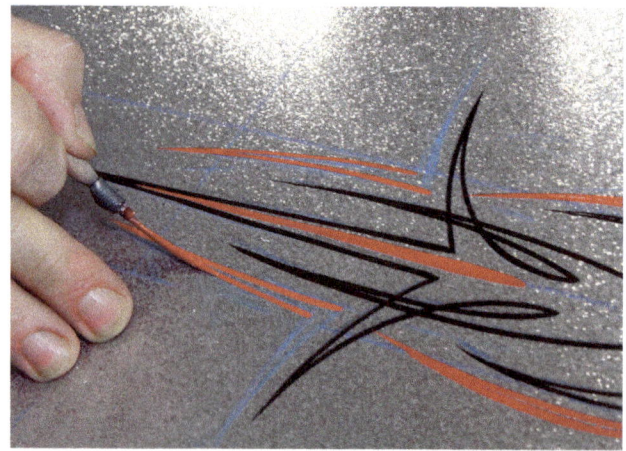

Here you see the same lines done on the other side...

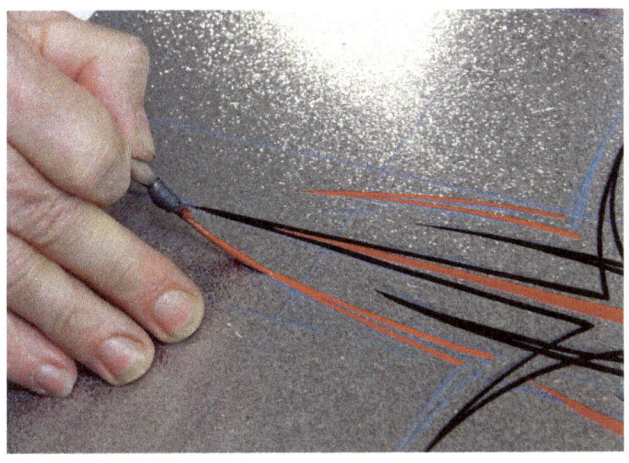

...and how they come down to a point.

Here I decide to add a red border stripe around the outside of the panel.

Next I connect these two lines at the top and swing each line with a slight curve outward to another point.

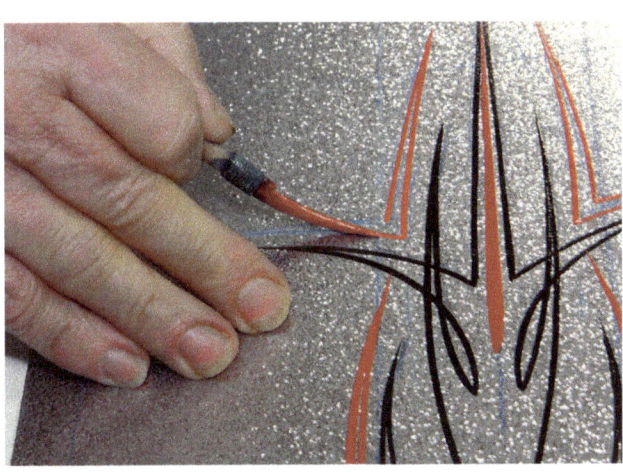

This picture shows the connection point on the inside and how it's pulled toward the outside. This also completes the design work.

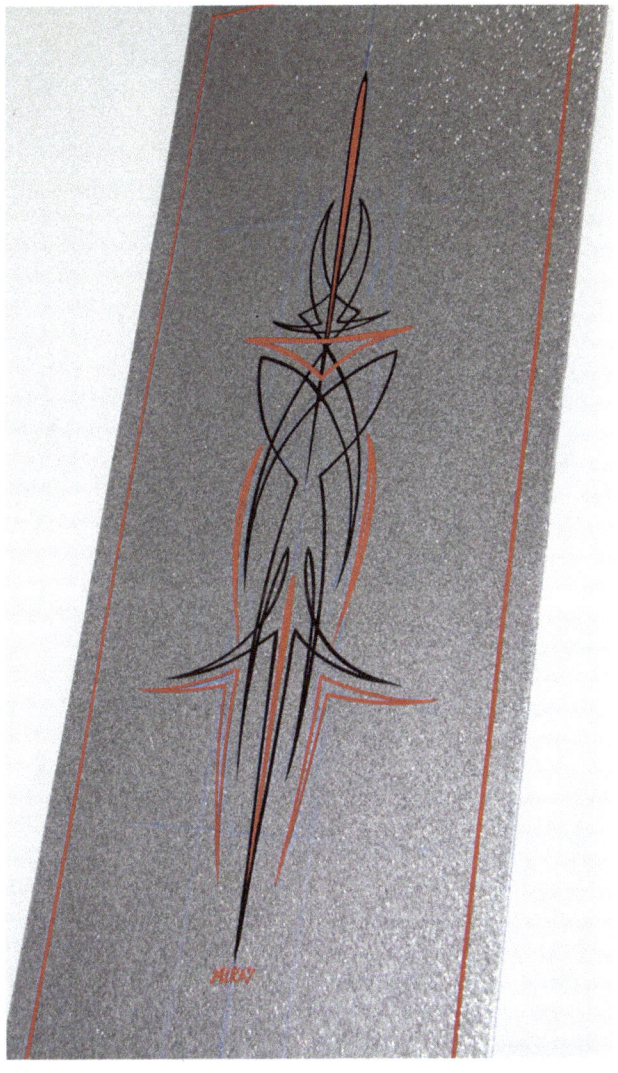

The completed panel.

Captions by Mikey

Chapter Five
Howie's Panel

And Now...

We could title this chapter with the cliche, "Now, for Something Completely Different," because this panel from Howie Nisgor is all of that. And, in this case, different is definitely a good thing.

Howie's panel is different in the sense that the design itself is unique and unlike anything seen in this book or any other. The panel is unusual in that it combines a wide range of techniques, from masking, to gold leaf, to shading, and pinstripes.

Howie didn't just whip this up in five minutes of contemplation. A professional, Howie planned this out ahead of time and showed up at our little "panel jam" with the design set in stone and the masking panel already created.

Once Howie had the base design sketched out, there was still a lot of work to do. First the creation of the multi-colored background panel. Next, the gold leaf - which he burnished, followed by the many steps needed to paint the two diamonds, followed in turn by various stages of pinstriping. This one is quite complex, much like the artist.

Using "Design Master" spray paint, I create a rainbow fade. This is followed by pearl "bagging." (Note the same technique shown again on page 56.)

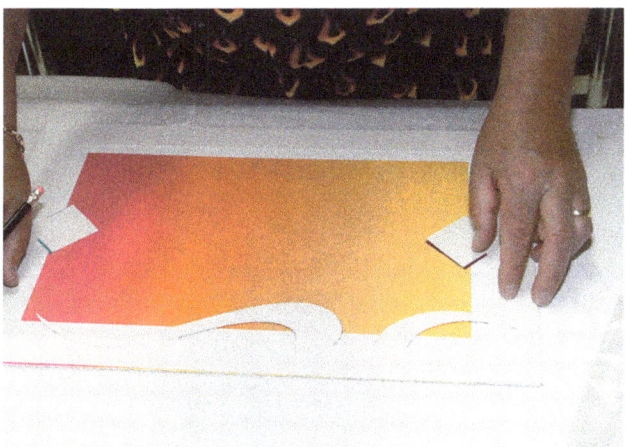

A tag board pattern is traced with a #8041 Blue Stabilo pencil to mark key design elements.

I mask a border for gold leaf with 3M painters tape...

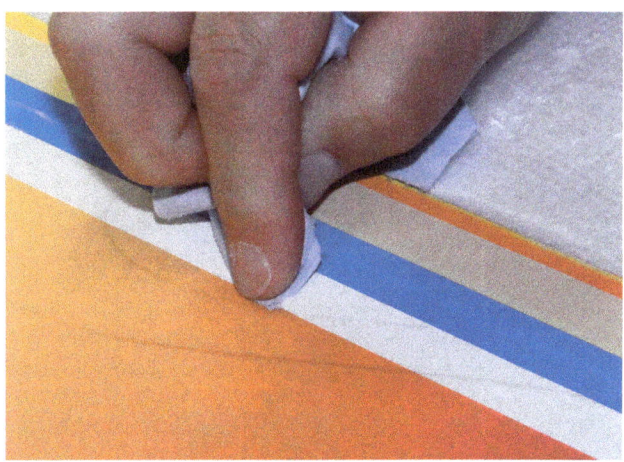

...and clean the area with alcohol before it is gilded.

Brushes: Kustom Shop SW-0, Mack 10 Series – 000, Dick Blick Eclipse – 1/16", Dick Blick Masterstroke Quill

Paint: Design Master spray paint, 1-Shot Lettering Enamel/Clear Overcoat, Kustom Shop E-Z Flow Fast Size

Wax & Grease Remover: DuPont Prepsol – 3919 S

Gold Leaf: Crocodile Double X 23K Gold

Artist Comments: I have used this style of panel with a color fade and involved black border many times. They are most often used for presentation type pieces, such as this one created for my friend of many years, East Coast Artie. Each time I have displayed one a fellow pinstriper says "I know a guy who paints panels like that!"

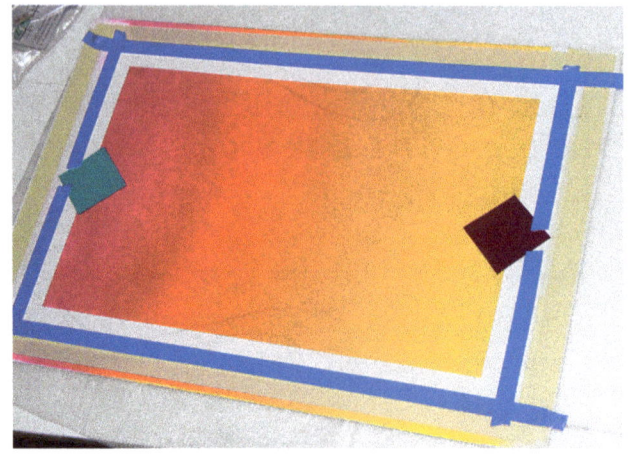

The panel is now ready for size.

Note the finished size application showing blank areas to be used for the overlay black border.

Gold leaf fast size from Kustom Shop is mixed with chrome yellow paint, for visibility.

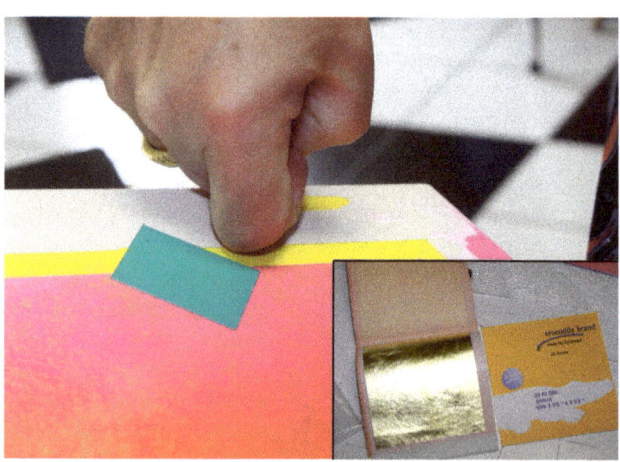

I check the size, with my knuckle - before applying the gold leaf, to ensure that it has just the right degree of tackiness. It should snap, but not lift off.

Applying the sizing with a brown quill.

Gold Leaf is applied one sheet at a time and will stick only to the "sized" areas.

There will be some excess gold leaf, and this is rubbed off with sterile cotton, rubbed in one direction only.

The colored jewels are masked and filled with K. C. Teal.

The swirls are done using a spinner made of padding covered with velvet, producing an engine-turned effect.

The tape is removed while the paint is still wet.

The finish should be made up of equally sized swirls, and then clear coated after 24 hours.

Mixing Pearl Powder into the clear.

53

The transparency of the pearl mix can be seen on my palette.

This shows the jewel masked for a beveled finish.

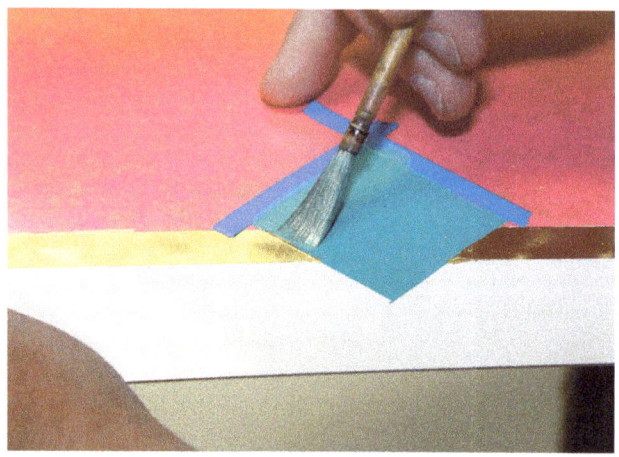

The entire "jewel", or diamond, is coated with the pearl mix.

A dark glaze is applied to the lower sides.

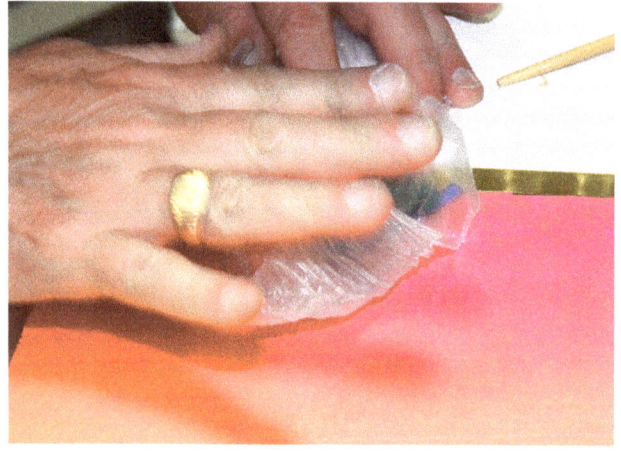

While wet, the jewel is "bagged" using a plastic bag, which leaves a marble pattern.

The pearl mix is ready for the marble finish.

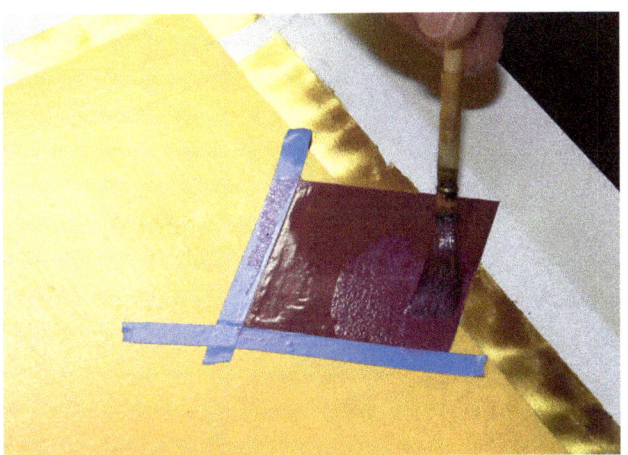

Pearl Glaze being applied.

Applying a blue-violet (created by mixing purple and peacock blue) inside the border of the gold leaf.

Bagging again with a plastic bag or Saran-type plastic wrap.

Outlining the border design in process blue, bridging the line with a Kustom Shop striping brush.

Time now to clear coat the gold leaf.

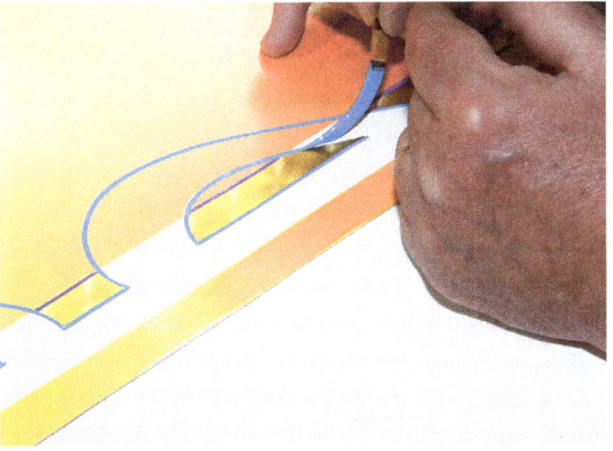

I roll the brush to maintain a consistent width of the stripe.

Continuing the outline, two-handed style.

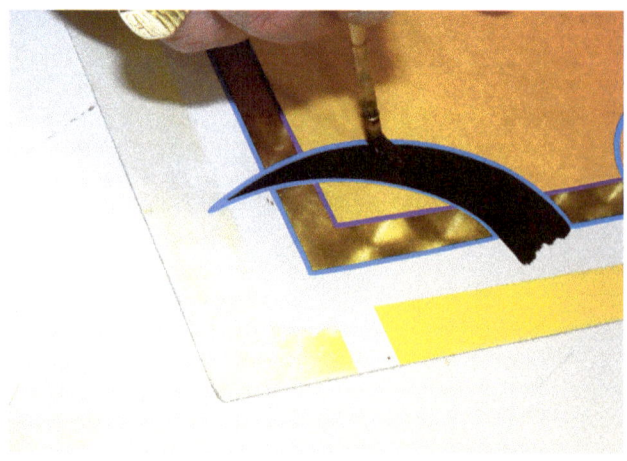
Starting to back fill the black border.

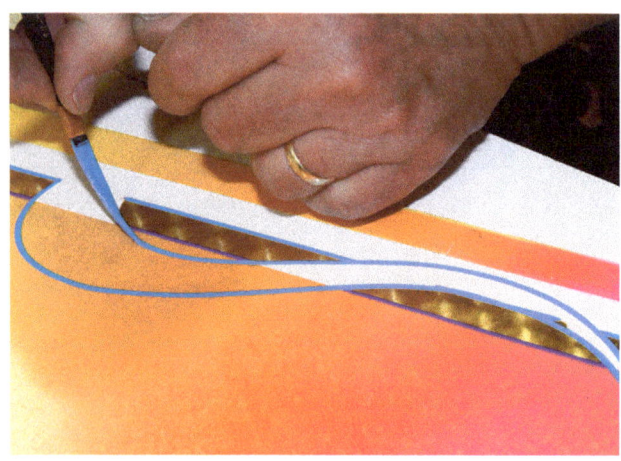
Rolling the brush again.

Here's the border as it continues to be filled.

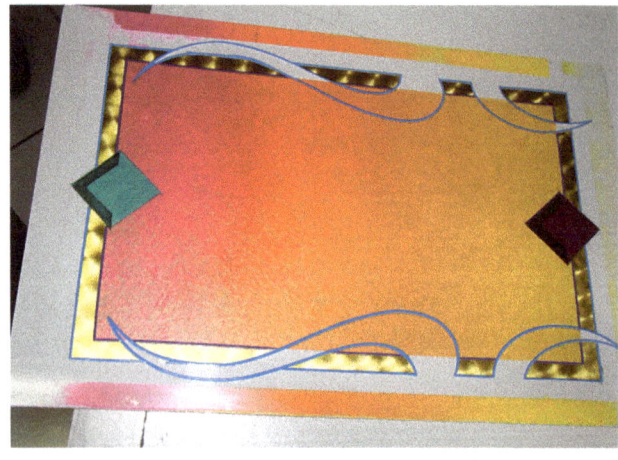
The completed outline showing the areas that overlap with the Gold Leaf.

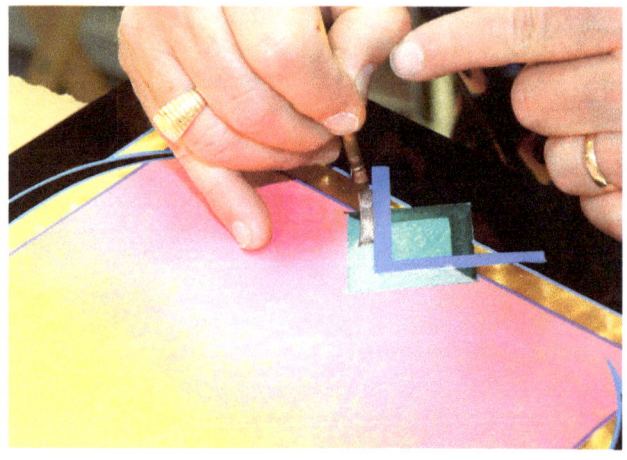
A white-tinted glaze is applied to the top sides of the jewel.

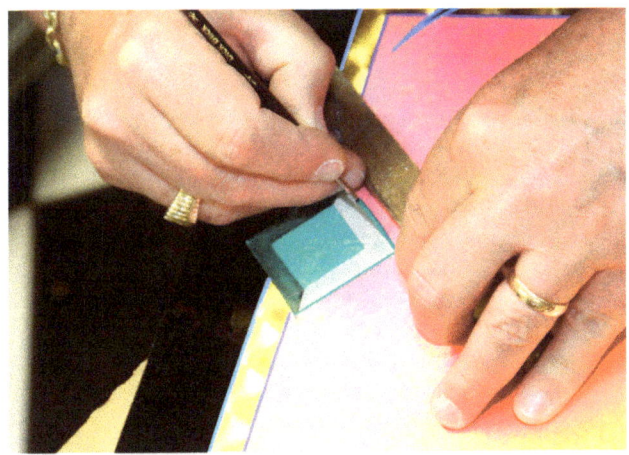

An outline is added using a 1/16 inch Dick Blick eclipse #4840002 brush.

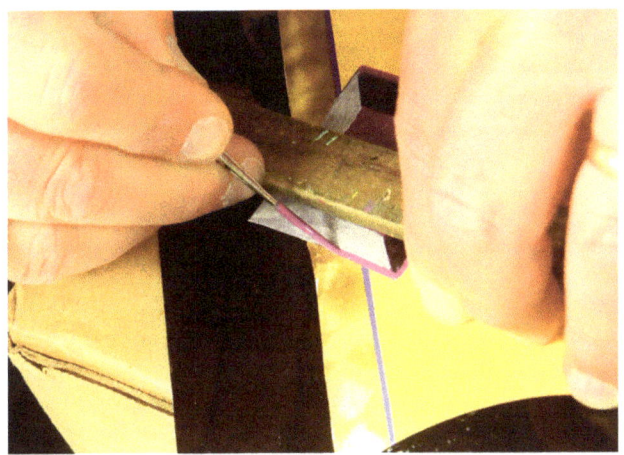

Here I begin to outline the jewel...

The outline stripe is done in the original K.C. Teal.

...then finish with white dot highlight.

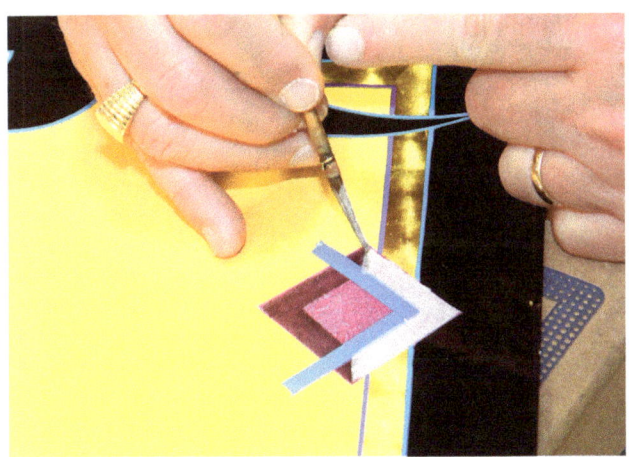

The dark magenta jewel gets the same treatment.

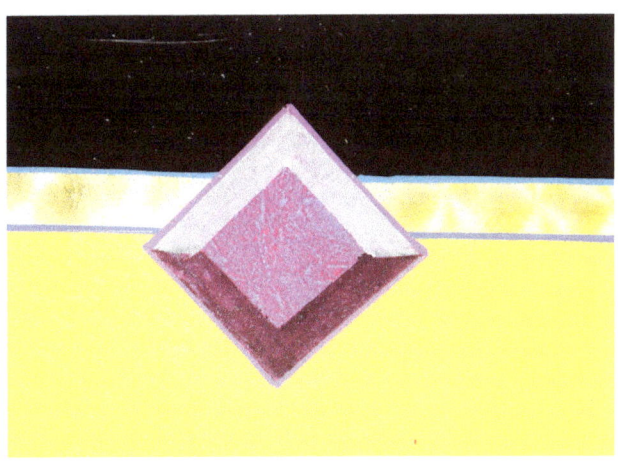

...to create the finished jewel.

Creating a center grid for a personalized design.

Here the Artie design is darkened with a Stabilo pencil.

The central design is a mirror image of "Artie" done in a #2 pencil on both sides of a piece of tracing paper (turn the page sideways to see the "Artie").

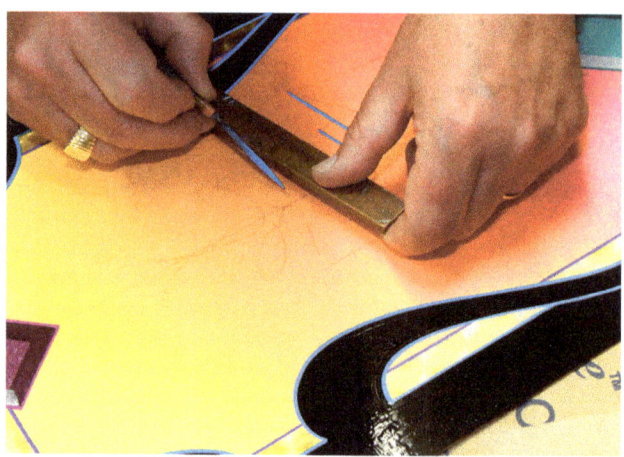

Now I'm starting to paint the design...

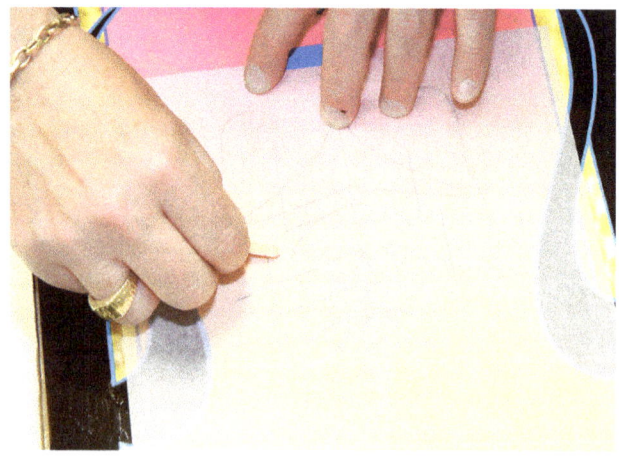

Design is rubbed from the back side using a wooden mixing stick. Transferring the design to the panel.

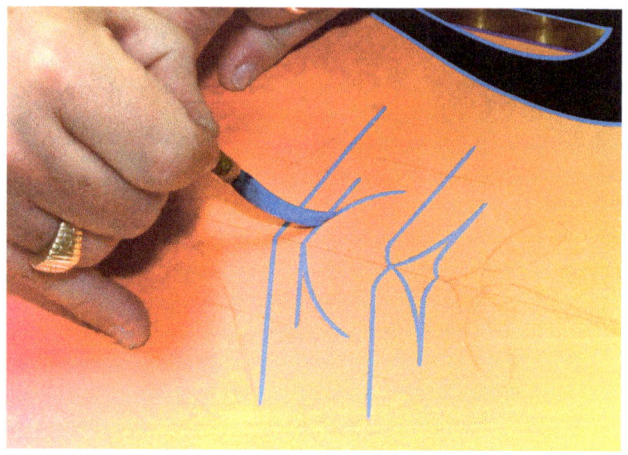

...using a striping brush.

The name is beginning to take shape.

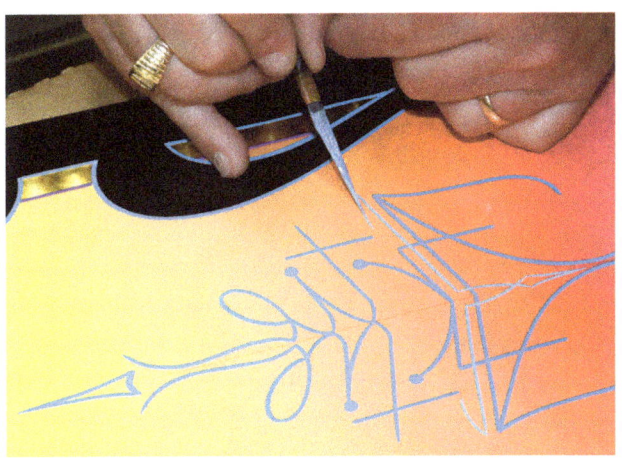

The new design follows areas already created.

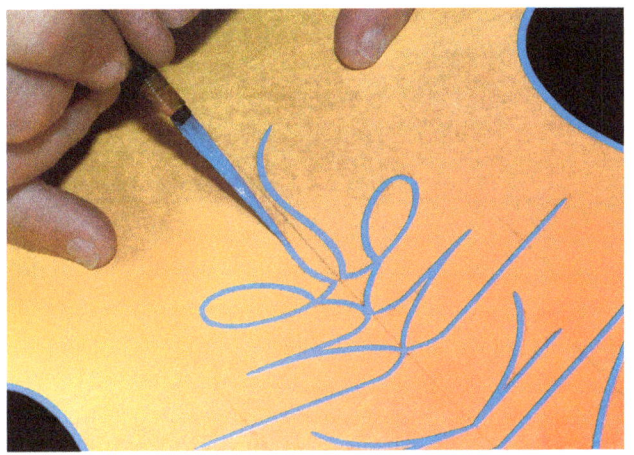

Finishing the central name section of the design.

The second color echoes existing shapes, and creates new ones.

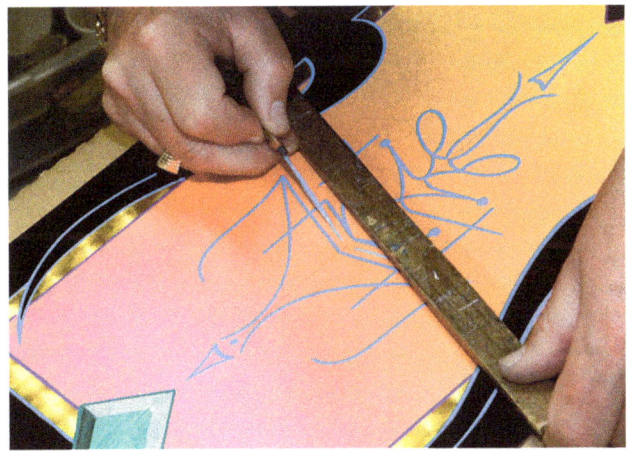

Changing to peacock blue, I weave a second layer of stripes.

Expanding the peacock design into the outer central panel area.

I continue to build the design.

…to allow for…

With the peacock blue.

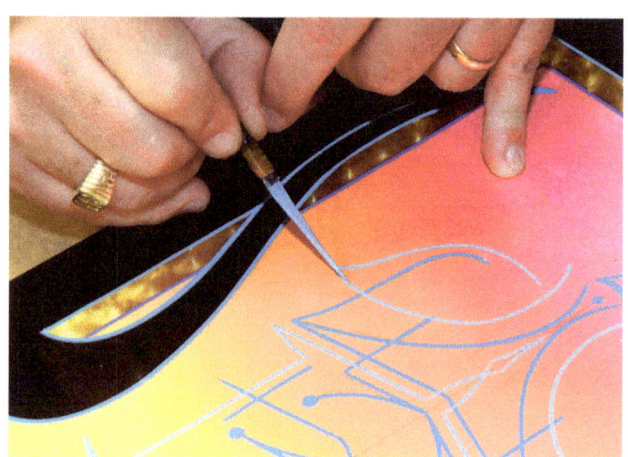

…more lines to follow.

Here I create negative open spaces…

I always pallet the paint with a little thinner to maintain the proper consistency.

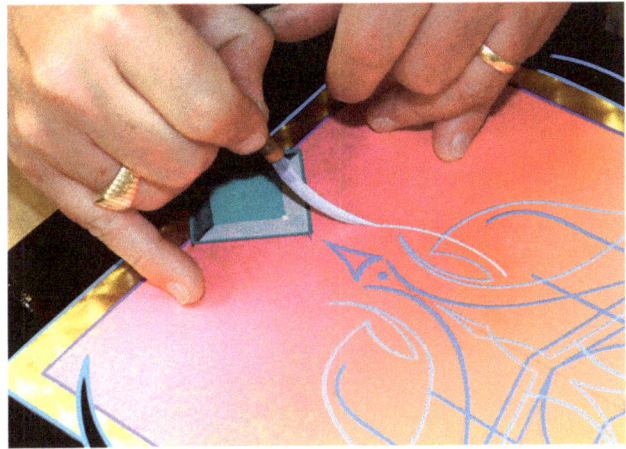

The third layer of the design is being done in robin's egg blue.

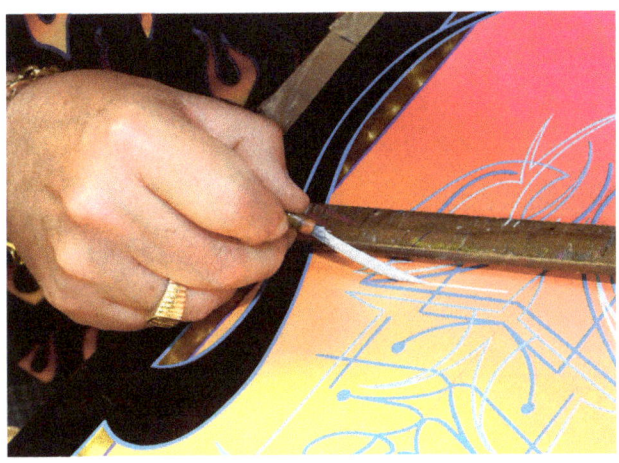

...outward...

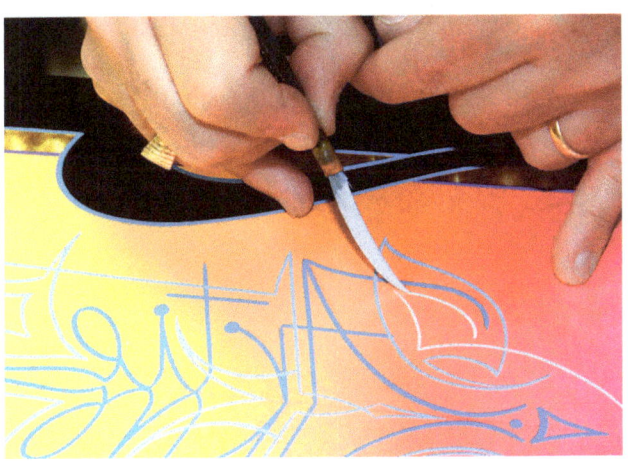

The beginning of this stage is more open in nature.

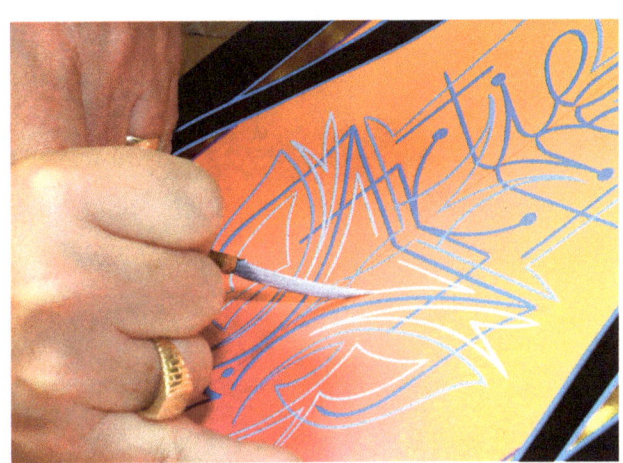

...with the...

Now I'm expanding the total design area...

...new robin's egg blue.

Here I move to the other side, creating new open areas...

Still working with...

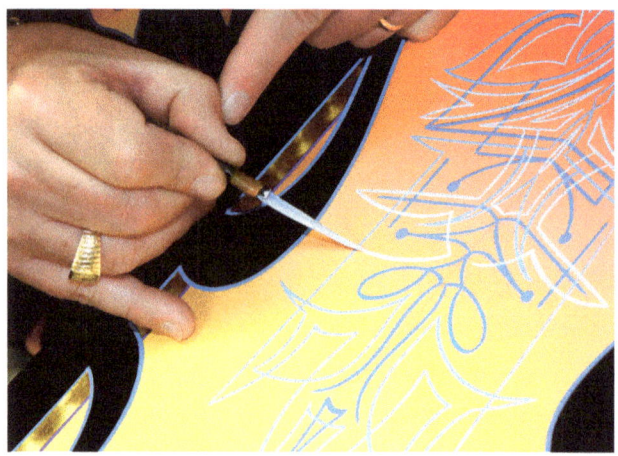

...and then weave in, out, and over the existing lines.

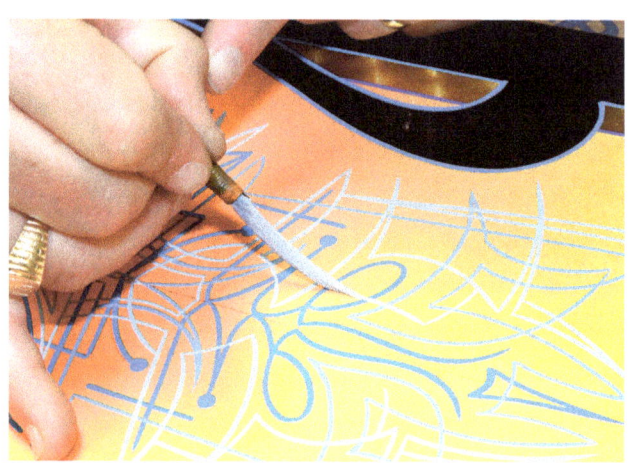

...the robin's egg blue...

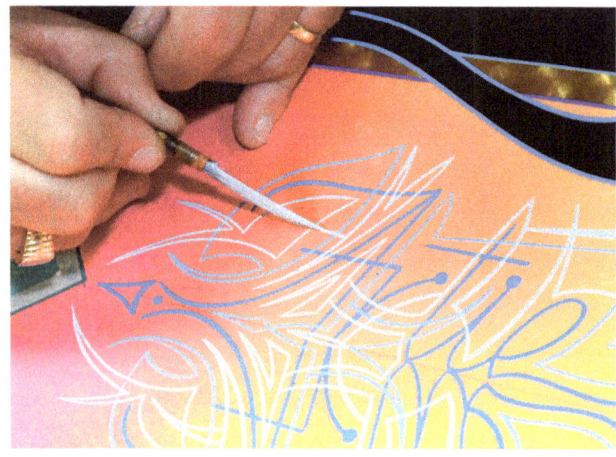

Then it's back to the other side.

...I work through the design, sometimes with rather small shapes.

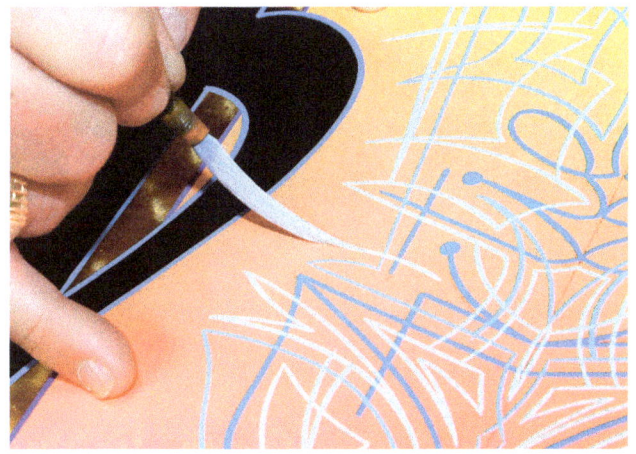

Some of my lines connect and cross other lines...

Here I run the line almost to the edge.

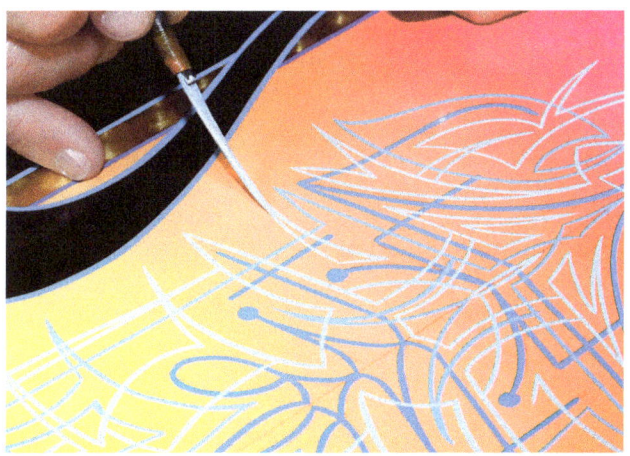

...some create small shapes that stand alone.

What I do on one side I come back and do to the other.

The completed panel, signed and waiting for a final clear coat.

Captions by Howie

Chapter Six

Howie's Gold Wing

Stripes for the Wing Nut

If the panel that Howie created in Chapter five seems a little over the top, the striping job seen here is the kind of day-in day-out project that stripers have always faced.

As is often the case, Howie grids out the area he's about to stripe, before any paint goes on. And like most stripers out there, he's careful to wipe down the whole bike with what he calls a "triple cleanup."

Other than the cream spears, this is a one-color striping job, done with an orange tint that compliments the bike's bronze color. It's a tasteful, clean design that flows nicely from the front to the back of this three-wheeled Honda.

Howie calls this a "bread and butter" job. It's also a good example of a design that's both simple and elegant, one that looks like it belongs on this Honda.

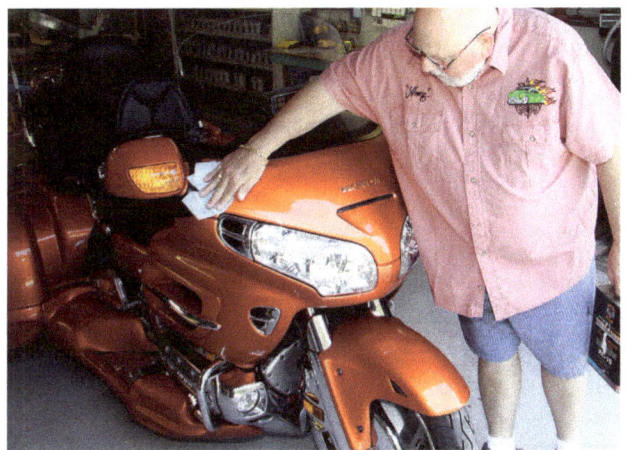

Following a triple cleanup of: 1) Windex 2) wax and grease remover 3) rubbing alcohol, I'm ready to start.

Brushes: Kustom Shop SW-00

Paint: One-Shot Lettering Enamels

Tape: 3M Painters Tape

Wax & Grease Remover:
1) Windex
2) Kustom Shop Prep-Sol
3) Rubbing Alcohol

Other:
White Stabilo Pencil #8052

Artist Comments:
This is an example of what I call a "Bread & Butter", standard striping job. I try to repeat elements of the design to maintain continuity throughout. In this case, I repeat the two color teardrops and basic shapes.

Using a white Stabilo pencil #8052, I find the center and create a grid.

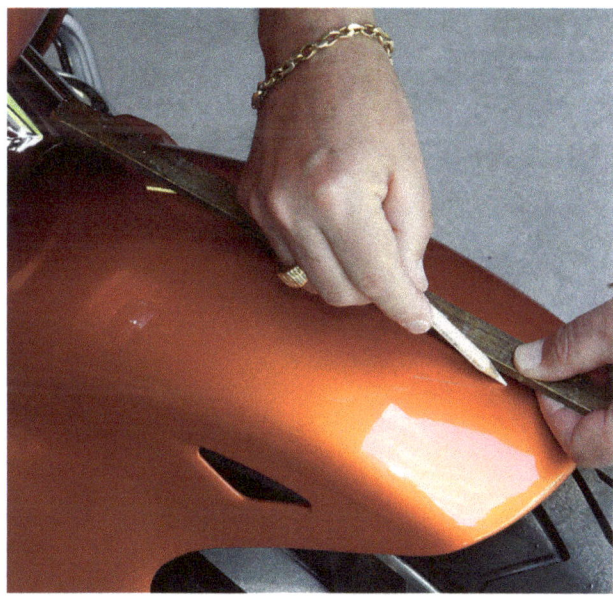

Grids are marked using: the GRD by Kafka, the Stripe A Line Grid System from Sign Technique, or my (20 year old) hand painting stick.

Here are the upper and lower finished grids.

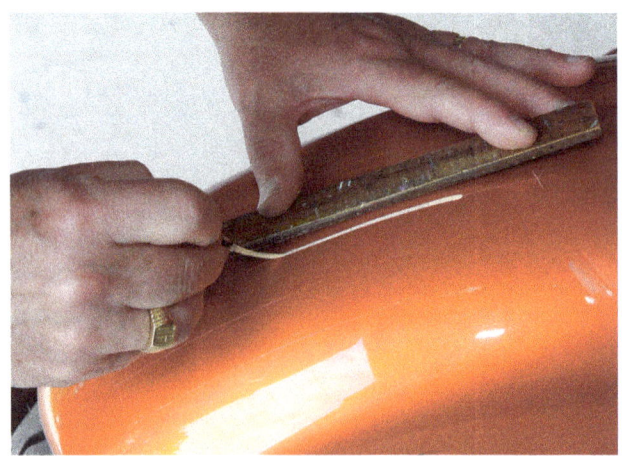

I'm starting an ivory teardrop on the fender by "bridging" the line.

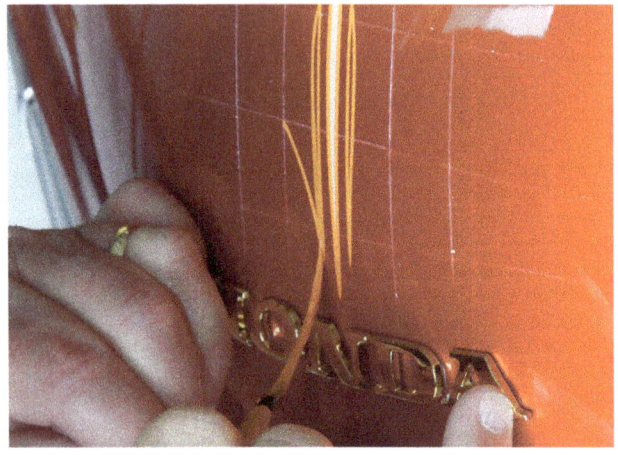

Being right handed, I try to always start designs on the left.

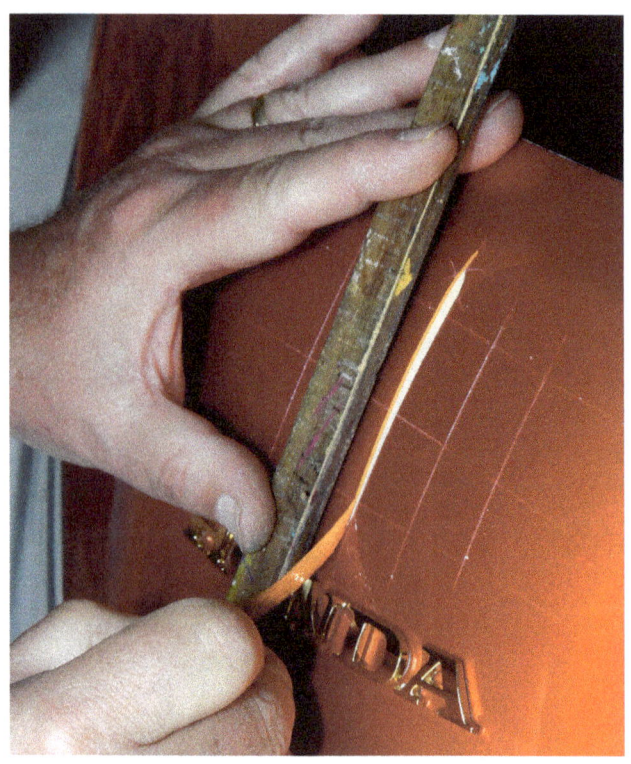

Outlining a teardrop on the fairing with a custom mixed, soft orange...

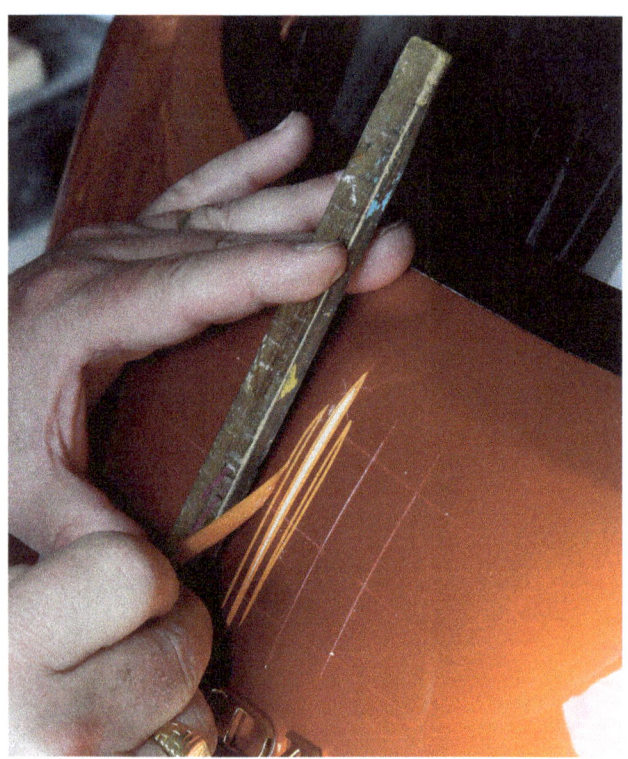

....creating a pair of teardrops to match those on the fender.

The design grows slowly - line by line.

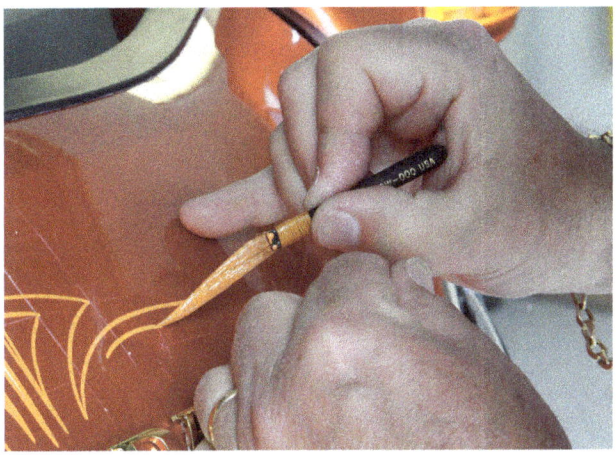

I'm using the two handed method for support.

First the left side, then the right.

Touching up the lower left corner.

Using the transition stroke to expand the design horizontally.

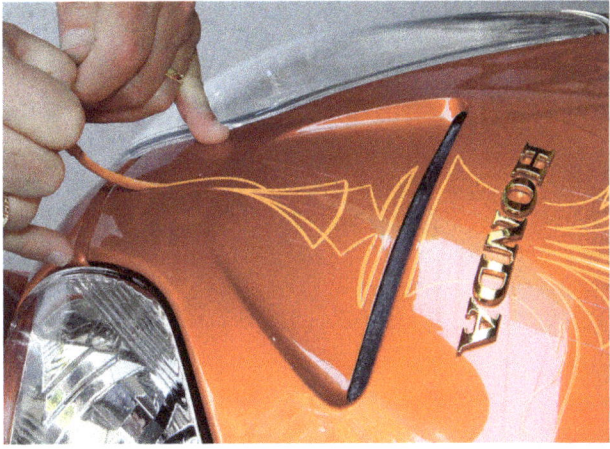

Adding a design to the lower half of the fairing using my pinky fingers for support.

Starting a marching teardrop for the front fender.

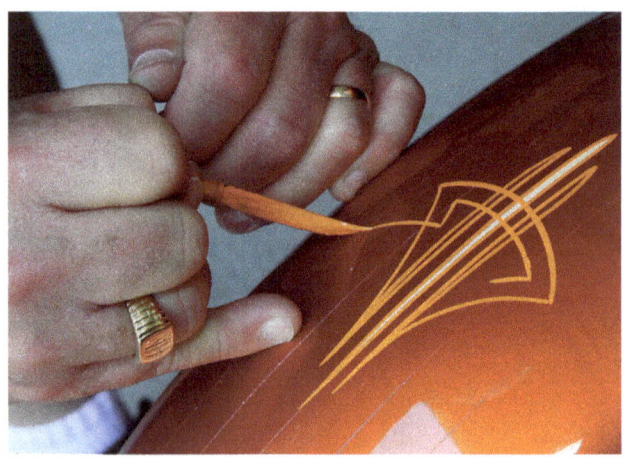

Continuing the design, I try to create an interesting negative space.

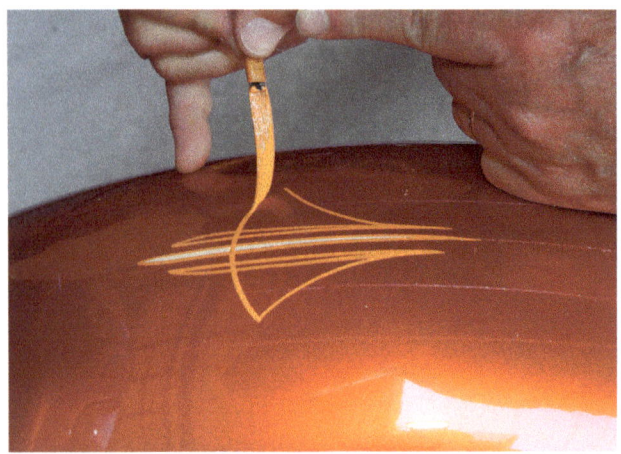

I keep the design similar to the fairing.

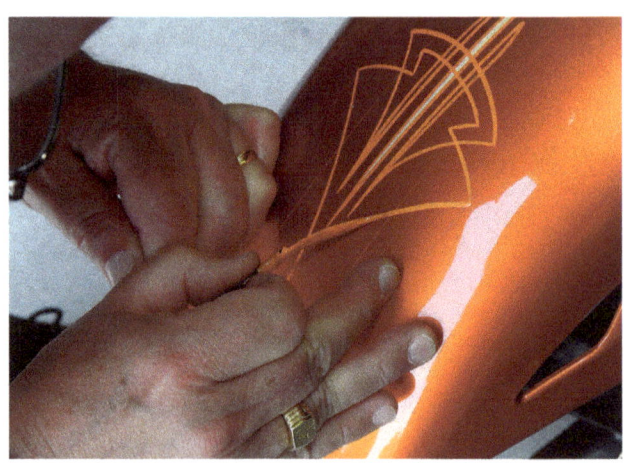

I am rolling the brush between my fingers to maintain a line of consistent weight.

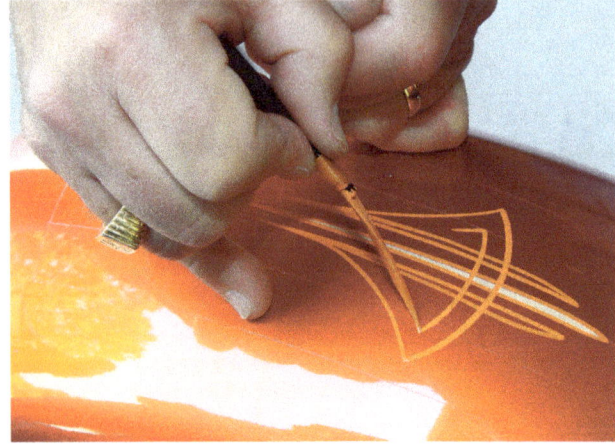

First the left, then the right again.

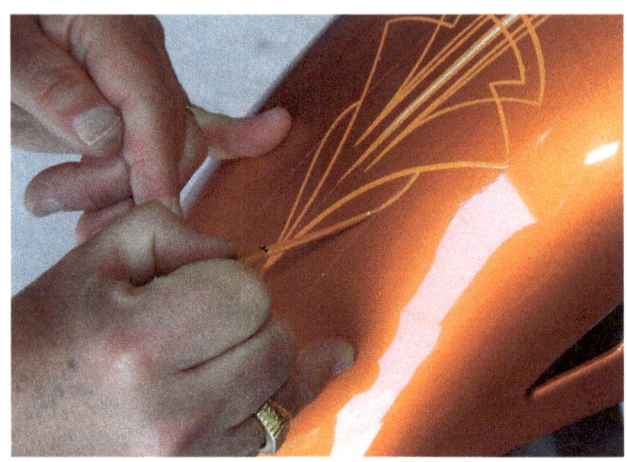

Almost done…

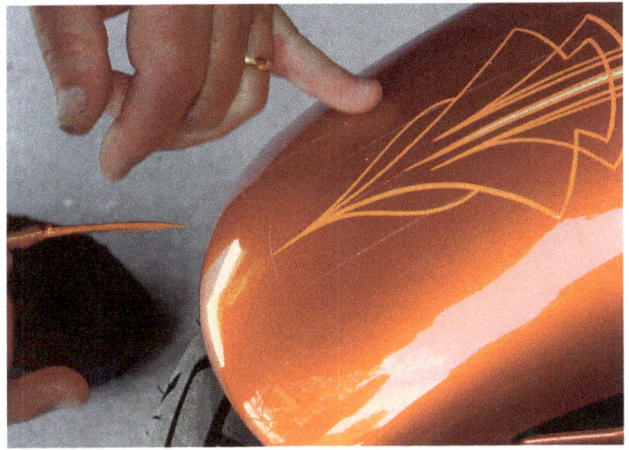
…done!

Matching open teardrops.

Starting the ivory teardrop on the rear fender.

Using the transition stroke to move vertically this time.

Orange outline.

Continuing to expand the design.

The rear fender designs are mirror images to each other, but are not symmetrical.

This time I used a straight line to create horizontal movement within the design.

Rolling the brush again for the finishing stroke to this design.

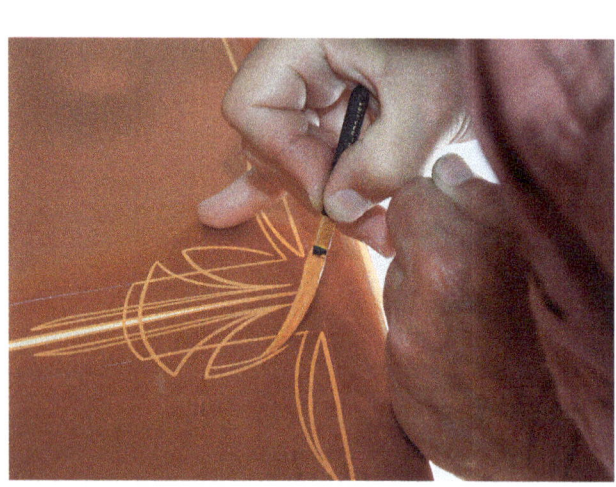

Symmetrical design on the top of the rear tour pack.

Here is the finished design on the lower trunk, located below a custom emblem done by East Coast Artie.

Captions by Howie

Q&A: Howie

Tell us a little about yourself, and how you became a striper?

I stared when I was 13 years old, I was drawing and drawing and trying to stripe. I found a #4 Mack brush early on that I liked, and that helped. I read what I could because, at that time, none of the stripers would talk to me. Eventually I progressed to T-shirt painting, and by 15 I was striping at car shows, by 17 I was in the magazines. I just kept practicing and improving. In addition to striping I was an art teacher for 35-1/2 years.

What do you like to do when you don't have a customer looking over your shoulder?

I like to go old skool, it's a nice rebirth. And just because it's old skool doesn't mean it has to be sloppy. Old skool work can be just as precise as modern striping.

What do you like to use for brushes?

I was a Grumbacher guy for a long time. Now I mostly use a Series Ten Mack, and also Xcaliber, and Dick Blick Eclipse Kustom Shop.

What do you like for paint?

I'm an old dog so I like One-Shot. I can stripe with anything, but One-Shot is my first choice.

When you're doing something like a panel, do you plan it out ahead of time or just work on the fly?

It depends on what I'm doing. With a gallery piece I plan it out very carefully. At a Panel Jam you can't plan at all. I always start with a grid though, no matter what.

Are there absolutes in terms of design, in terms of placement and how many times a line can cross another line?

I would say there are no rules, or if there are, they were made to be broken. I often start with a teardrop, work on the left side first, then replicate that on the right side. It's easier for me this way because I'm right handed. The design should have enough negative space so there's background showing through. Otherwise you can't see the stripes - all you see is the color behind the stripes.

Who inspires you, where do you get your ideas?

Early influences were Von Dutch and Larry Watson. Closer to home, there's Andy Southard, one of our local heroes, also Kenny the Mad Striper, and Vic Kessler.

How do you pick colors, and how did you learn to mix colors to match a certain color?

I use the strongest color first, the color with the greatest degree of contrast, and then follow with any additional colors. In terms of mixing colors, the color wheel is one of the best tools in the world. The other way to mix color is mono chromatic; that is, you tint the color lighter or darker with white or black.

Any final words of wisdom?

If you're trying to learn how to stripe, take advantage of stripers who will talk to you, I couldn't do that. Whenever I teach pinstriping classes I use a series of seven basic strokes. And practice, practice, practice. Master each step before going on to the next.

Howie Nisgor started pinstriping in high school, and all these years later he's still a pinstriper at heart.

Chapter Seven
Artie's Paint Kit Case
Four-Sided Art

The fact that Art Schilling - aka East Coast Artie - is the master of many different styles of "pinstriping" is well documented in this project, which is really five projects in one. That's because Artie, being Artie, did each panel of this paint kit in a different style. Yes, the side panels all have gold leaf - which ties them together, yet the panels are as different as they are alike. Each is beautiful not only because the application of the leaf is done correctly, or the because the striping is perfect, but because the underlying design is terrific. Also illustrated in this project is the importance of details, and no matter how minute - Artie gets 'em exactly right.

Like five projects in one, Artie did each side of the case in a different style, to create the nicest paint kit case anyone has ever seen.

photo: East Coast Artie

I lay out a nice design on masking vinyl and cut it out with an Xacto knife.

Next, I position the mask on the case.

Brushes: Xcaliber 0000, Mack Bobbo Super Quad, Mack Virus Striper

Paint: Kustom Shop EZ Flow Paint and fast sizing

Tape: R-tape yellow masking vinyl, variegated leaf from Coast Airbrush Supply

Wax and Grease Remover: House of Kolors wax and grease remover

Artist Comments:
This new, "traveling" style paint kit is constructed of composite aluminum/ PVC sheeting. We ground the designs into the surface of the panels, then Jimmy shot the candy yellow, orange, red, and blue paint. After clear coating, I went to work on it.

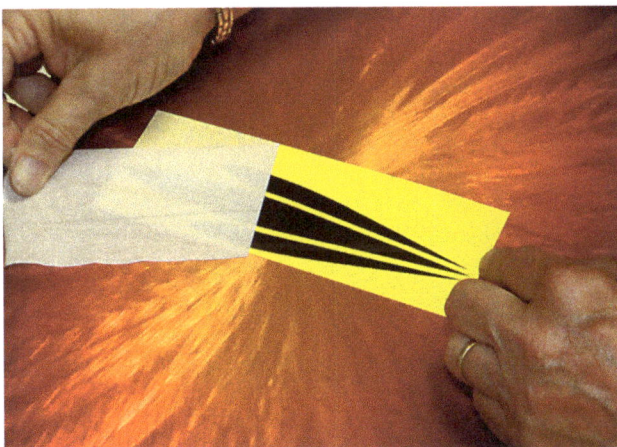

After the mask is squeegeed down, I remove the transfer paper, leaving my exposed pattern.

I apply the sizing with my bobbo brush for long, smooth coverage.

I remove the mask while the size is still wet.

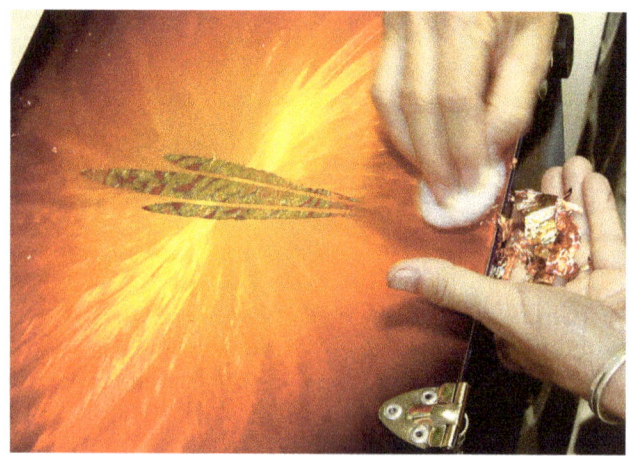

Once all the excess is removed, only the design is left.

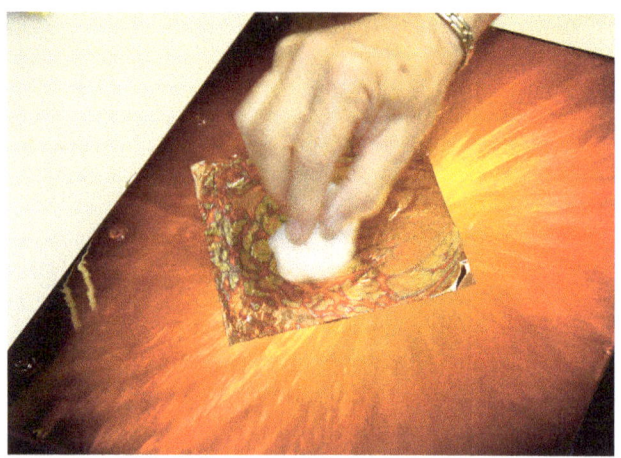

After the size is set, I lay the leaf and pat it down with cotton.

This imitation leaf is a lot more durable than real gold, so you can get away with applying more pressure.

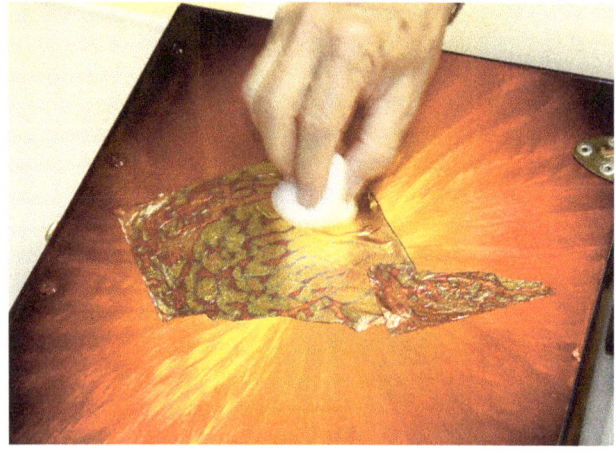

I start to break the excess leaf away with the cotton ball, so as not to contaminate it with the oil on my skin.

I then burnish the leaf down with my cotton ball to smooth it out.

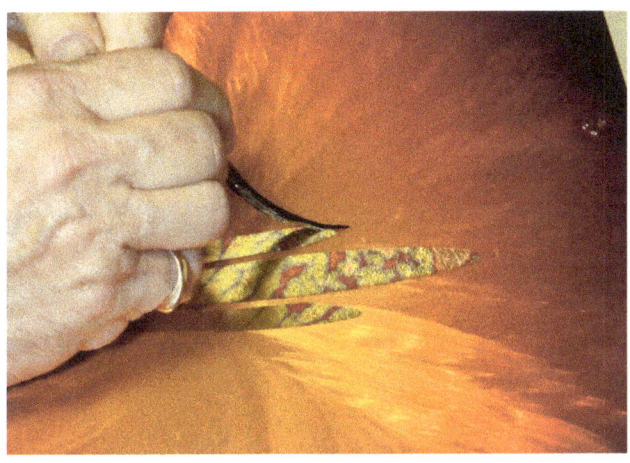

1. Using my Xcaliber brush, I start to outline the leaf.

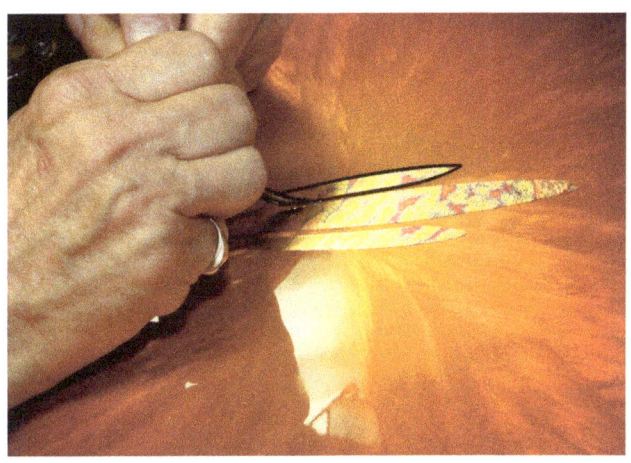

2. I overlap the leaf edge with the black paint to hold it down.

3. At this point I lay a coat of clear over the leaf and the black outline, to seal it.

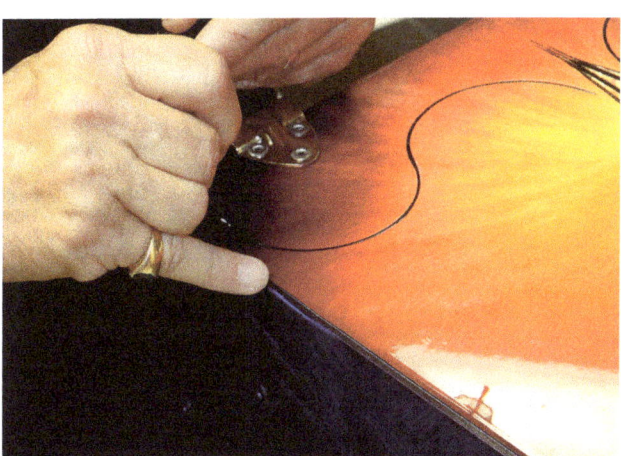

4. After my clear dries, I start my design.

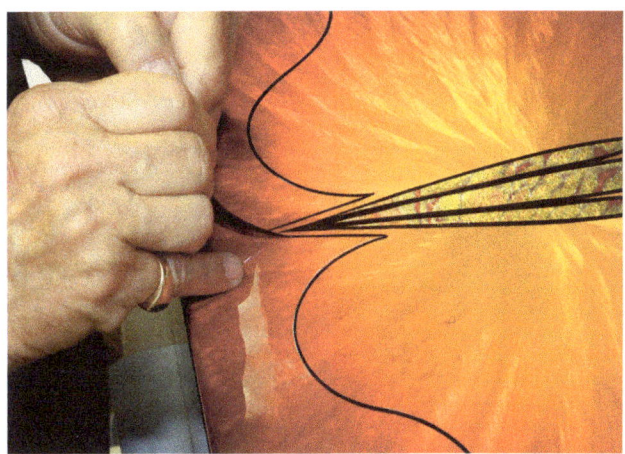

5. I'm going to keep the design simple, so it isn't distraction from the paint finish.

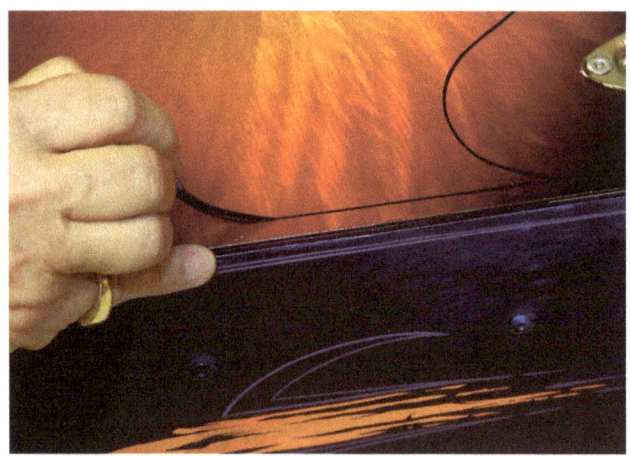

1. I carry the design up the sides to frame the front panel.

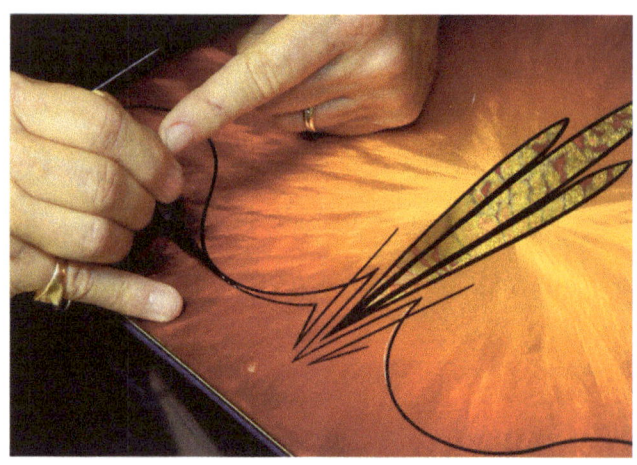

3. Almost there…

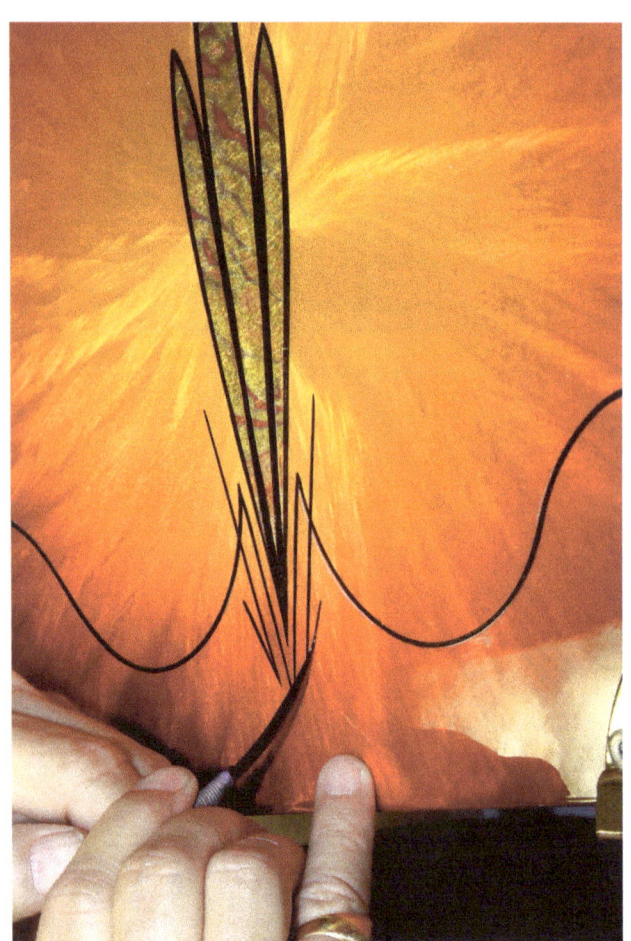

2. Now I tie things together.

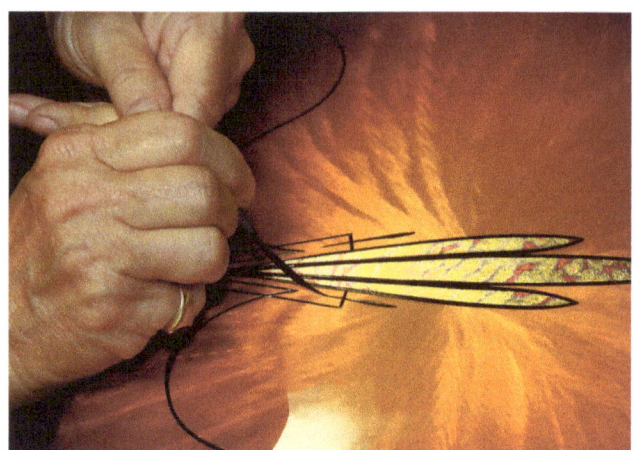

4. …Ok, ok, stop!!!

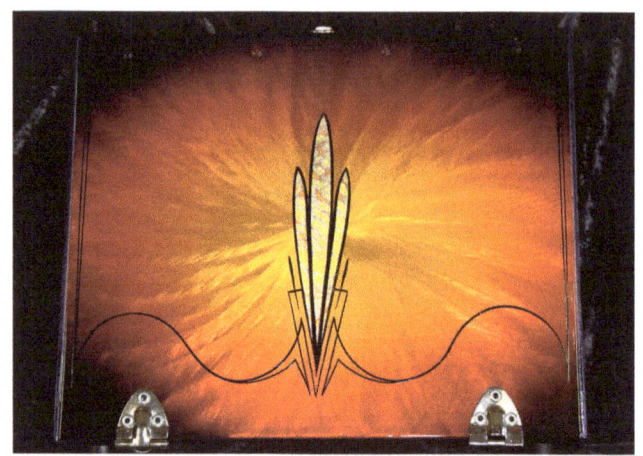

5. That's it.

Now I can get loose on this side. I free form a design and add a little yellow paint to my sizing so I can see it more easily.

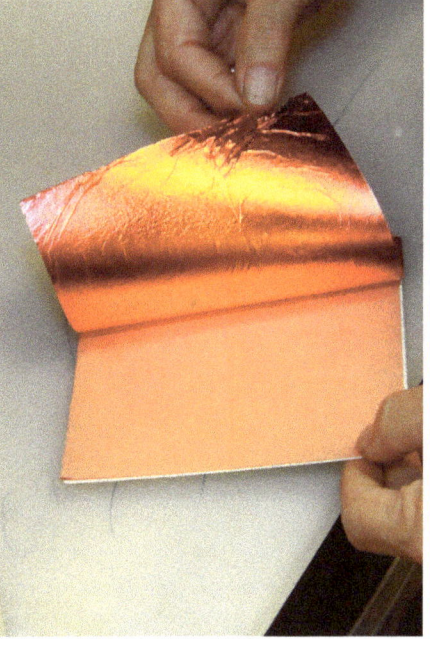

This cranberry colored leaf from Coast Airbrush Supply is pretty stuff.

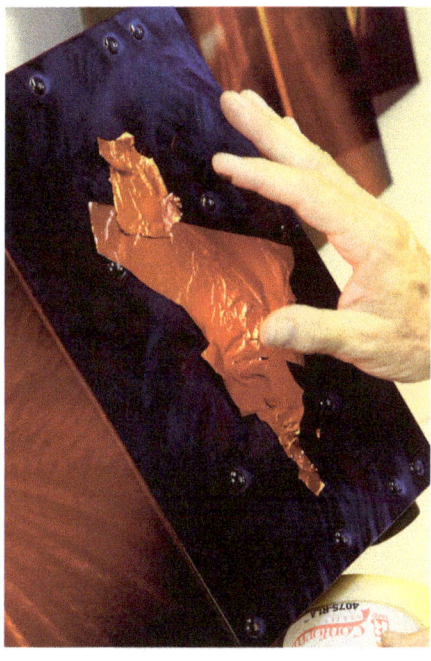

When the sizing is "squeaky" I lay the leaf into it.

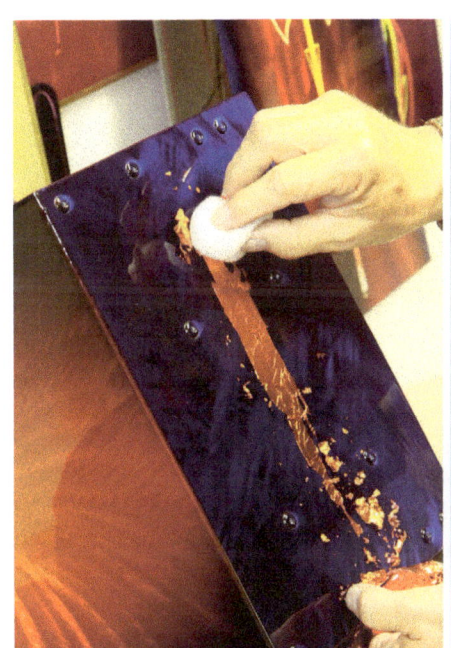

Clean off the excess leaf and burnish again with a cotton ball.

I use a paint eraser to create some breaks in my design...

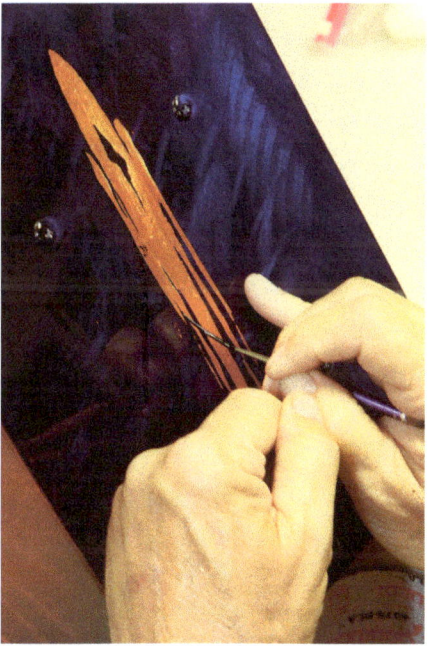

... then I use black paint and a virus brush to do the outline.

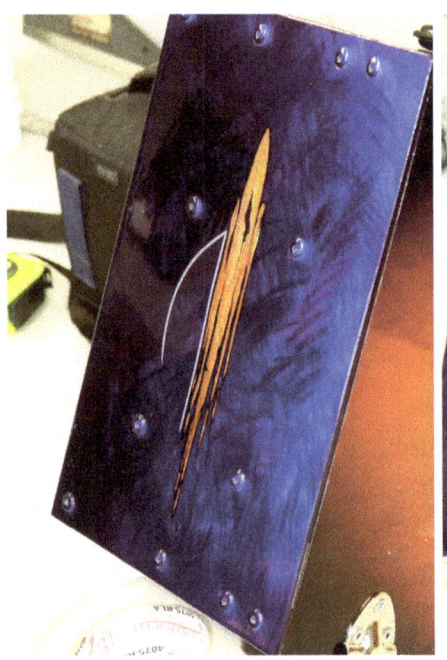

After coating with clear, I start my design.

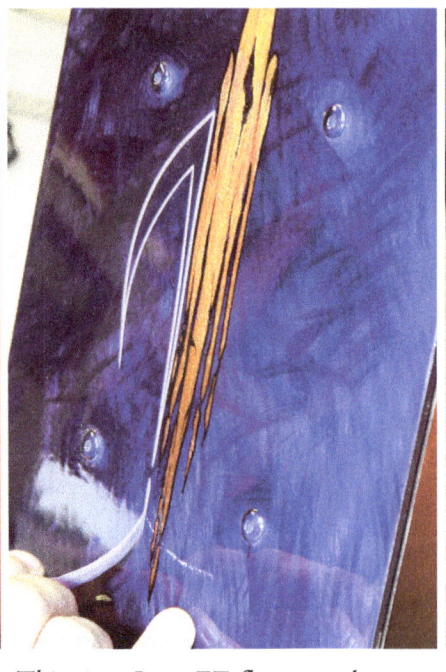

This time I use EZ flow purple.

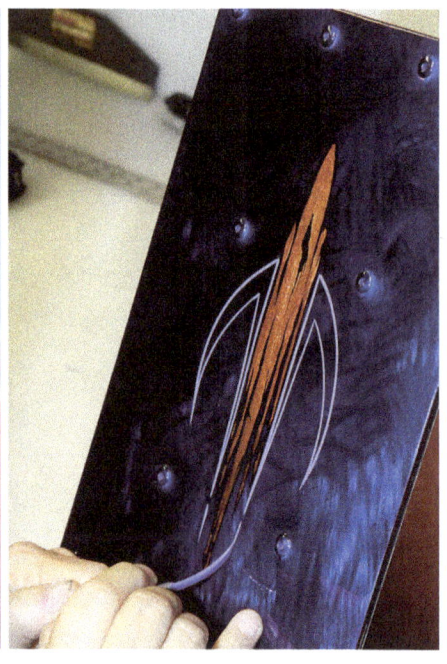

"Keep it simple." I say it time and time again. It works.

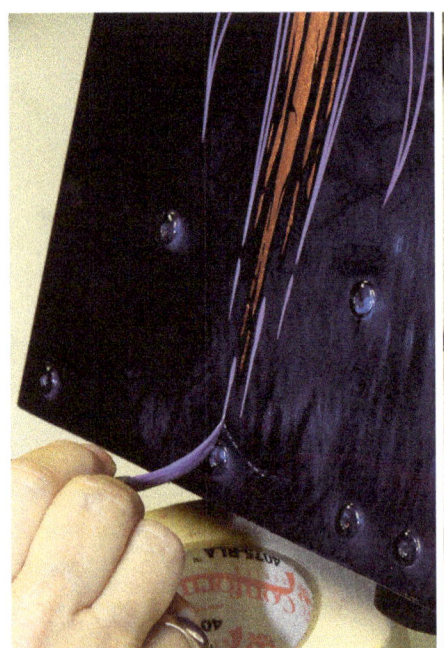

I make this an asymmetrical design by adding some off-center spears.

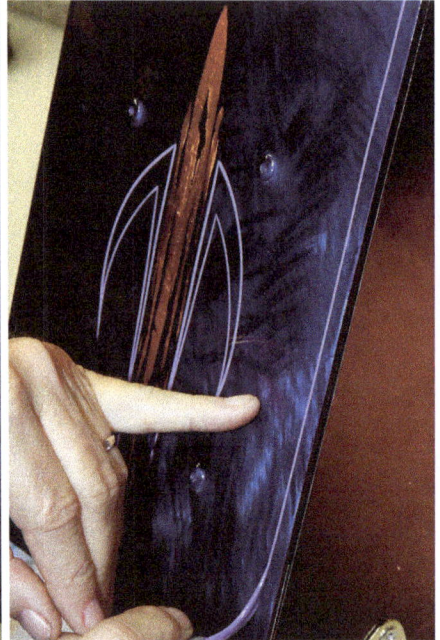

A couple of long torpedoes run down the side.

One more side finished - three to go.

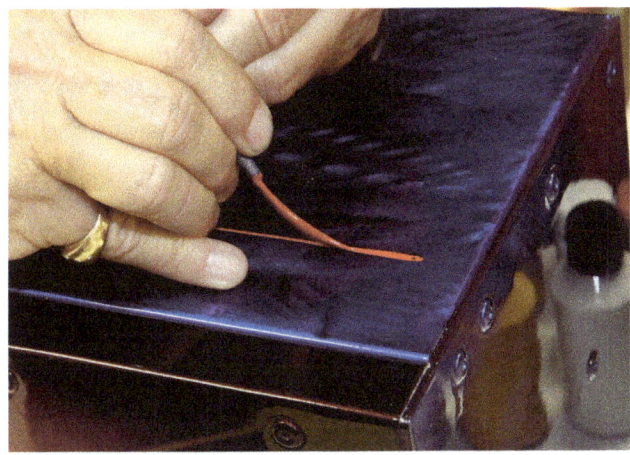

I start my top design with a couple of spears done with EZ flow indian red.

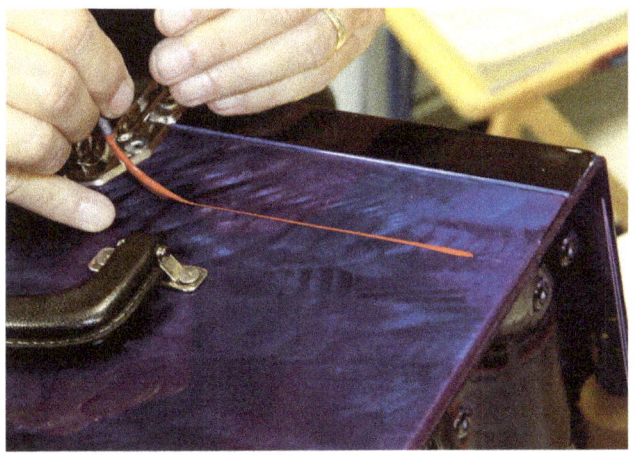

I lay my brush down, and then lift it back up as I pull this line.

Now I blend some California orange into the stripe.

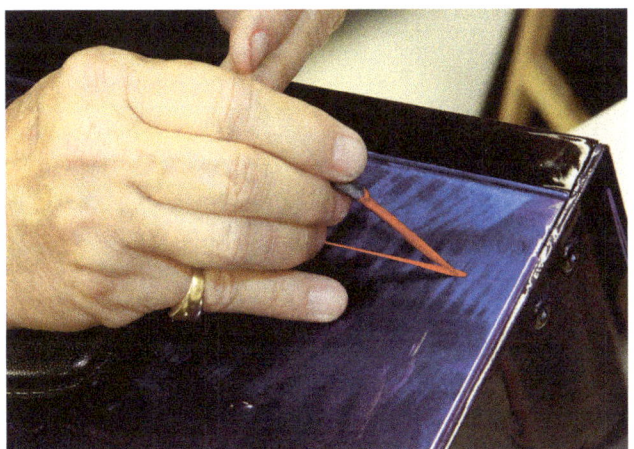

I repeat this on the other side of the handle.

A little bit of yellow in the tip lights it up.

Dry brush the yellow back into the orange while it's still wet.

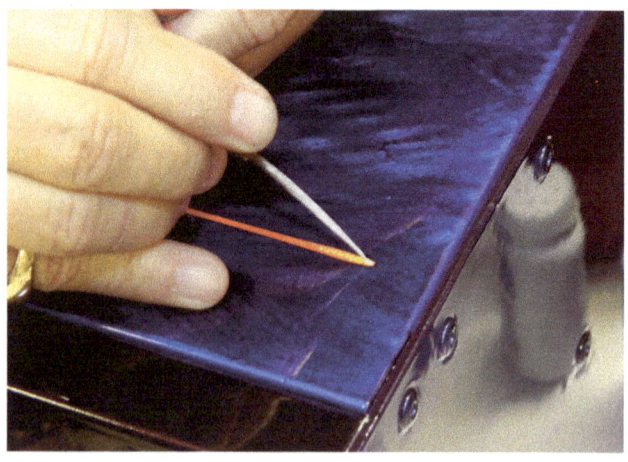

A drop of white adds a spark to the tip of the spear.

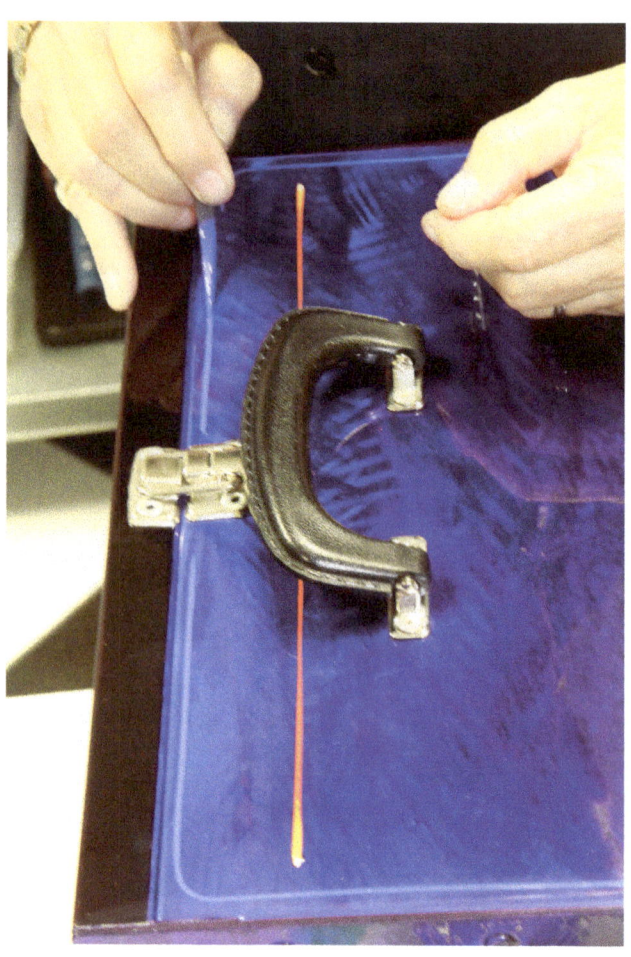

A border stripe ties the design together.

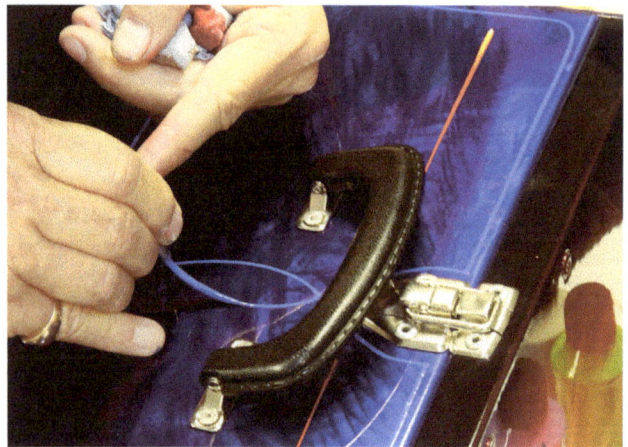

I switch over to process blue for the center of the design.

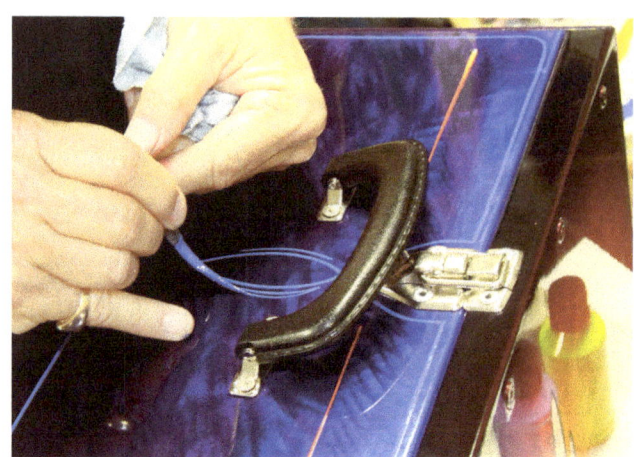

A couple of accent lines add to the central part of the design.

I add three red spears to the center of the design.

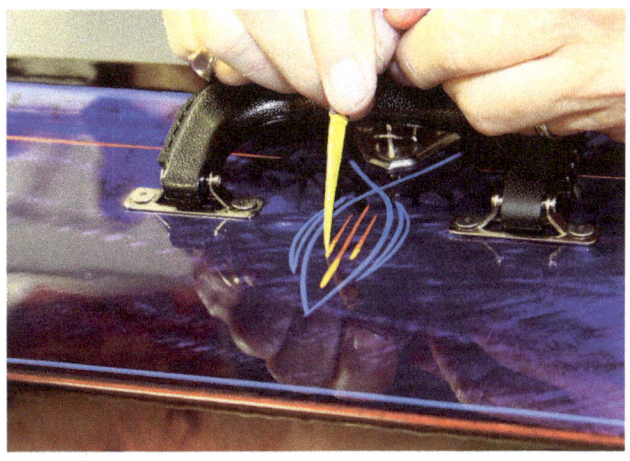

The white "sparks" finish it off.

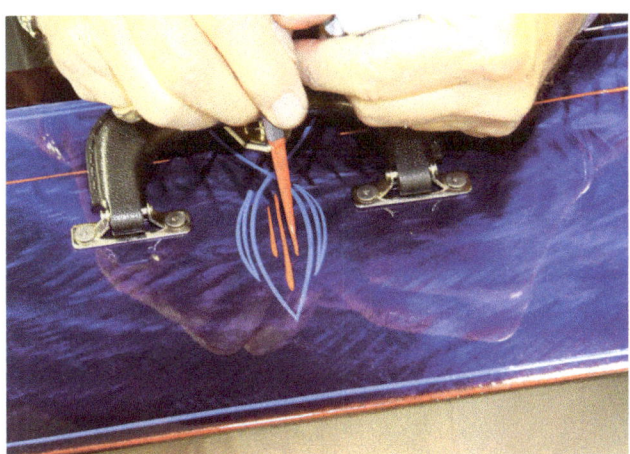

Add the orange blend…

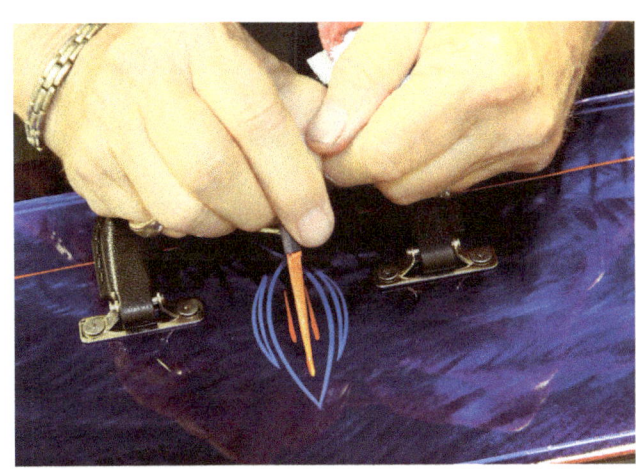

…and the yellow dry brush.

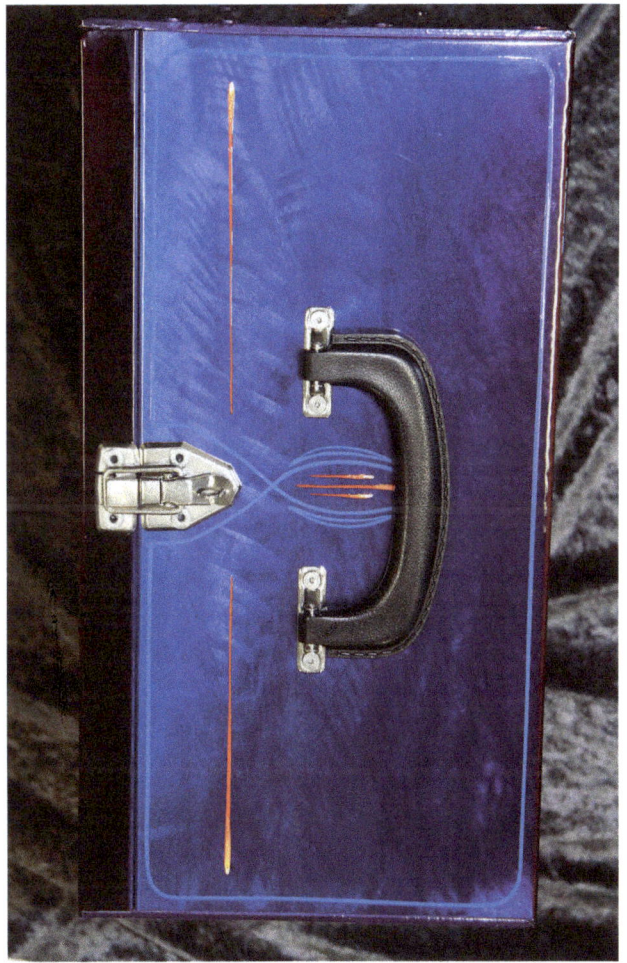

The top is done, two sides to go - can't stop now!

With a stabilo pencil, I lay down a free form splash.

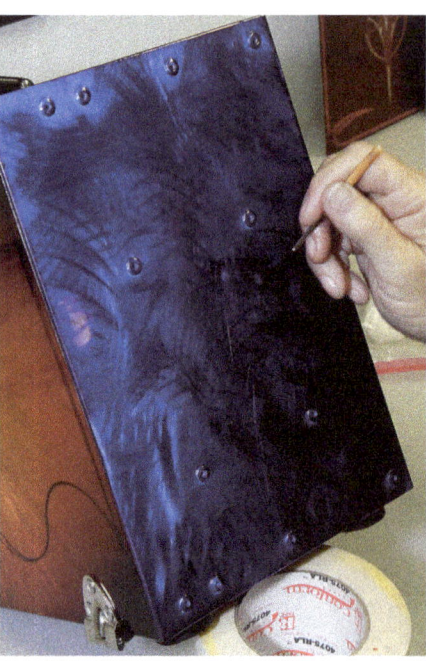
I paint the sizing over my layout...

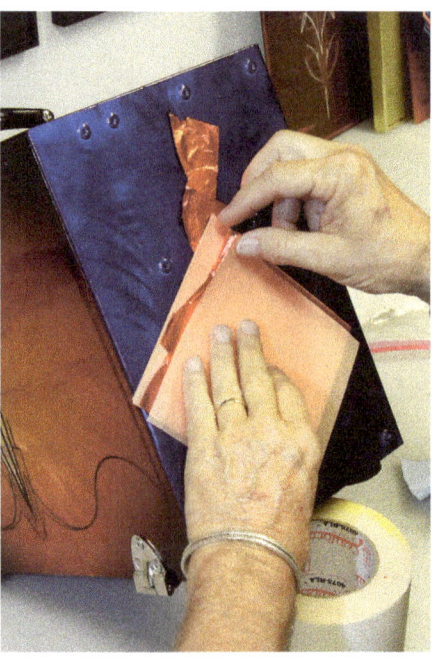
...let it set up just enough and transfer the leaf from the paper sheet to the surface.

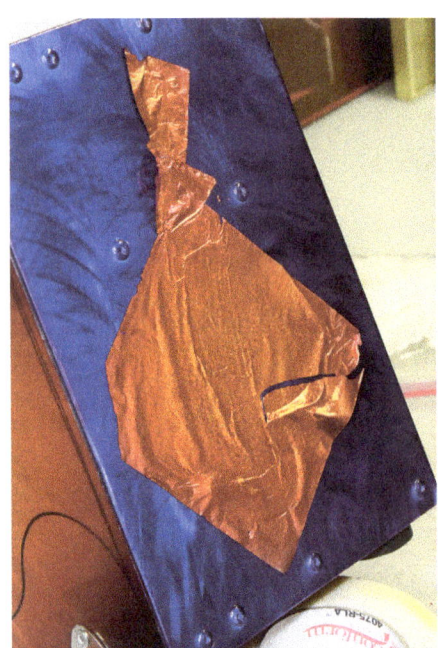
Here's the leaf, ready to be burnished.

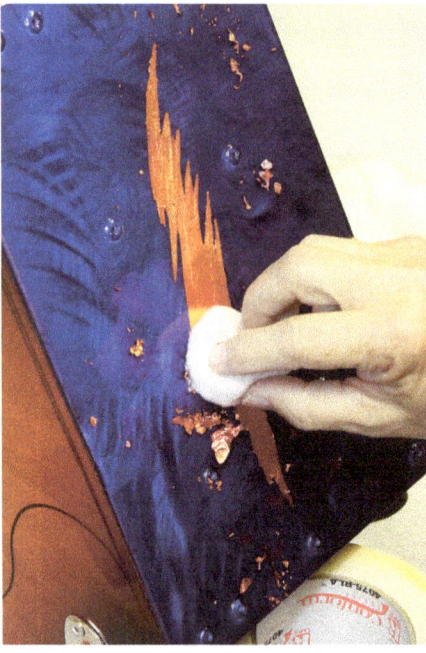
If you use this cotton ball method, do it lightly so you don't tear the edges of the leaf.

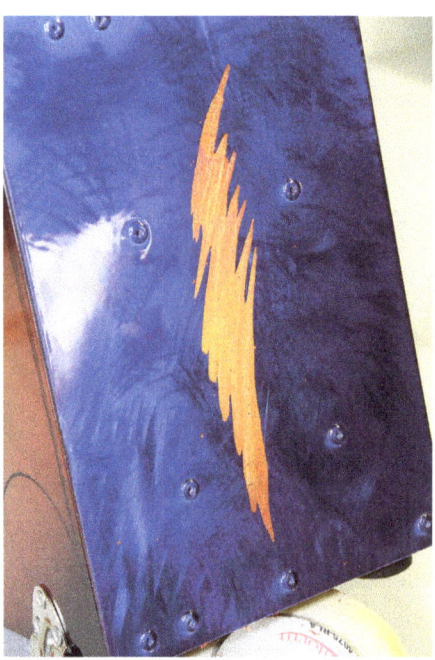
Here it is - ready to outline.

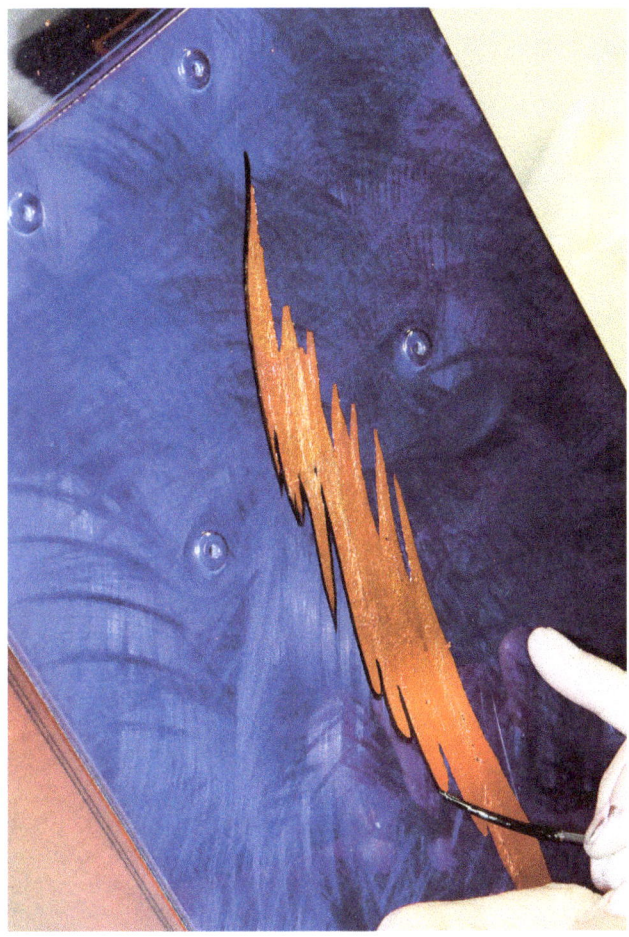

Black paint and the Dave Jeffries virus brush are used again for the outline.

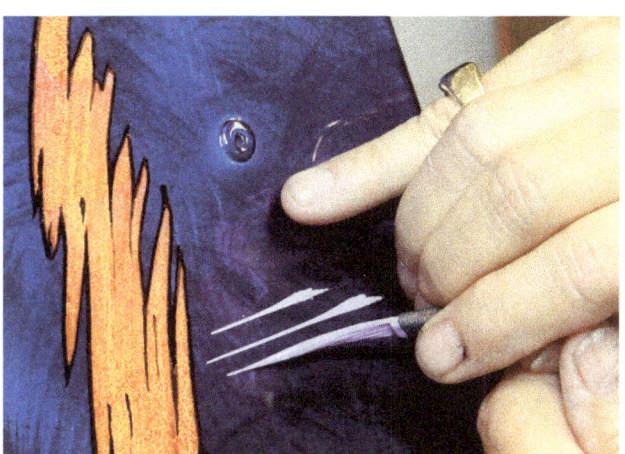

I reverse, and start at the point. Then I lay my brush down to fatten the end. I twist the brush to make the end of the line ragged.

A little white added to the purple, and I highlight the top edge of the stripes.

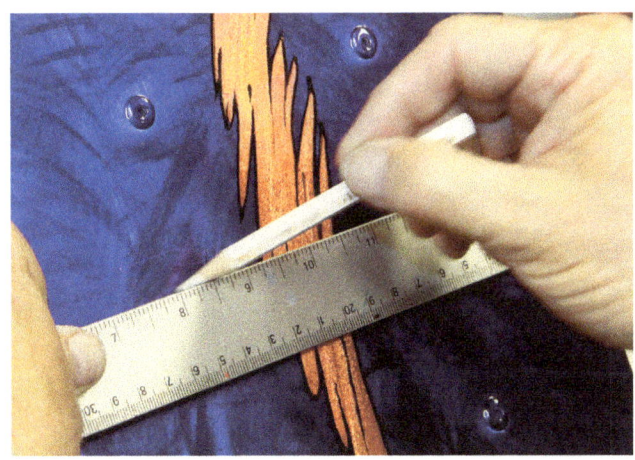

I get a horizontal reference line. (Should have done this in the first place!)

Just enough of a line to add an accent.

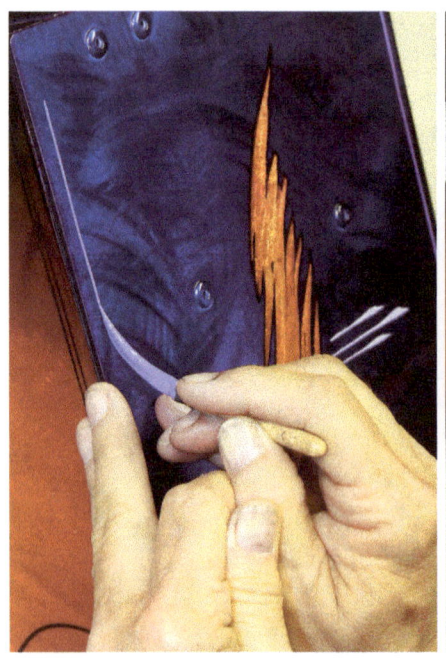

I pull some long spears down the sides....

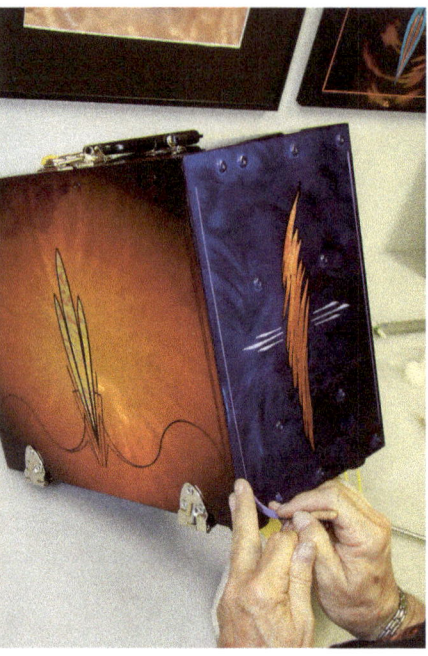

...to border the side panel.

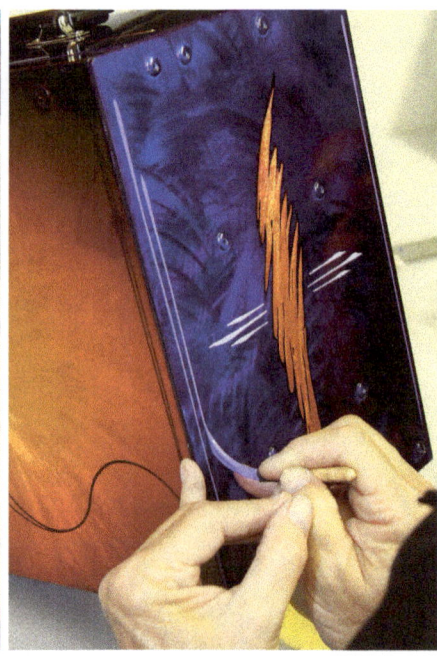

A second border looks even better.

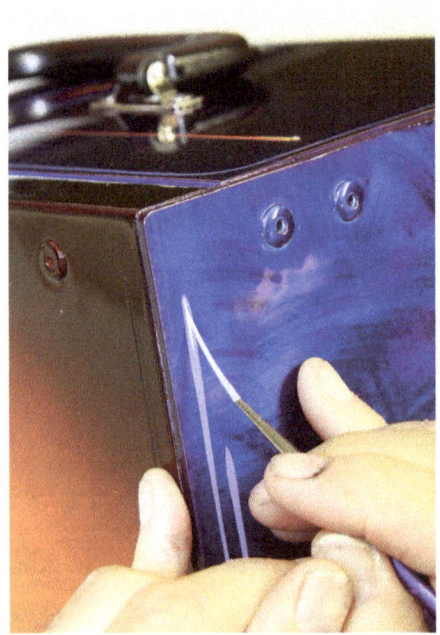

Some white blending for that highlight effect.

Dry brushing blends it together.

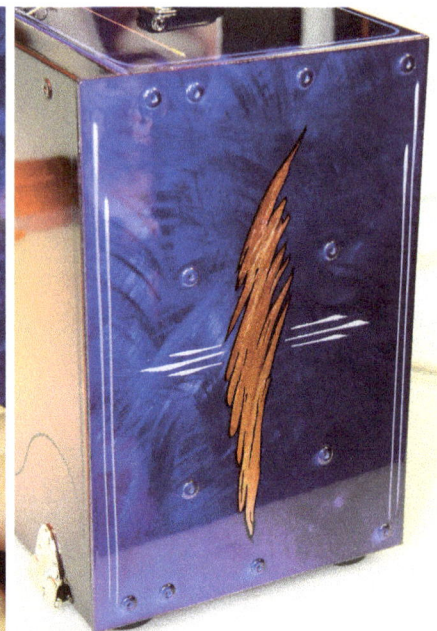

How many more sides do I have to paint?!

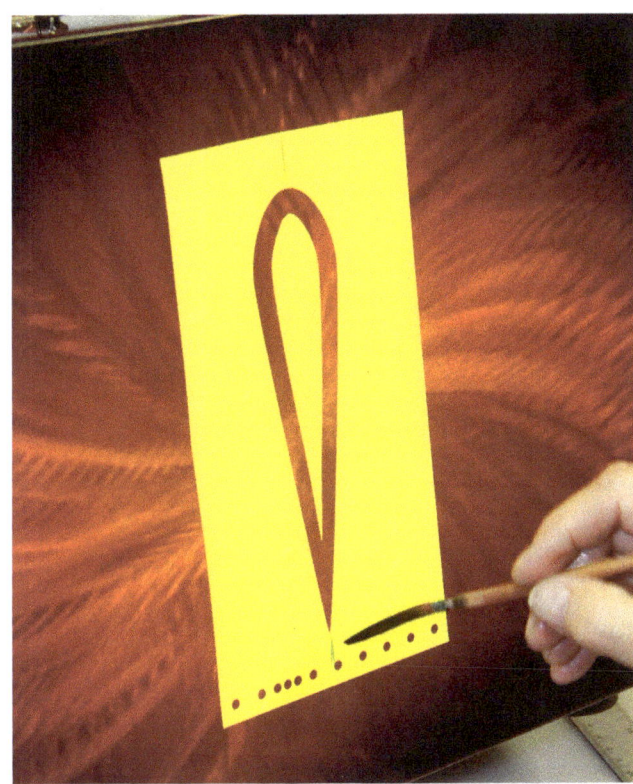

Using the masking technique, I lay down a pattern and paint in the sizing.

Off comes the mask. Don't forget to do this while the size is tacky.

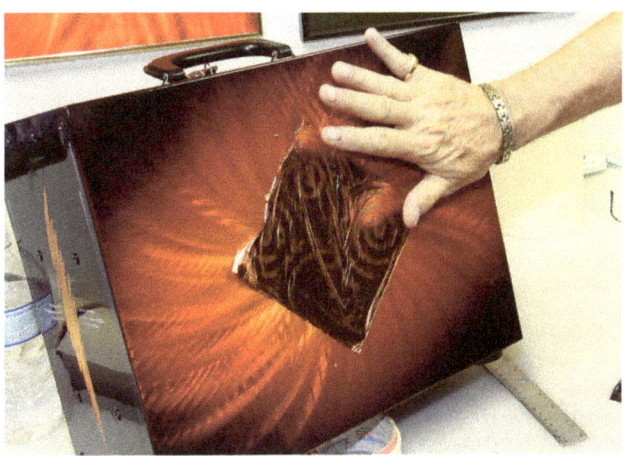

This is variegated leaf with a blue swirl pattern.

I brush and burnish, as before...

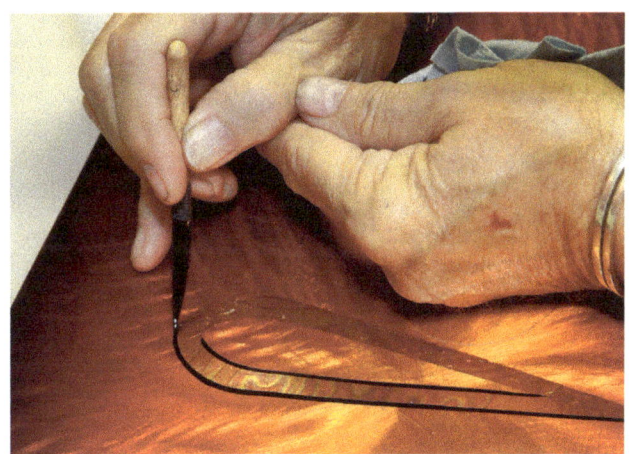

...then outline the design with black.

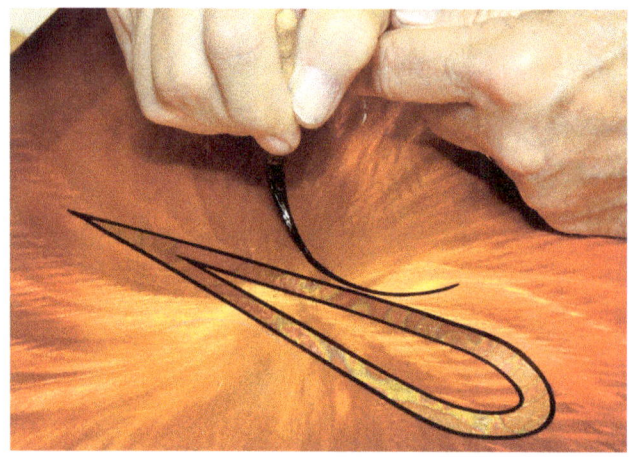

I start to build a design off of the leaf.

…then the other.

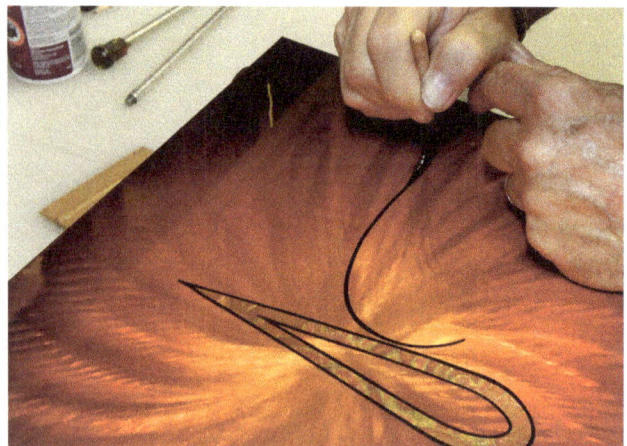

This one's going to be really simple.

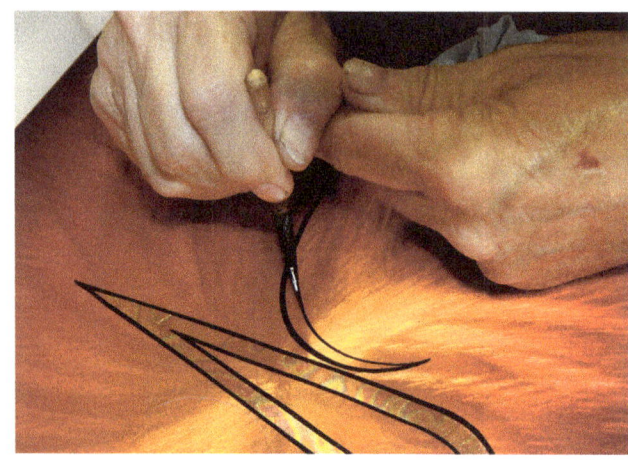

Just an open and closed design going one-way…

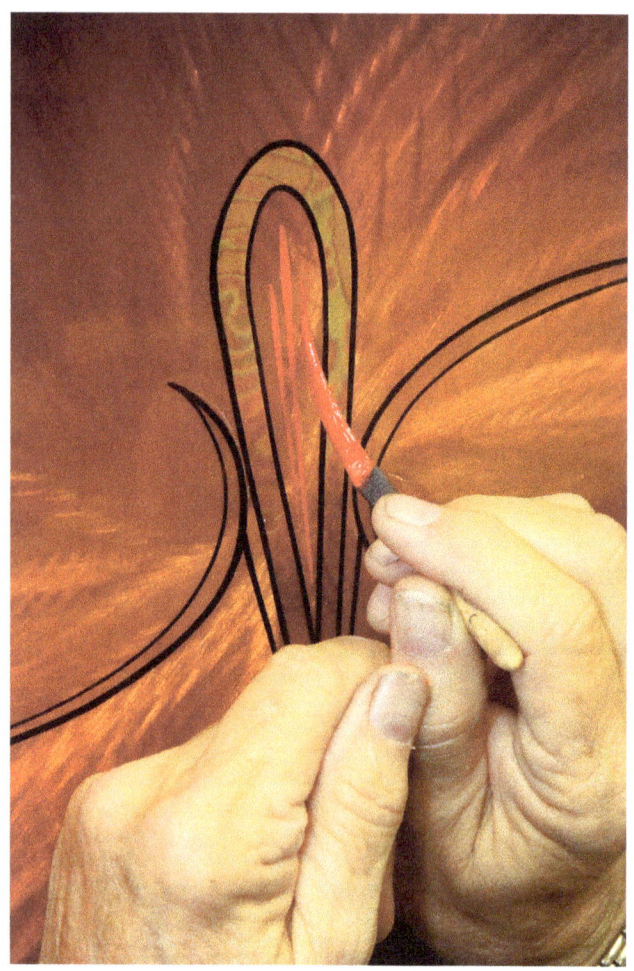

I add some indian red color spears in the center of the design.

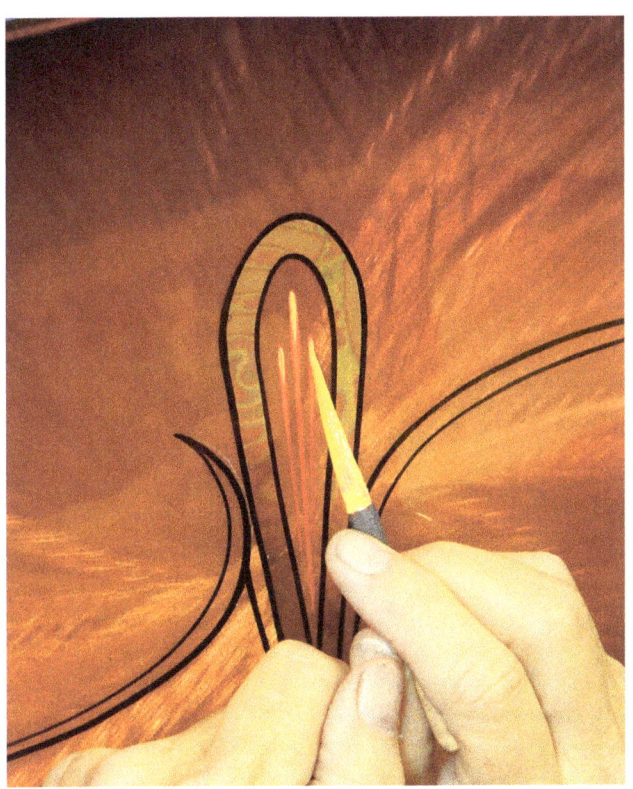

I add some yellow highlight blends...

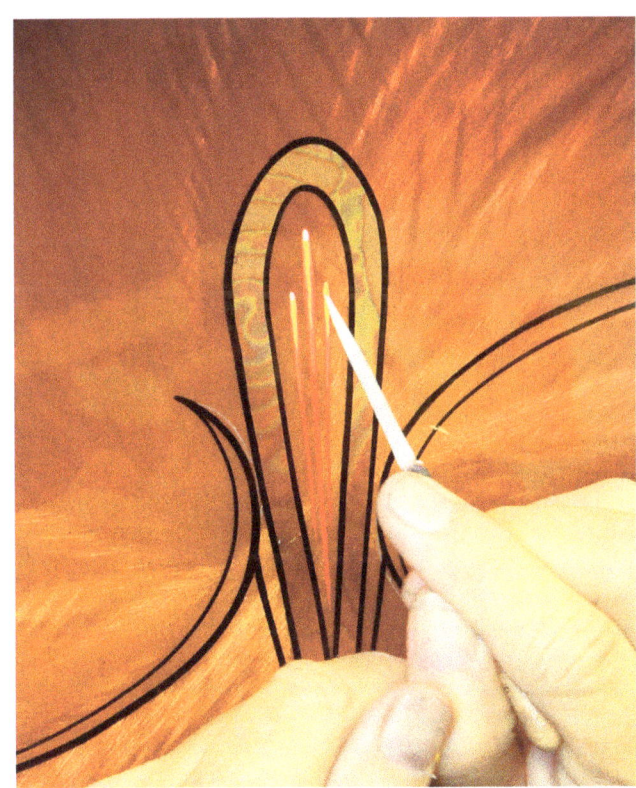

...and little white tip, then dry brushing away.

It looks good, but it still needs something...

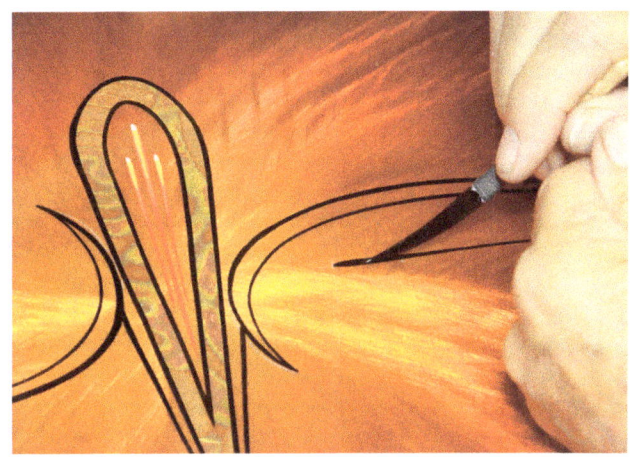

...this will do it.

All done. Thanks to Rodney for a cool box and Jimmy Jackson for the killer paint job!
Captions by Artie

Q&A: Artie

Tell us a little about yourself, and how you became a striper?

I was 13 years old, and worked at a body shop after school. The body shop built custom cars and I was fascinated by the striping that Kenny the Mad Striper did on cars. One day when Kenny came in to stripe a car, the owner of the shop said, "show Artie how to do that," and Kenny did. At the end of that session he gave me the brush I'd been using and that became my brush.

I did my first car 2 weeks later, for free. A month later I striped a car for twenty dollars, a '57 Ford. And by the next year I was doing cars in my driveway and in the high school parking lot.

In high school my art teacher saw me lettering a Pontiac in the parking lot, so he taught me sign painting. For the next eight months I practiced doing Helvetica on graph paper, it was just amazing what I learned. Pretty soon I was doing all the banners for the school. I learned how to do scripts by putting names on continental kits. Those kits were very popular at the time. I had a girlfriend with good hand writing, so I would have her write it out - and then that would become my pattern.

What do you like to do when you don't have a customer looking over your shoulder?

Something that's off the wall, I like to find a different way to approach it. I feel like I approach pinstriping as an art form. Generally though, my customers want traditional looking, Von Dutch style striping. But for myself I want to stretch it, be more abstract.

What do you like to use for brushes?

Xcaliber, in fact those brushes had a lot to do with changing my style. With their quad-zero I can really get down to a fine line. I also like the Bobbo quad brush, especially for flames. One other that I like is the virus brush, designed by Dave Jeffries, for fine work.

What do you like for paint?

I like the Ronan or Kustom Shop EZ Flow striping paint.

When you're doing something like a panel, do you plan it out ahead of time or just work on the fly?

On a panel I work on the fly, even when I start with a plan I end up changing it part of the way through.

Master of many styles and techniques, Artie's personal work is on the simple and elegant end of the spectrum.

Q&A: Artie

Are there absolutes in terms of design, in terms of placement and how many times a line can cross another line?

No, in my opinion pinstriping should be a very personal thing. I encourage people to develop their own style and come up with their own rules as they go along. The trouble is, the public wants one thing and you may want another. But if you gain potential customers confidence, they will let you have more freedom in what you do for them. It helps to not be stuck with just one style. I work at that, I try to pull things from different styles so it gives me lots of versatility.

Who inspires you, where do you get your ideas?

Music. Especially Jackson Browne, Poco and Doo Wop music.

How do you pick colors, and how did you learn to mix colors to match a certain color?

I kind of base the color selection on the customer, I ask, "what color don't you like," so we eliminate that color right away. The trouble is, when I think of a color I'm thinking of a line that's 1/16th of an inch wide, and the customer is thinking of a wall in that color. I might suggest teal with purple and lime green and they look at me like I'm nuts.

In terms of mixing colors, I just figured it out over the years. Sometimes it doesn't' work and I end up with a lot of brown. As the paint technology has changed over the years though, it has affected how we mix paints. There are some things we can do now that we couldn't do before, because the pigments are different now.

Can you talk about the business part of pinstriping?

The reason I've been successful in the business is that I treat it as a profession. Consequently, I'm always looking for tools, things that make my job better and easier, and looking for ways to make the relationship with the customer easier. You are putting paint on their pride and joy, and for a lot of people it's a traumatic experience. They have an idea in their mind and I take all that into consideration to make it work. Gaining customer confidence takes time, they have to trust you.

Any final words?

Being the kid who was never going to amount to anything, I feel OK with what I do and what I've accomplished. I'm one of the old guys now and that's OK, the pressure is off.

What does the studio say about the artist? That he enjoys a wide range of art from various artists, and that he's a very neat man.

Chapter Eight

Artie's Victory

Sometimes Less Is More

With minimal accessories and solid black paint, the Victory 8-Ball is the perfect back-to-basics American V-Twin. Despite the bike's popularity, or because of it, Coastal Victory Motorcycles in Myrtle Beach, South Carolina, decided to separate one of their new 8-Balls from all the others.

Thus the call went out to East Coast Artie, with a mandate to make this particular bike really jump - visually. And do it without loosing the feel of the stripped down Victory. Artie chose bright colors, and a simple design, to achieve exactly what the dealer desired - a new Victory. Different from the others, but still black and still an 8-Ball.

This is a new Victory 8-ball that the dealer asked me to "trick up" for the show room. I use a different style of striping on these new bikes, more of a "tech" look than old skool striping. I make a mask on the computer. For a fast and tight focal point to my design, I use r-tape yellow paint mask, first printing the design on my Gerber edge. Printing makes it easier to read and align on the bike. I then cut it out on my plotter.

I start by prepping with wax and grease remover. Then I lay down a center point to align the mask.

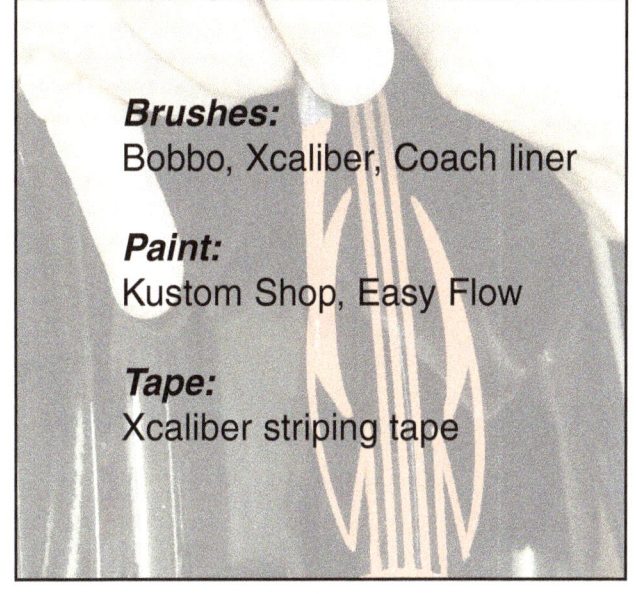

Brushes:
Bobbo, Xcaliber, Coach liner

Paint:
Kustom Shop, Easy Flow

Tape:
Xcaliber striping tape

I lay down the mask and squeegee it in place.

I'm using enamel paint from Kustom Shop.

Now I remove the application paper.

I use a coach liner to paint in my base color, it hits all 3 stripes at the same time!

I blend orange into the end of the stripes.

I use my Bobbo Dunn, super quad brush from Mack to pull the yellow into the orange.

I also highlight the circle for some added dimension.

I dry brush the yellow out into the orange, and add some stippling to blend it in.

I'm going from Indian Red, to California Orange, to Lemon Yellow. These are all Kustom Shop, E-Z Flow, striping colors.

I put a dot of white on the tip of the center stripe, then pull it dry.

Removing the mask, you can see the base from my design. Notice how the blended colors add a little flash.

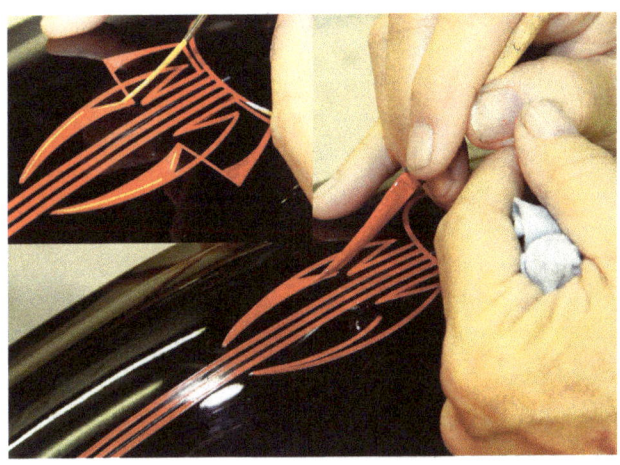

I keep building the design until it strikes me - to stop! That's the hard part, knowing when to quit.

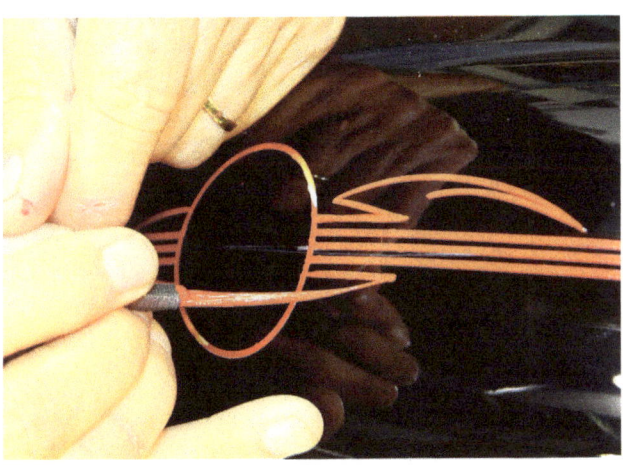

From here I'm on my own.....using my Xcaliber 0000 striper I keep it simple and clean. Less is more!

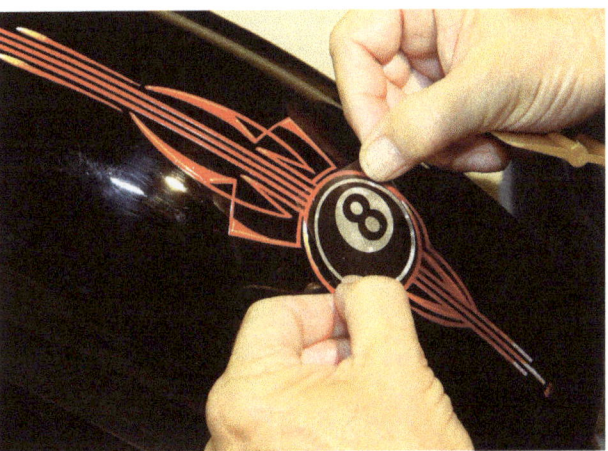

I printed an 8-ball on silver leaf vinyl, using my Gerber edge. Remember, this is a dealer bike, so price is a factor. Otherwise, I would hand lay silver leaf.

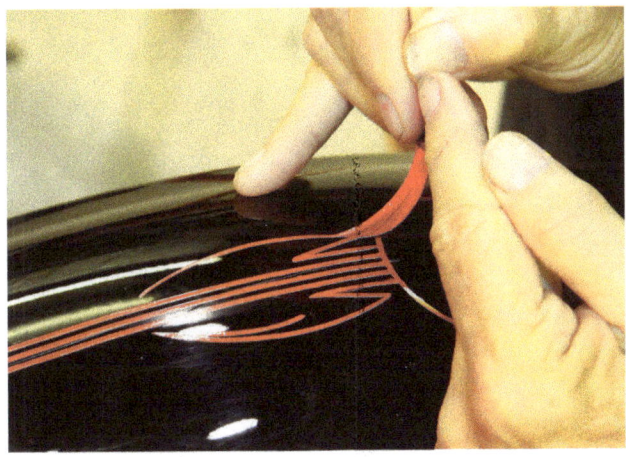

I didn't plan this part, I just start building off my base design.

I lay a triple stripe down the tank, using Xcaliber striping tape.

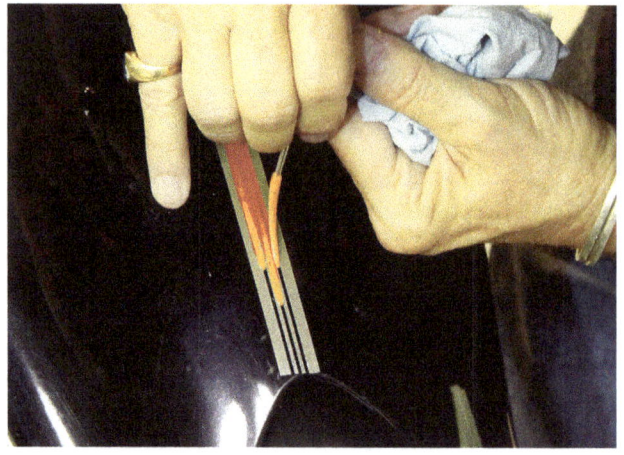

I repeat the blending technique I used on the front fender.

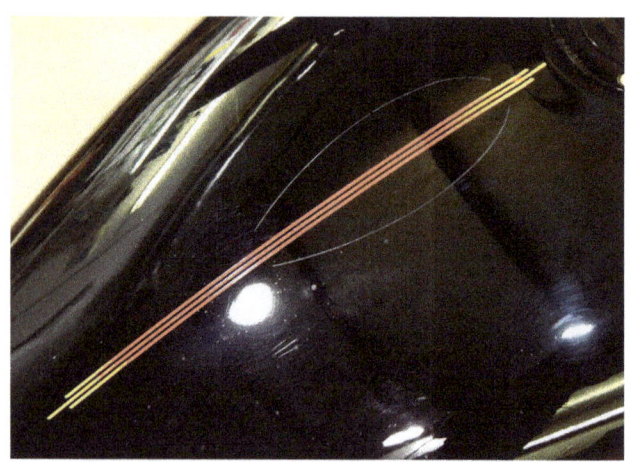

Using a stabilo pencil, I mark out a design shape.

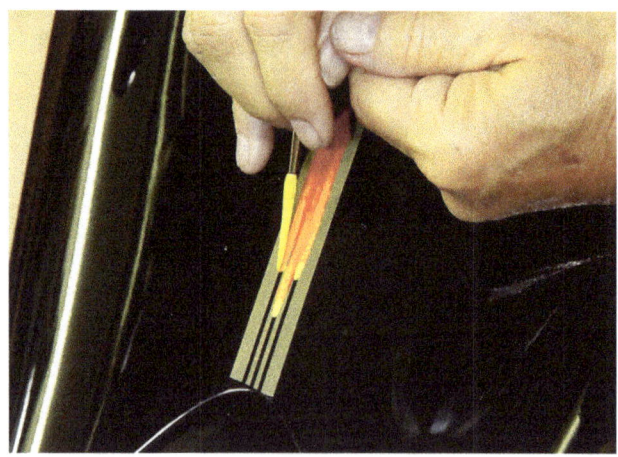

This works with a lot of color combinations. Making some sample panels has helped me build a "catalog" of these combinations.

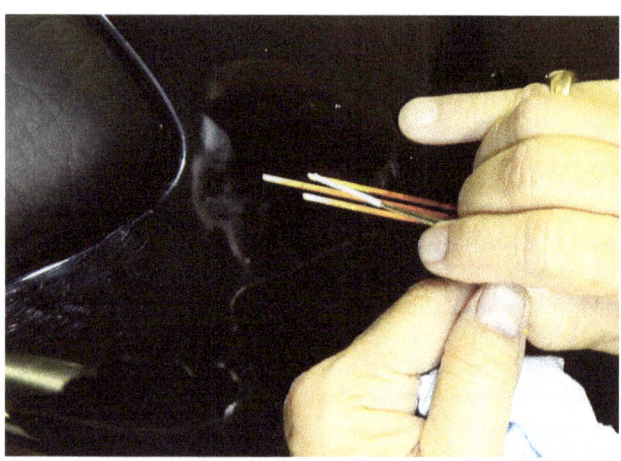

Oops…forgot to put the white highlighting down the center line.

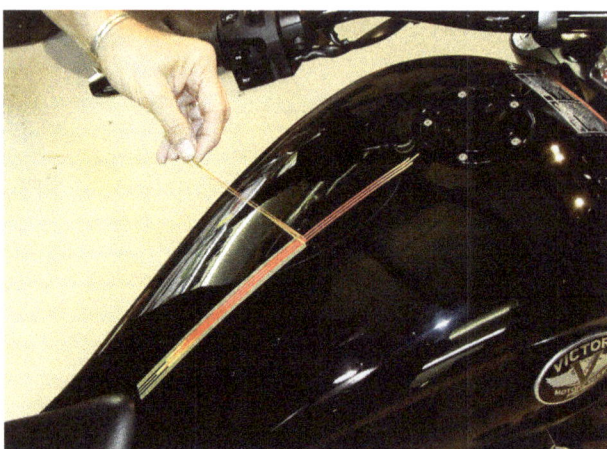

I pull the center tape and have a nice, tight center point to work with.

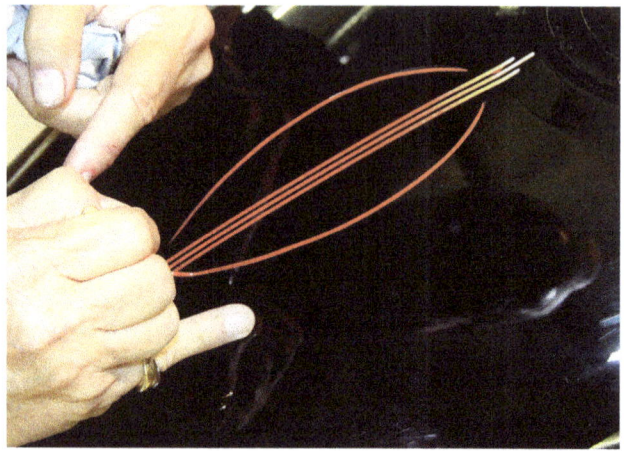

Now the design will start coming together. And I'm back to winging it.

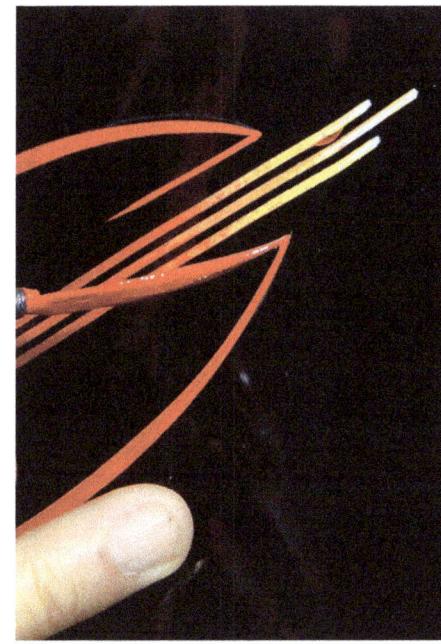

While doing the tank design, I start on the back fender to carry the design theme on.

A couple shorter lines on the rear fender get things started.

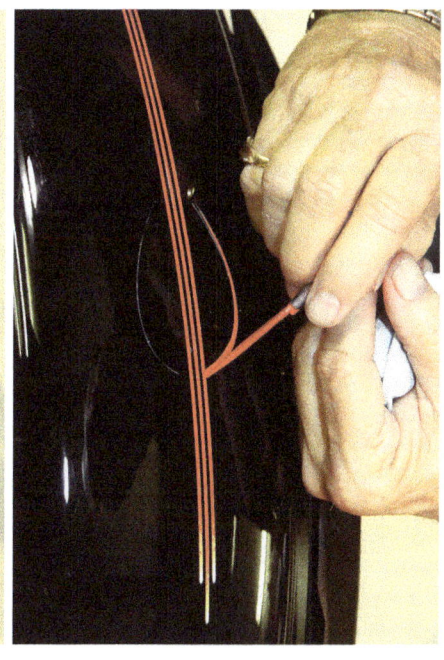

Following the basic tank design, I build the rear fender design.

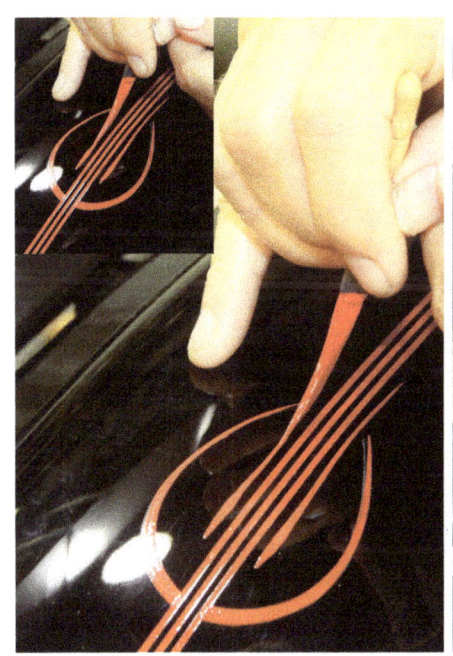

These "spears" add a nice fill, and you can shade them too.

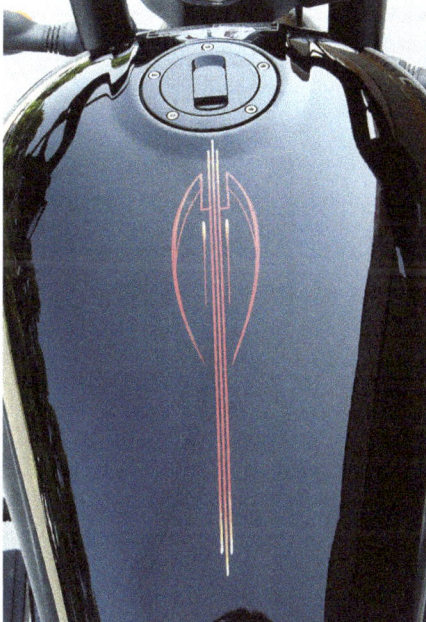

That's it! It took about 45 minutes to do. I like it... and so does the customer.

Here's the finished front fender design with the 8-ball logo.

Artie Paints the Blues

Dwayne Farmer wanted some flash added to his Fender Tele. Here I'm using my "color guide": plastic strips I painted with Kustom Shop EZ flow paint.

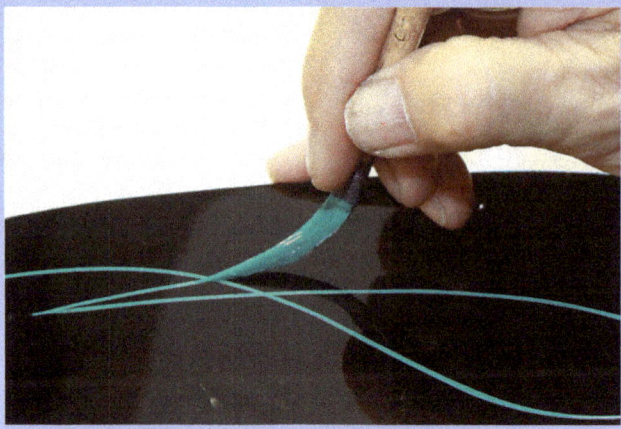

Sometimes the easiest things are the hardest to explain. I head back with my brush along the bottom of the guitar. Why? Because it looks right to me.

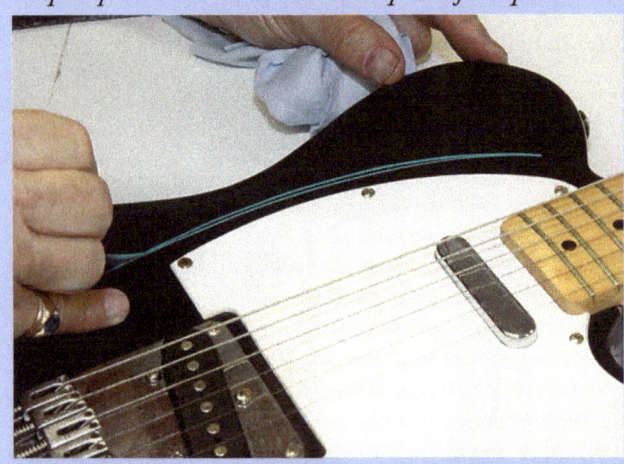

I start with teal and pull a line along the pick guard and continue down the guitar body.

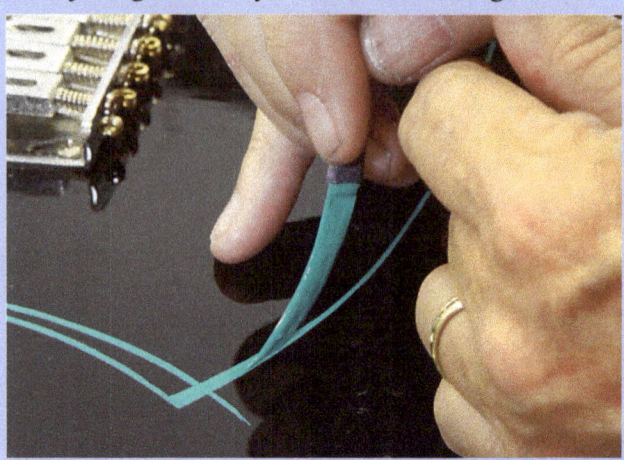

I thicken this line to add some weight to the design. This comes in handy if your line needs fixin'.

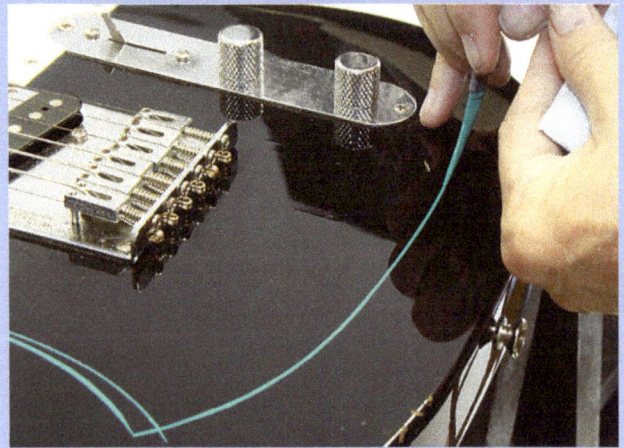

I come off that line across the bottom of the guitar to the control panel.

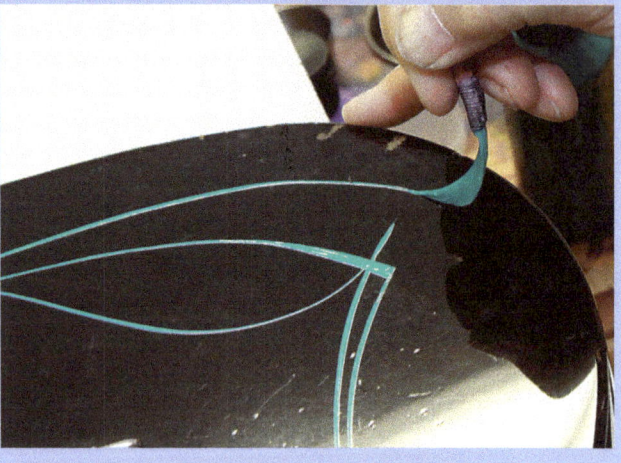

Now I come back around the edge of the guitar body to tie it all together. You are following this - right?

Artie Paints the Blues

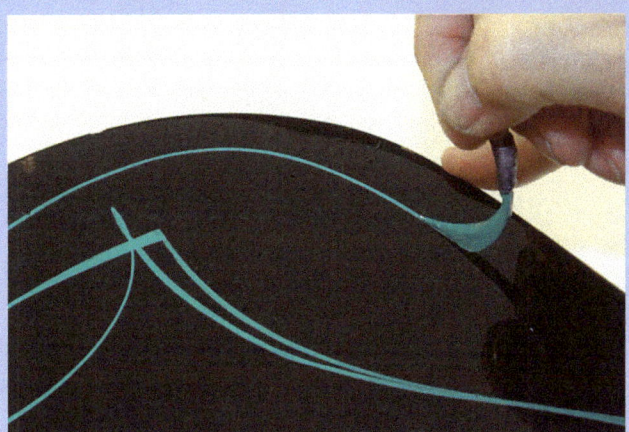

I continue striping around the body to "border" it. Because the guitar body is asymmetrical, I can be pretty loose with the design.

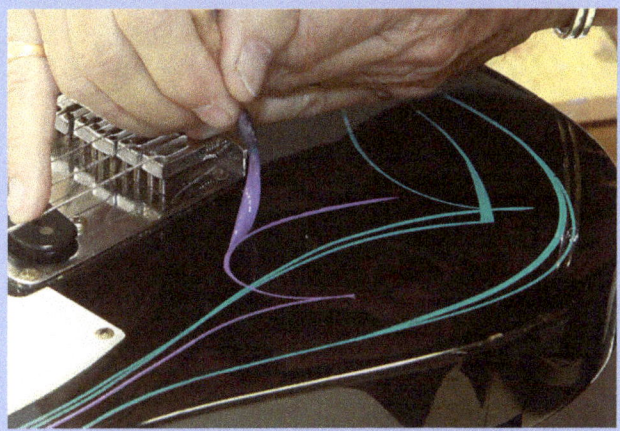

Now some purple lines, in and out of the teal.

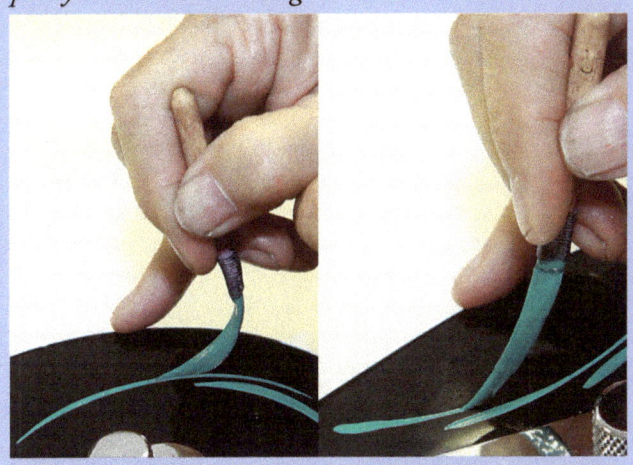

See how I torque the brush in the corner. This keeps it from spinning out and messing up my line quality

A few more purple lines and...

A couple of spears finish up the teal part of the design.

...done! I'd like say I planned this all out, but the truth is I was listening to The Last Laugh Coming Down by Van Morrison and got lost in the music.

Chapter Nine

Artie's Computer

Pounce Pattern Outline

There simply isn't anything that someone, like Artie, won't embellish with pinstripes. The owner of this laptop wanted it dressed up a little, and in the end it got dressed up a lot.

There are numerous ways to transfer a given design onto almost any surface. The pounce wheel and pad may not be very sexy, but the method is certainly tried and true. It requires nothing more than a handle with a wheel - one that looks like a mini spur from a cowboy's boot, and a box (or bag) filled with chalk. In this low-tech way, anyone can create a design and then transfer that design as many times as they like onto a fender, a hood, or your favorite computer.

A simple pattern that repeats, done in three colors. Considering the fact that I used a pounce wheel and pad to transfer the design onto the computer, you could say that it's old sign painting technology being used on a new, high tech computer.

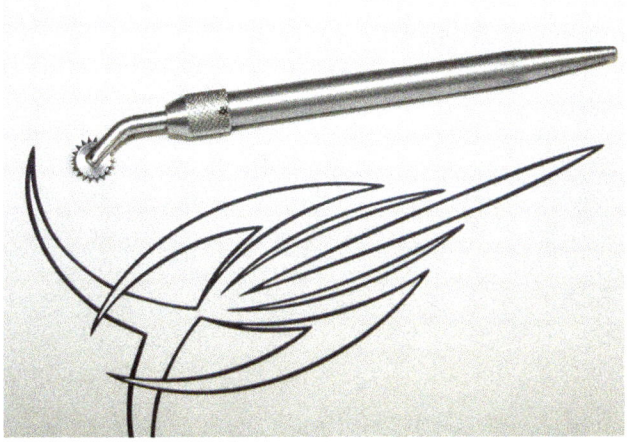

1. I draw the design on paper with a fine sharpie marker.

2. Using my pounce wheel from Grifhold, I perforate the paper so the chalk can flow through.

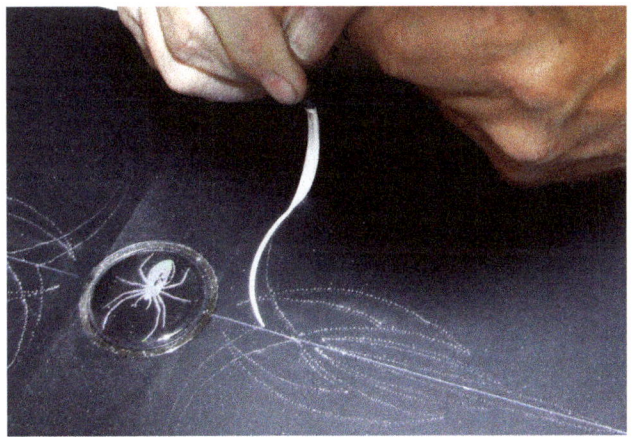

4. I now start to paint the white parts of the design. The chalk dissolves into the paint.

Brushes: Xcaliber 0000 striper

Paint: DuPont Hot Hues striping paint

Wax & Grease Remover:

Other: Han-See chalk box, Grifhold pounce wheel

Artist Comments: This is a computer I did for a customer who wanted some "old school" striping on it. I used the pounce pattern method for uniformity.

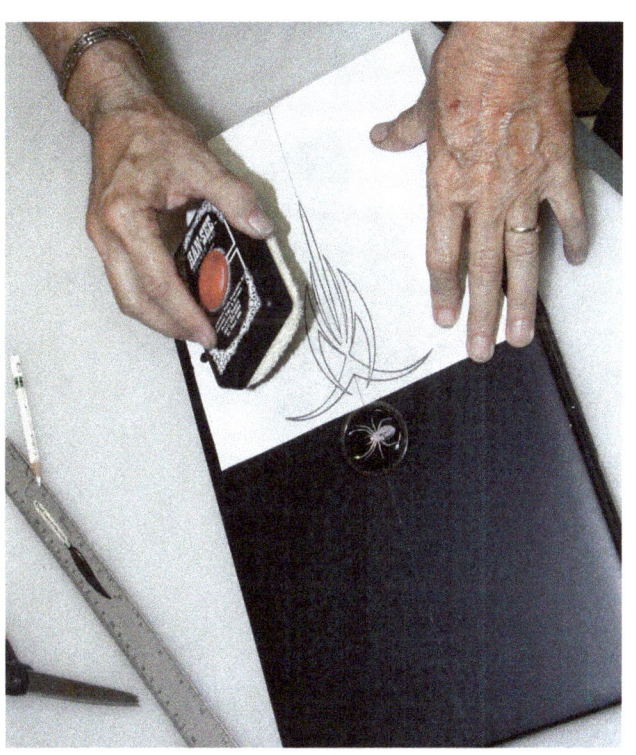

3. I place the pattern on the computer surface and pat it with the Han-See pounce box to transfer the design onto the surface. You could also use a sock full of chalk powder instead of a chalk box.

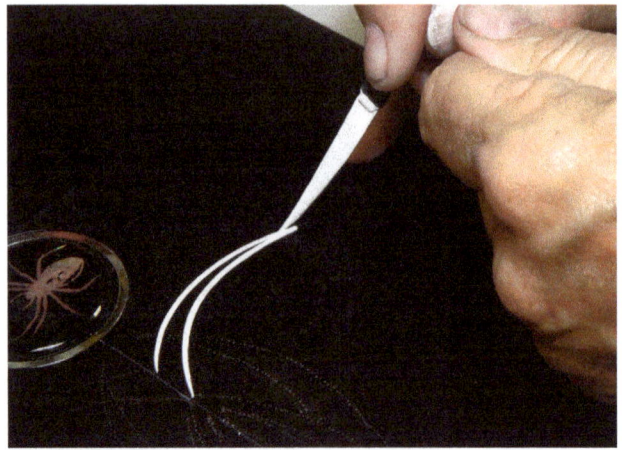

I get the base of the design on one side.

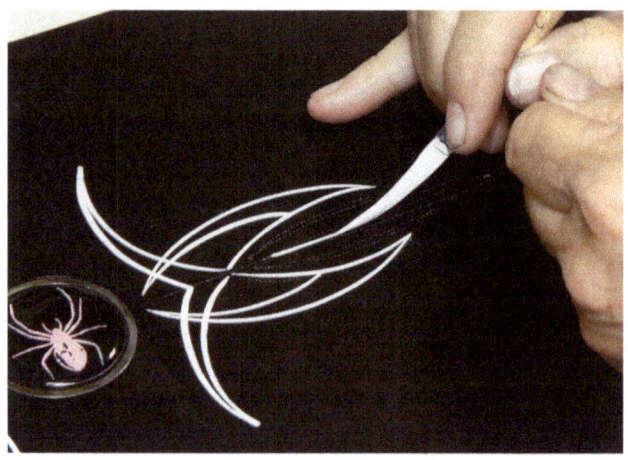

I leave a lot of open space, as I will be adding more colors.

I move to the other side of the emblem and duplicate the design.

Now I connect the 2 side designs with an outline around the emblem.

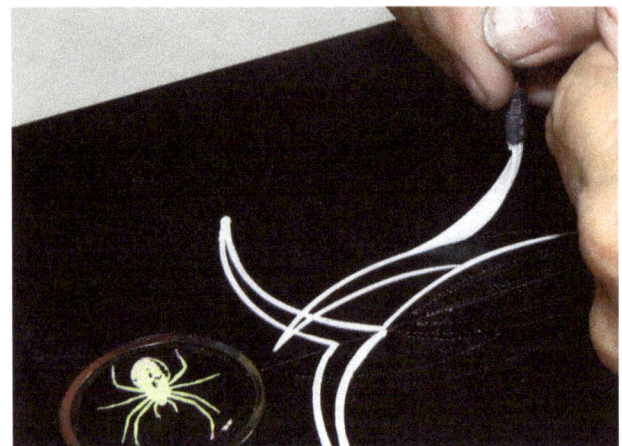

Going side to side, the design starts coming together.

A couple of "torpedoes" tie the design together.

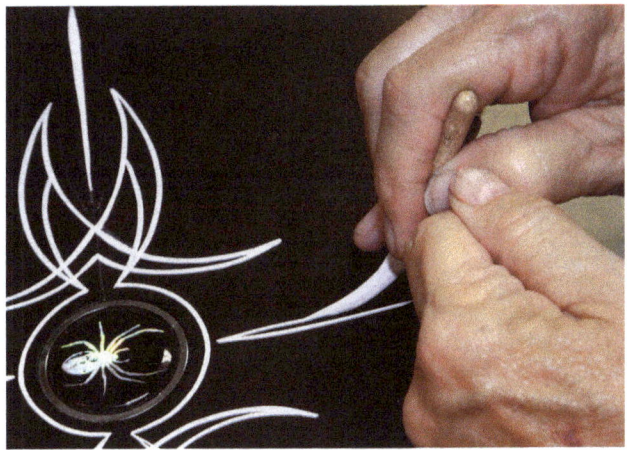

I repeat the torpedo on the top of the circle.

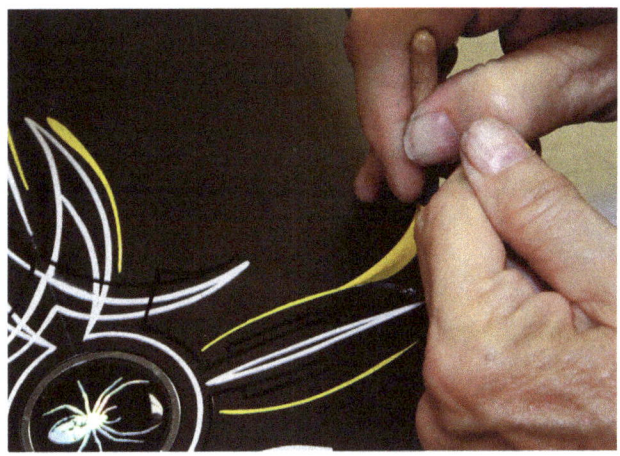

Keeping the yellow parts simple, I work around the white and black.

Because the computer has a satin finish, I can add gloss black to the design, working in and out of the white.

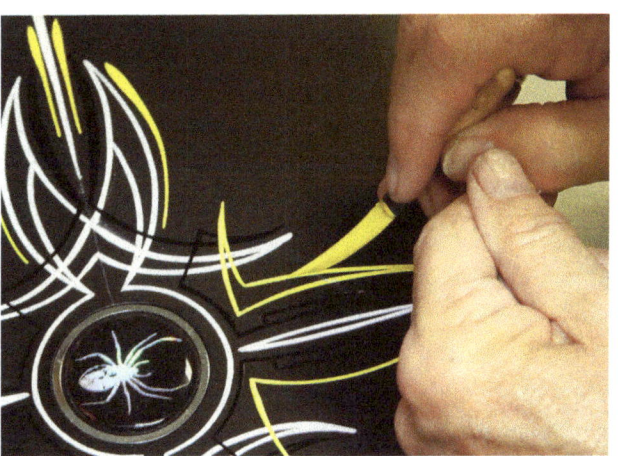

Don't overdue the yellow, or it will become too busy.

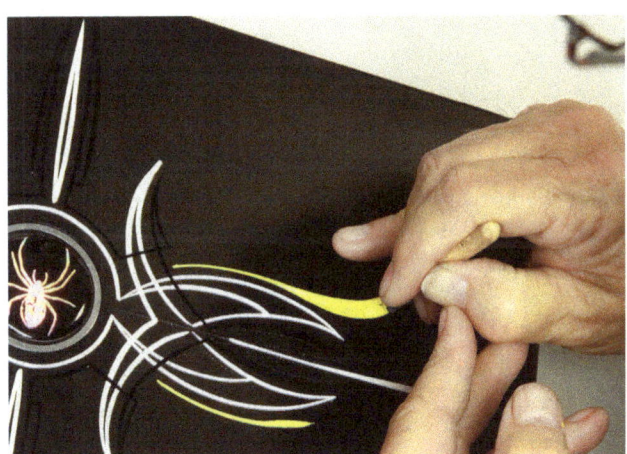

With the black completed, I start adding yellow accents.

A couple more licks and it's a done deal…don't forget to sign it!

Chapter Ten

Mr. J's Ranchero

Old Skool Scallops

Who better to put some old skool scallops on a primered Ranchero than a man who started striping when what we now call old skool was new? Back when the magazines were little, but the talent, like Von Dutch, was huge. It was all bigger than life to a young man like Julian Braet, who bought his first striping brush at the age of twelve.

For the project seen here, Julian was armed with nothing more than two cans of enamel from Ronan, a striping brush from Xcaliber and a roll of tape when East Coast Artie said, "why not put some old skool scallops on that thing?" As you can see, Julian did indeed give character and color to a vehicle in desperate need of both.

We all love primered cars, but sometimes a bit of color can do a lot for an object that's one big flat canvas of grey. Mr. J wisely chose cherry red with ivory highlights to spiff up this Ranchero and give it a bit more character.

Here's my project, a 1965 Ford Falcon Ranchero, in primer paint.

Brushes: Xcaliber, and a lettering quill

Paint: Ronan, ivory and cherry red lettering enamel

Tape: Fineline

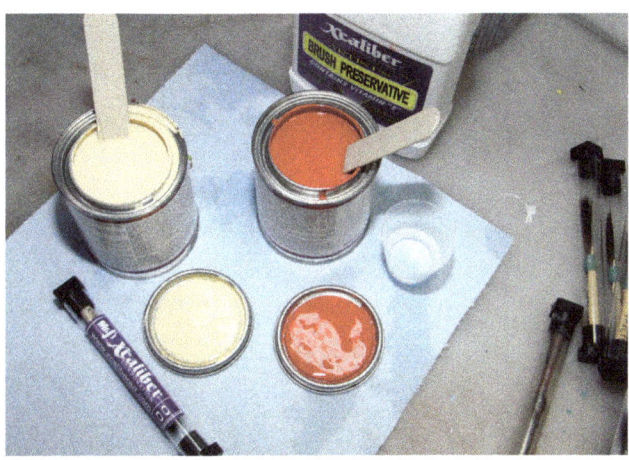

I'm using Ronan's ivory and cherry red lettering enamel for the scallops and striping. To reduce the paint I'll add a small amount of enamel reducer (never use mineral spirits).

To layout the guide lines I use a white Stabilo pencil (water soluble) and a yardstick.

On the "sail panels" I paint the scallop lines freehand.

103

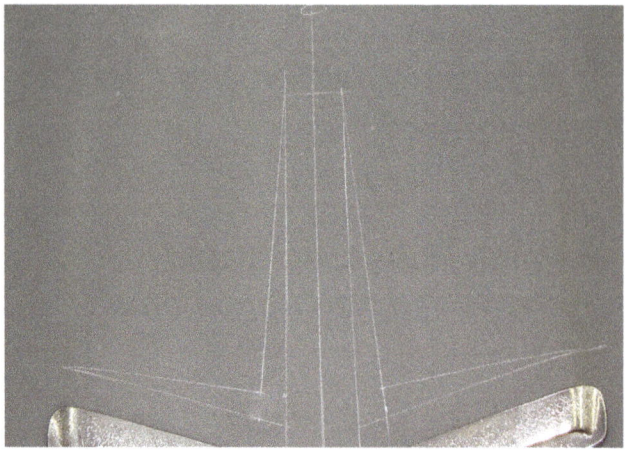

The hood and all of the other scallop designs are done the same way.

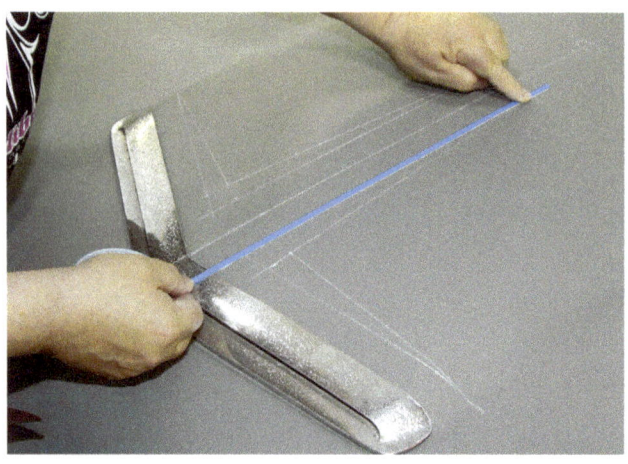

I lay down some blue fine line tape, but decide to continue using the green fine line tape.

...so I trim them with a razor blade. Be careful here, you could ruin a great brush. My first color is cherry red.

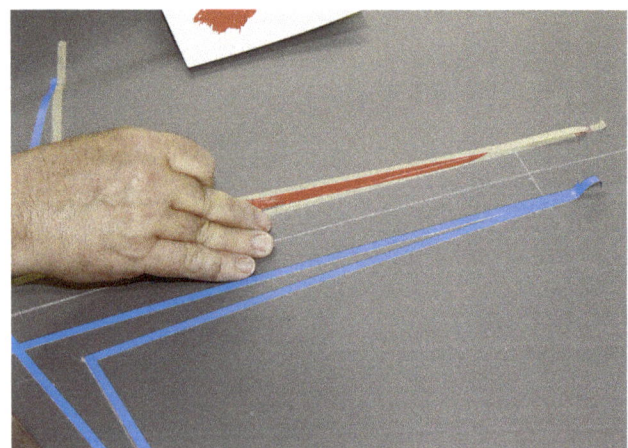

I decided to use a new Xcaliber 00 striping brush. After I start to pallet my brush I notice a couple of long hairs extending beyond the tip...

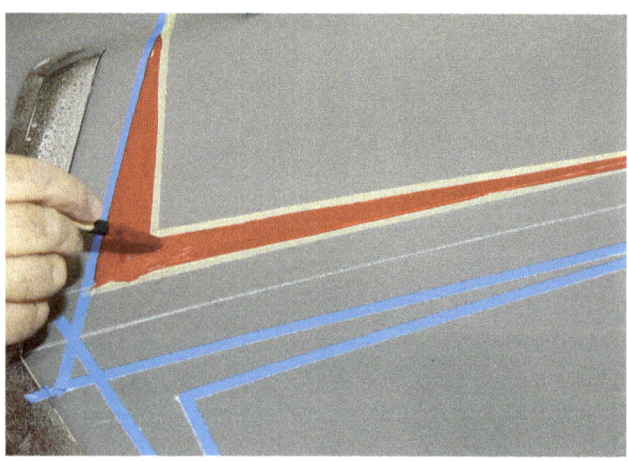

I fill the design in with my Xcaliber brush to show that you can use it for this purpose.

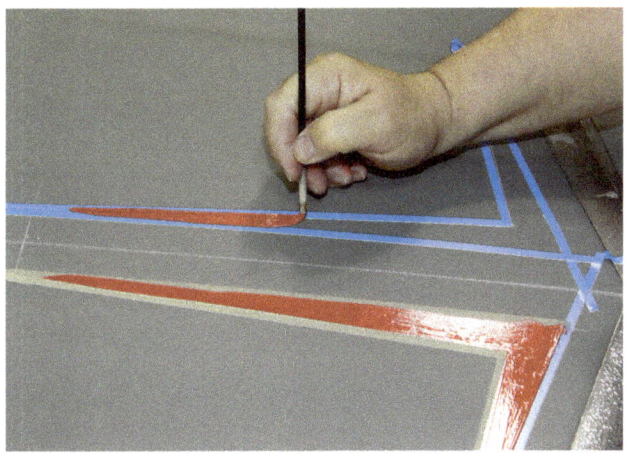

I switch to a #8 brow lettering quill because it makes the job go faster.

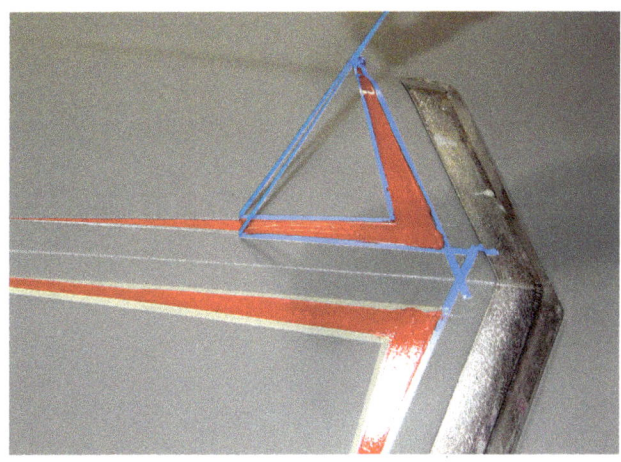

I wait about ten minutes and remove the tape.

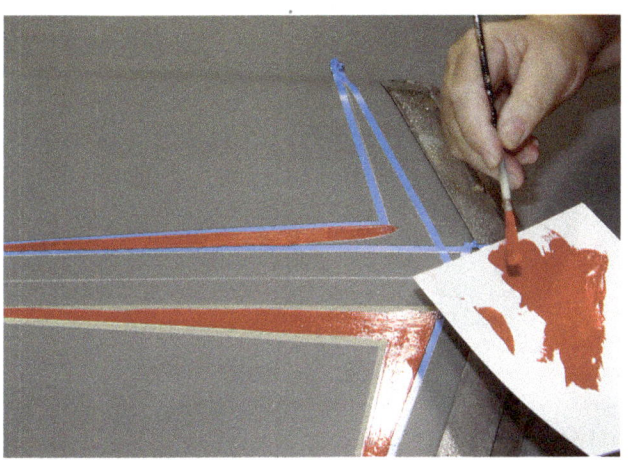

I pallet my brush on smooth, slick card stock.

The lines turn out very clean and neat.

Avoid obvious brush strokes by brushing in the same direction.

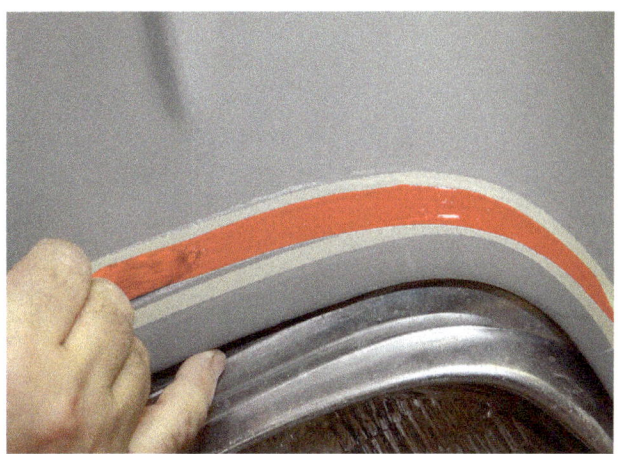

Here I paint the scallop on the hood.

The first part of the hood is complete.

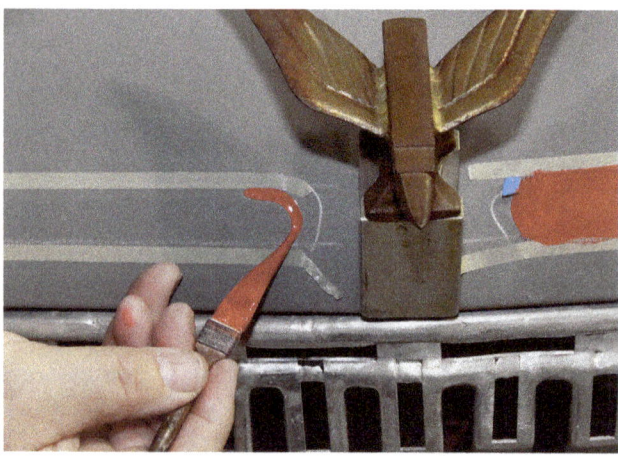
Note the position of my fingers. The higher up you hold the brush, the tighter the curve.

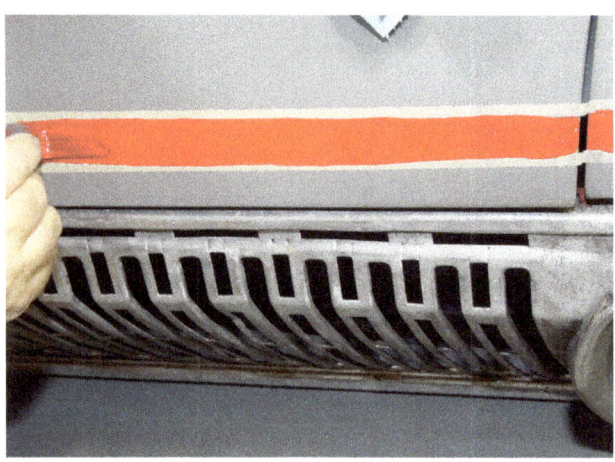
Filling in the long part of the hood.

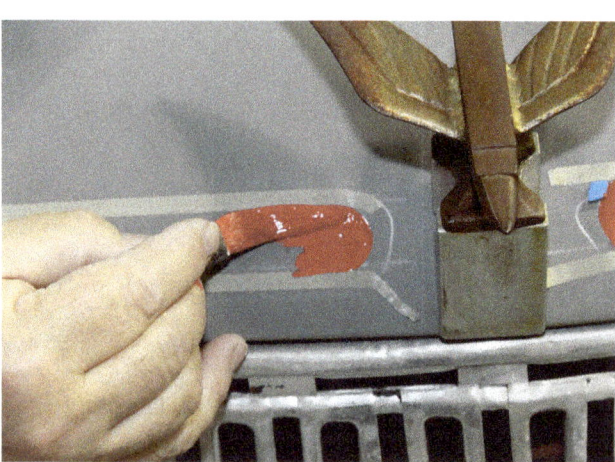
I continue to fill in the scallop.

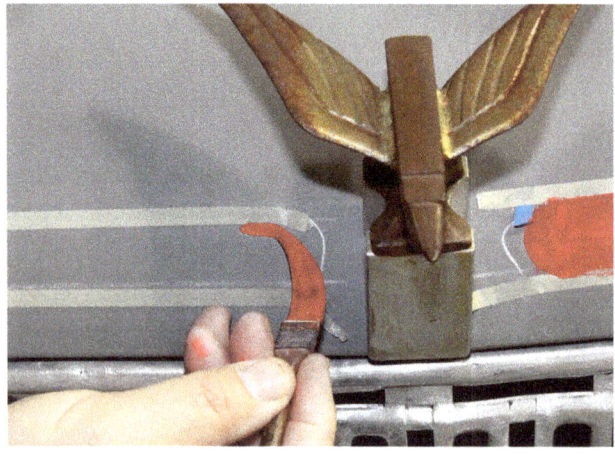
I break out a monster Mack brush #4 to fill in and create the round parts.

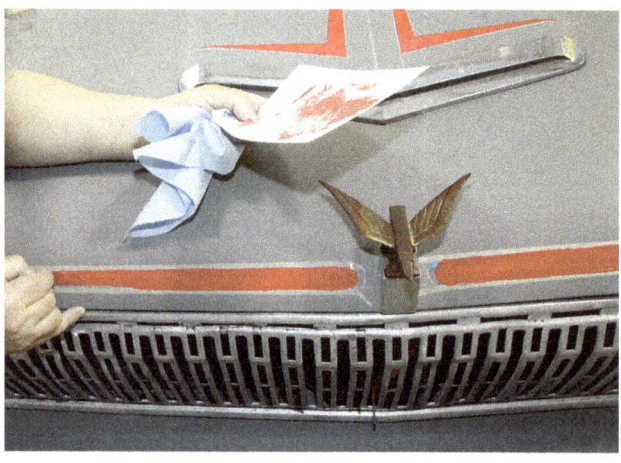
Here I pull the stripe together to create the long fill.

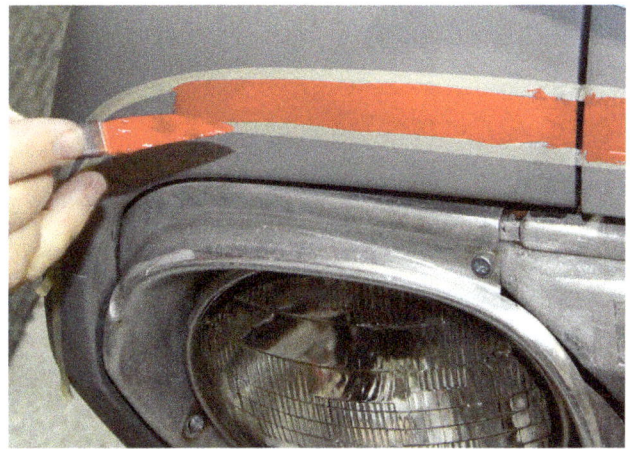

Now the last part of the hood is striped.

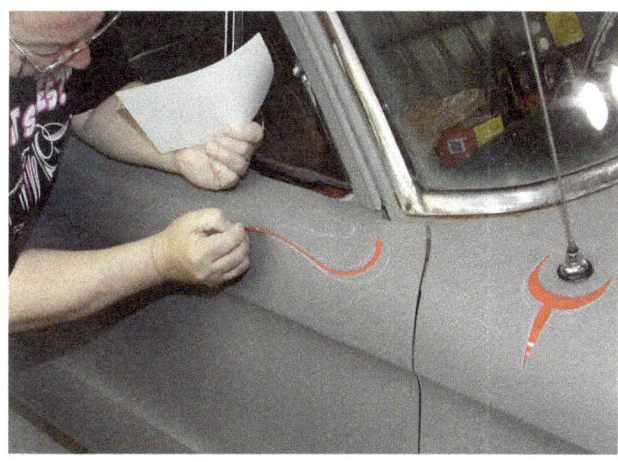

I lay down the first stripe, wrapping it around the mirror.

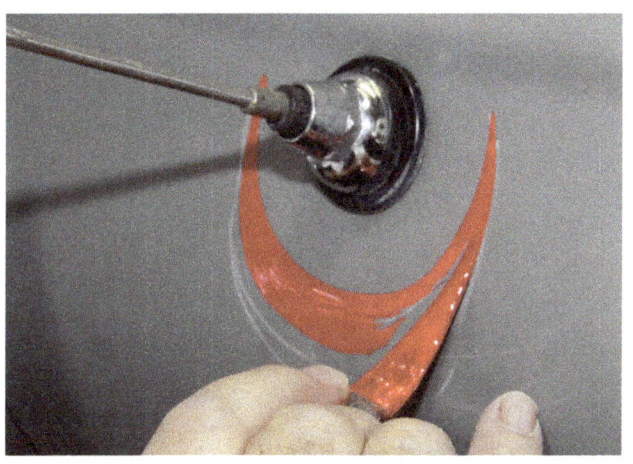

I penciled some art work around the antenna and the places where the mirrors will go.

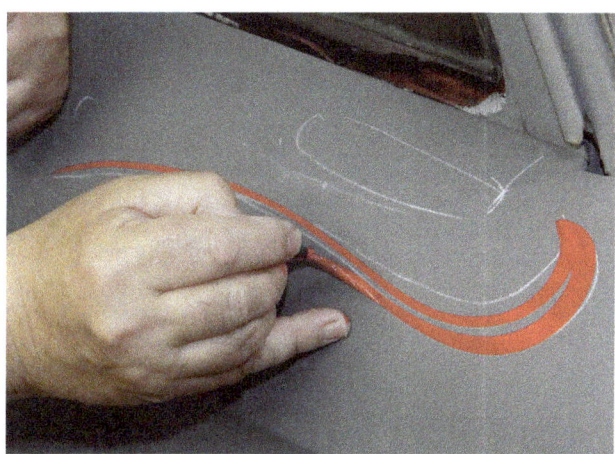

Now I stripe the second line. You see I use my pinky as a way to steady my hand.

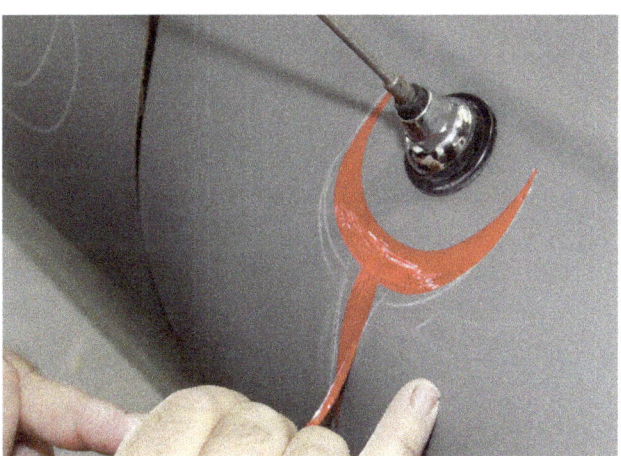

I stripe the design using my Xcaliber 00 brush.

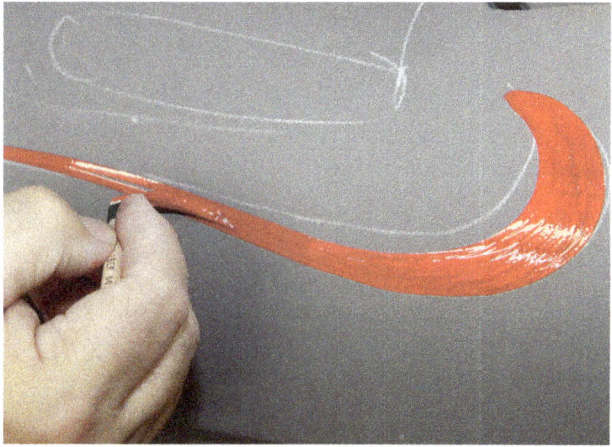

Using the same brush, I fill in the design. I allow the red to tack-up and then apply a second coat later - this is because the truck's paint is porous.

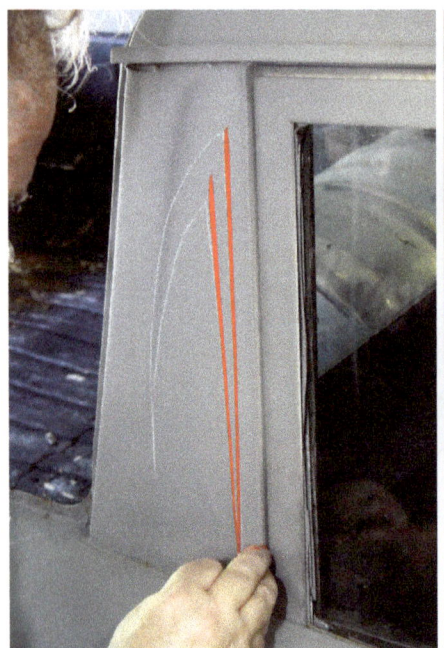

Moving to the sail panel, I stripe the first lines.

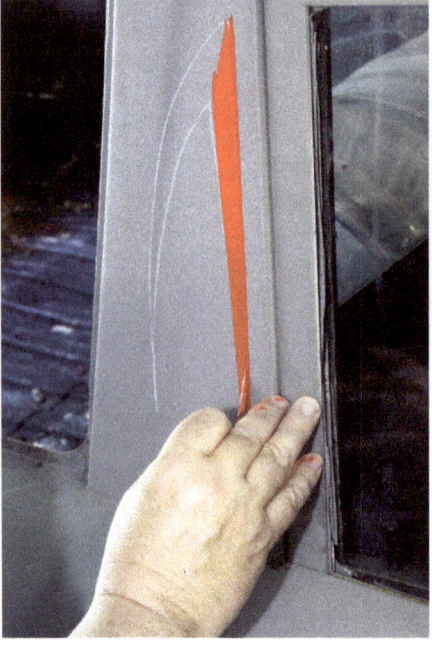

Then I fill in theses lines.

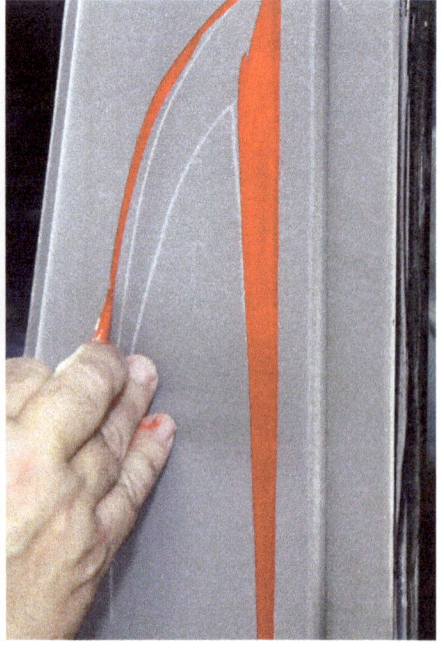

Next I start to work on the arch that tapers back and down.

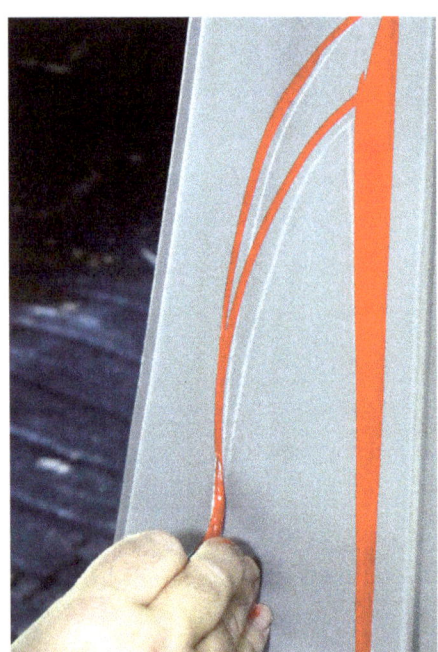

With the arch, or scallop, finished I can fill it in with solid red.

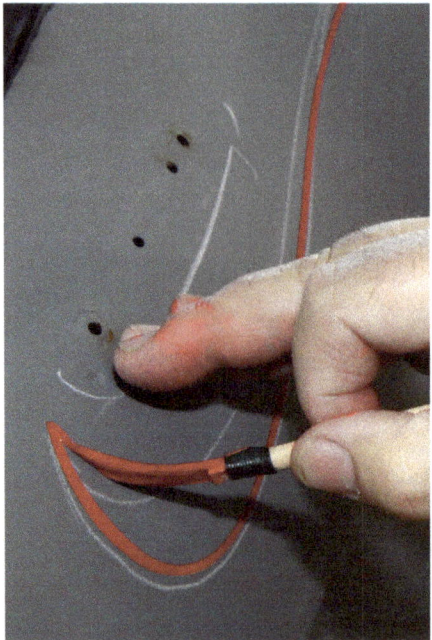

You'll notice that I lay the 00 striping brush on it's side.

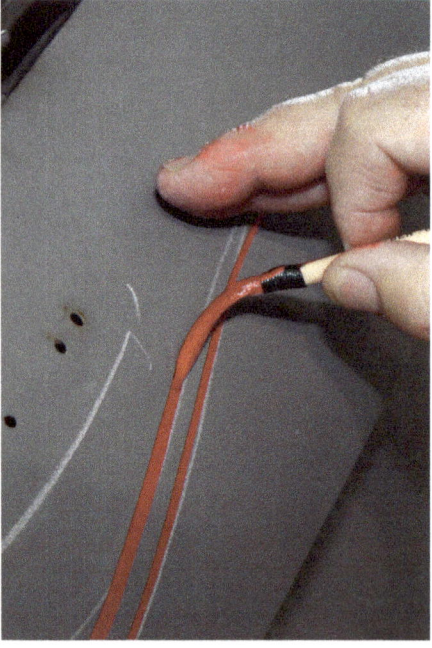

Using my pinky again, I continue the outline.

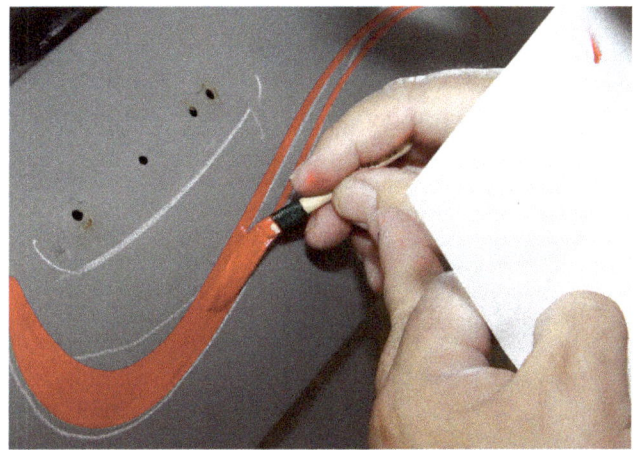

Time now to fill in this part of the design.

A #8 brown lettering quill is used in the larger areas.

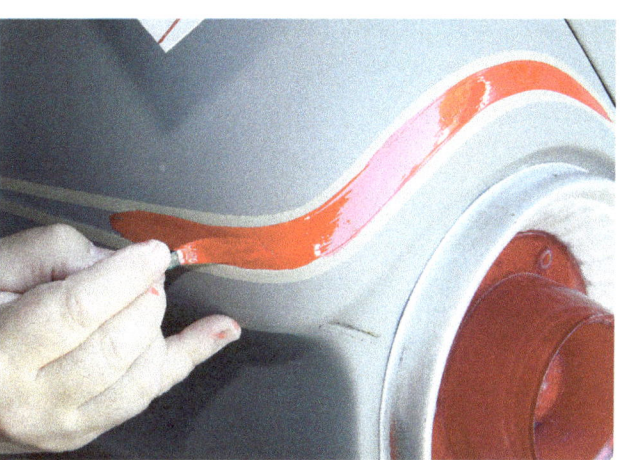

I allow the paint to tack up for about 10 minutes before removing the fine line tape.

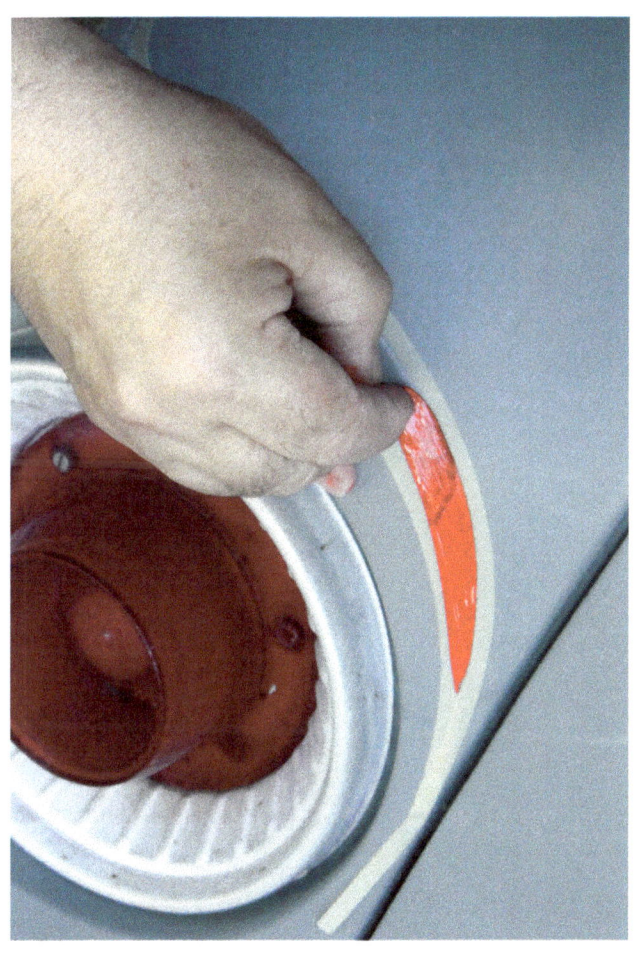

This scallop starts at the lower part of the taillight and wraps up and around.

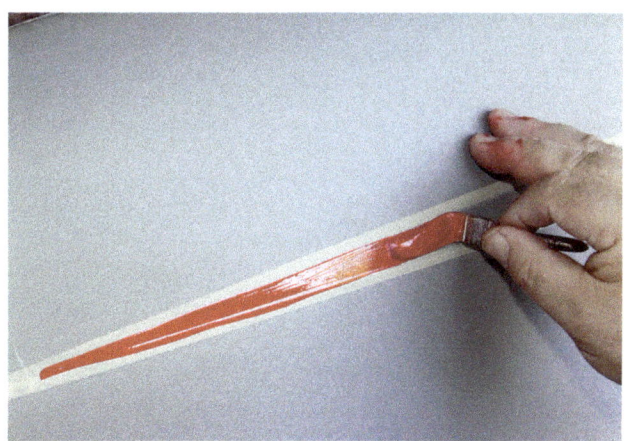

This is how I hold my brush when working on a perpendicular surface.

Xcaliber Brushes

They say that if you build a better mouse trap the world will beat a path to your door. In the case of Julian Braet (aka Mr. J), it wasn't a better mouse trap but a better pinstriping brush; the Xcaliber brand. Better, at least in certain situations. And while the world did not beat a path to Julian's door, more than 20 years after designing the first prototype Xcaliber brush, Mr. J is still selling Xcaliber pinstriping brushes, along with an entire array of pinstriping accessories and necessities.

If you ask where the design spark originated from for the Xcaliber brushes, Julian explains, "Every one of us would buy a brand new brush from Mack or whom ever, and the first thing we did was trim it down, to shorten the bristles and thin them out. So I thought, 'why not make a brush like that, shorter and thinner, so you could work more easily without having to modify the brush?'"

Mack manufactured the first Xcaliber prototypes for Mr J, and the response was immediate. "At first we just made the double-zero brush," recalls Julian, "and that model sold OK, but when we brought out the quad-zero brush - they really took off."

Today, Xcaliber brushes come in four sizes, from single to quad-zero. All feature a brush that is about a half inch shorter than a standard Mack brush, and a handle that's a little smaller as well. "Because these brushes are shorter" explains Julian, "it's easier to make tight turns, you have better control. Because it's easier to control, it's also a good brush for new stripers."

Xcaliber brushes are still hand-crafted by the company that made the first prototype, Mack. The bristles are made of 100 % blue squirrel from Russia, there are no synthetic fibers or filler hairs used on these top end pinstriping tools. Each comes with its own carrying case, "so the hairs don't get bent and beat up in the little brush case," says Julian.

Stripers who click onto Julian's site, www.xcaliberart.com, will find the full range of Xcaliber brushes as well

As shown, the Xcaliber brushes are available in 4 sizes, each a little smaller than a comparable Mack brush with the same size designation.

Xcaliber Brushes

Most painters have a brush kit or case. Mr. J has gone you one better by providing a protective tube for each brush.

Genuine squirrel hair is the only material used to make these brushes, no filler hair and no synthetic hair is ever used.

as the entire line of Mack brushes. In addition, Julian and Linda, (Mrs. Braet, whom Julian refers to as "the brains of the outfit") offer their own brush preservative and accessories. They carry everything from small waxless cups to various types of clip art. New digital clip art and fills - some reminiscent of paint effects from the '60s - will be available soon.

Does the success of Xcaliber mean that one of the best known stripers in the country has "retired" from striping. Not a chance. Mr. J can still be found in his shop on any weekday, and at various car shows on many weekends. The day to day running of Xcaliber is left to Linda, with help from various other family members.

I allowed the paint to set up to the touch, in this case about 1 hour, and then I applied my second coat of cherry red.

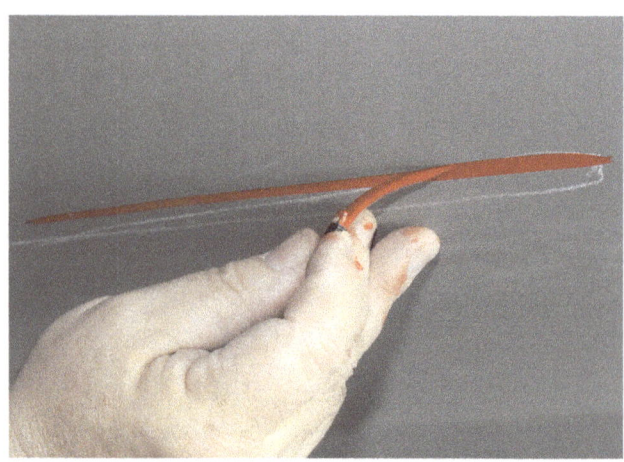

This is a nice little spear of color on the side.

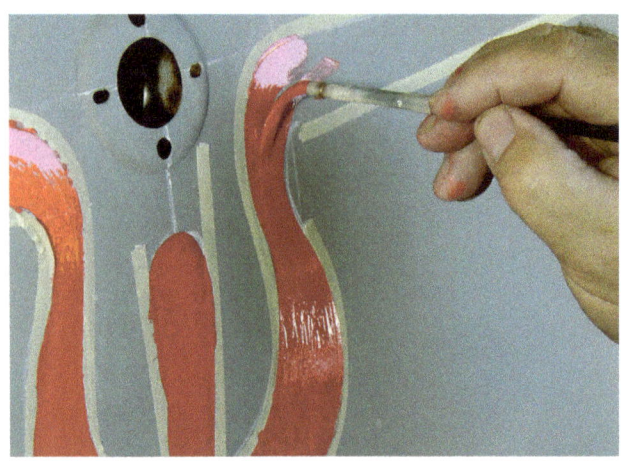

I continue to paint in the design, working to the right.

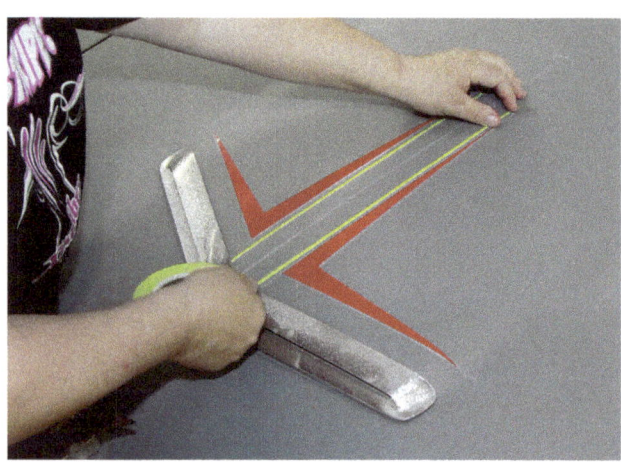

I use some green masking tape as a guide for my fingers to follow for this next step.

I pull the tape before the paint is fully dry.

Time to bring out the big gun, a #4 Mack striper. This is the ivory color that I talked about earlier.

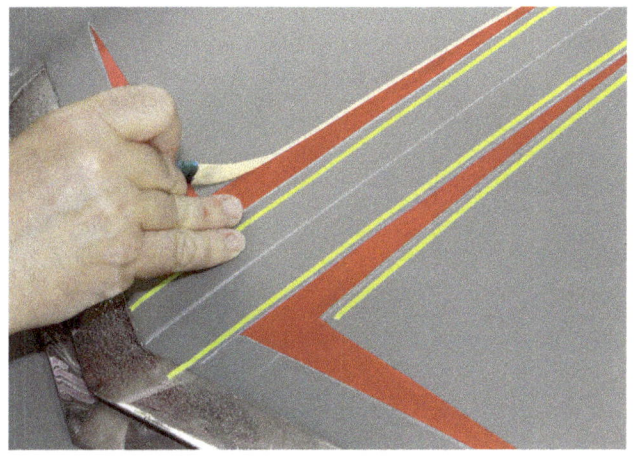

I begin by striping the right side.

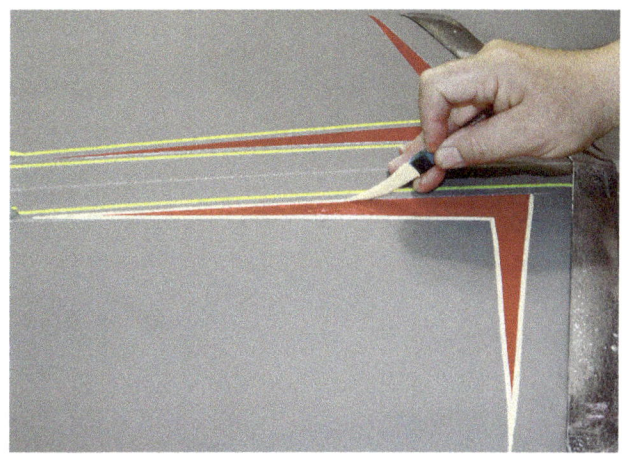

Coming down the back stretch. There's that pinky again!

A close up.

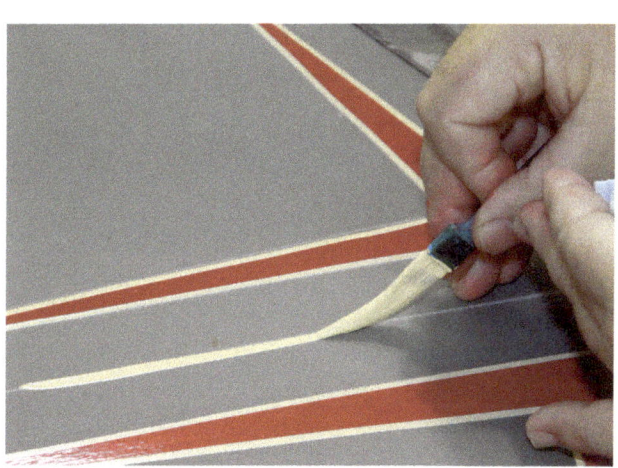

You can see my finger on top of the green tape guide.

Here I join the corners together.

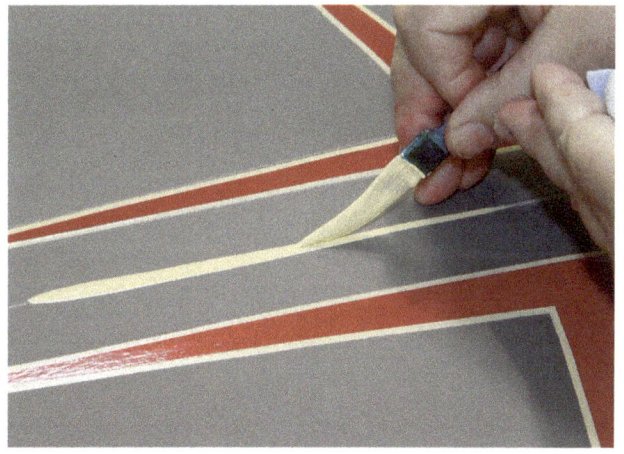

I start a teardrop in the center of the scallop design. I use the two-handed method.

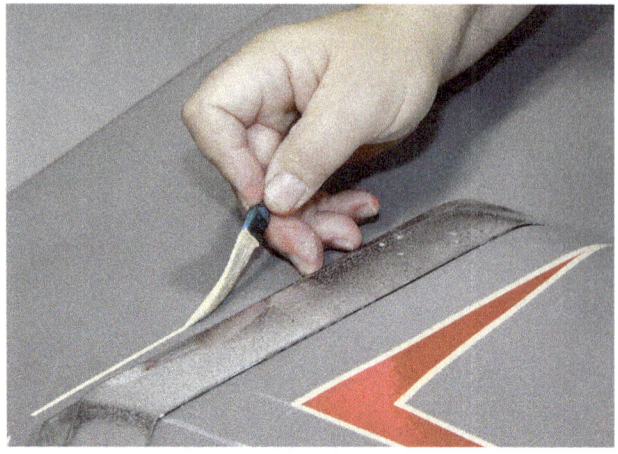

Using the hood trim as a guide, I start another part of the design.

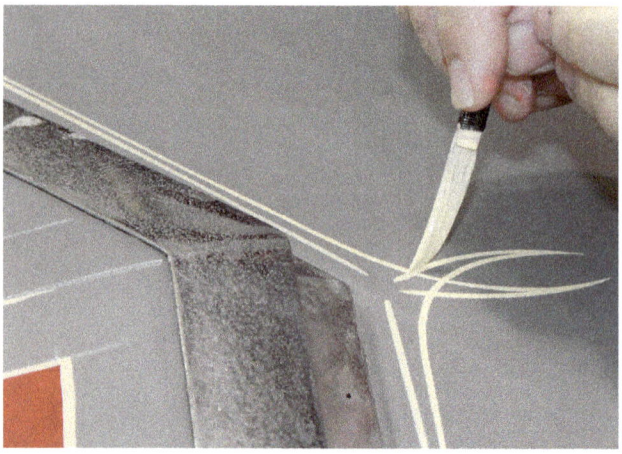

I bring the design down with a slight arc. Notice how high up the brush is. It's easier to create the arc or curve this way.

Here I add a second line almost parallel to the first.

On to the front of the hood. I outline the scallop.

Bringing them together.

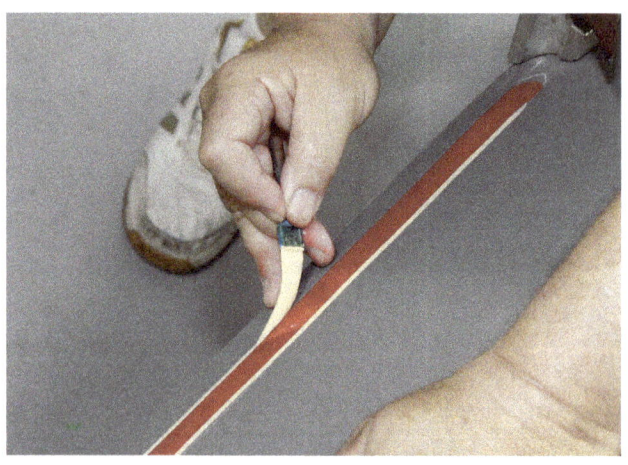

Seen from above, I'm finishing up the outlining of the scallop that runs across the front of the hood.

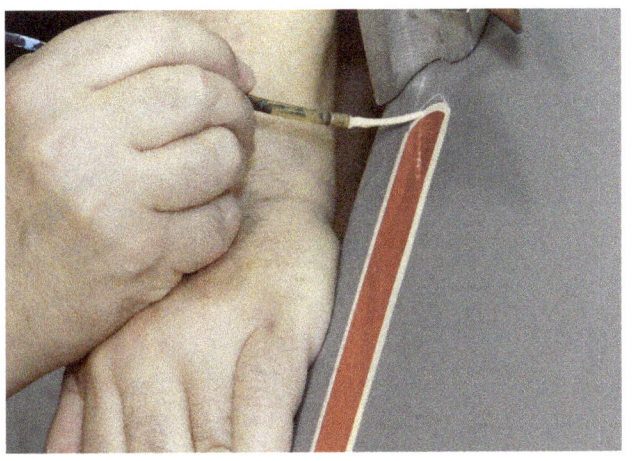

An overhead shot showing the position of my hands again as I round the bend.

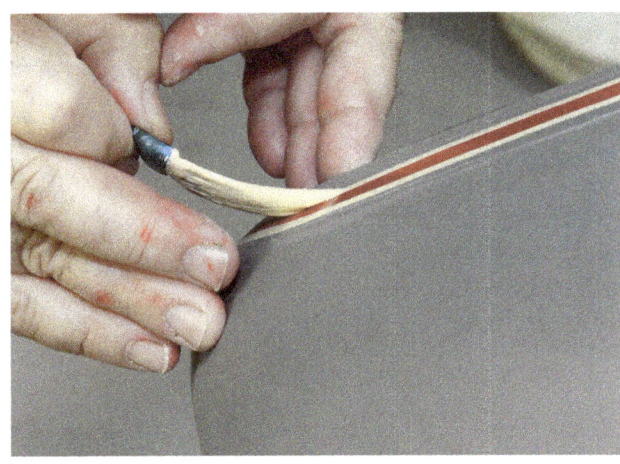

Another close up showing how to hold the brush.

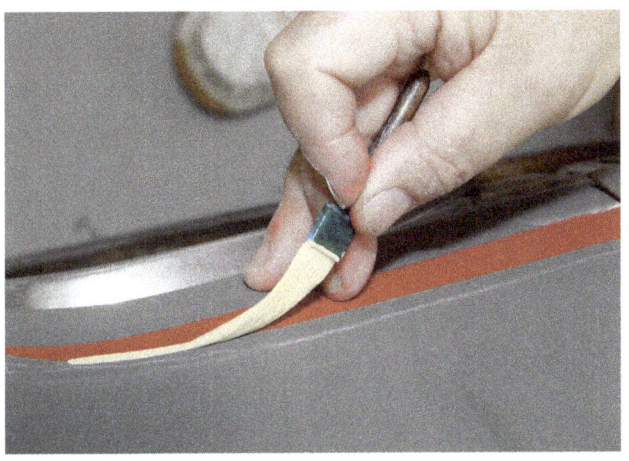

To stripe the corner's, I use a #4 Solo-Horton liner.

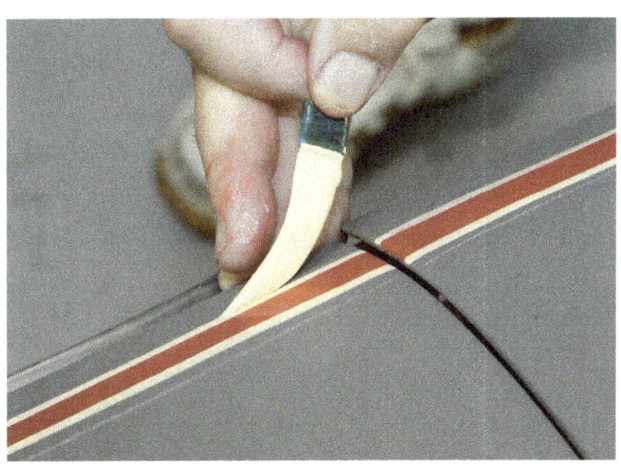

I switch to a Mack blue wrap #00 to connect the stripes over the head lights.

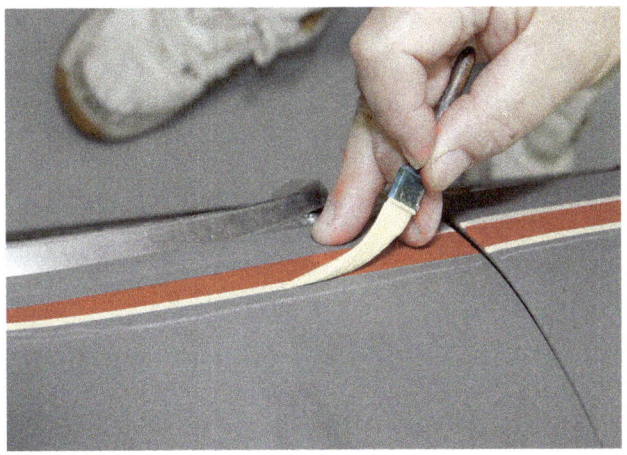

Striping over the head light area.

Back to the #4Mack, I make sure that the stripes connect with each other in a smooth line.

A shot of the completed hood outlining.

I add a small design to balance it off.

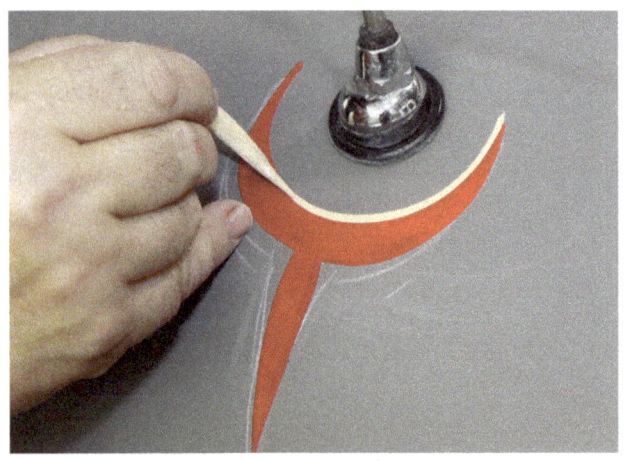

Outlining the antenna design.

Using the big dog brush again, with two hands.

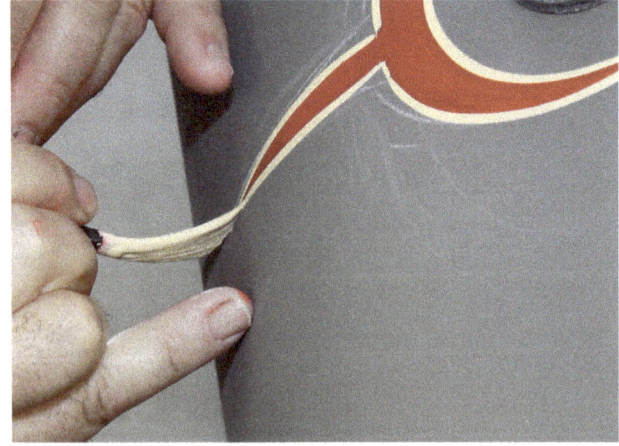

Finishing up the design. I come back with a small quill (#1 or #2) and square off the inside corners.

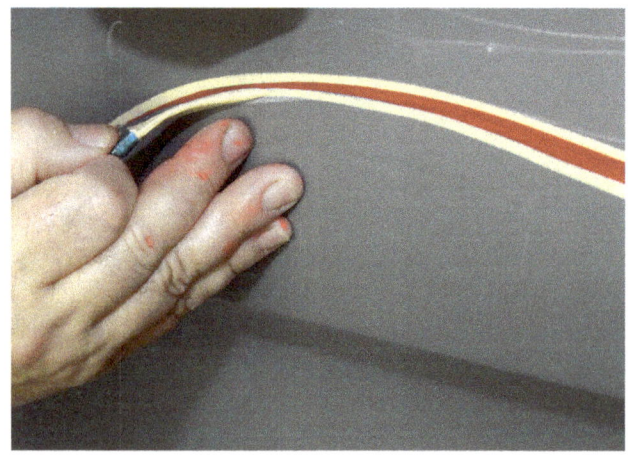

Switching to my Xcaliber #00 to bring the stripes together.

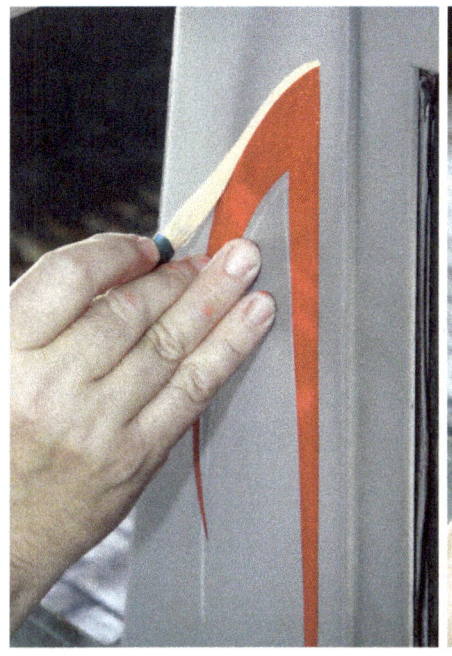

Moving once again to the sail panels I stripe left to right so that I don't put my hands in the wet paint.

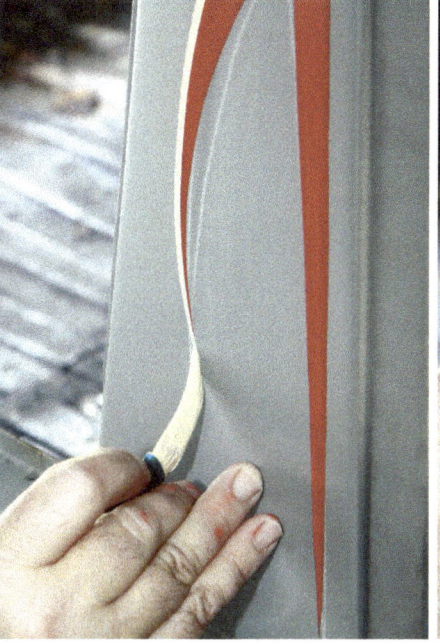

Pulling the line in one stroke.

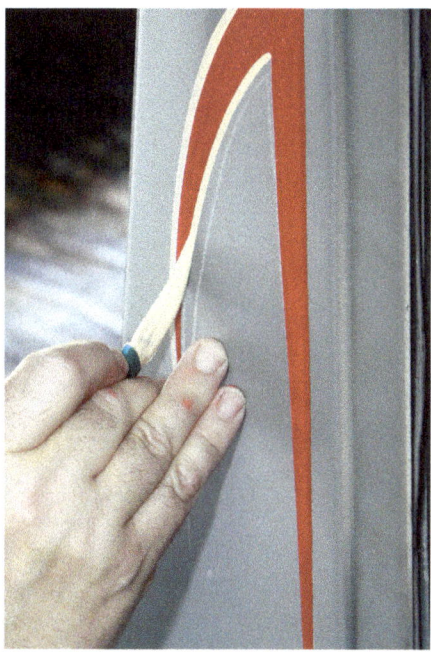

Now, the inside line.

The design is outlined.

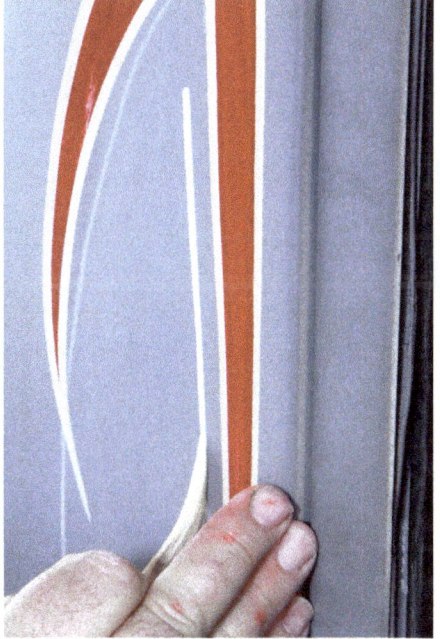

I add a line to the inside...

...then another to create the completed design.

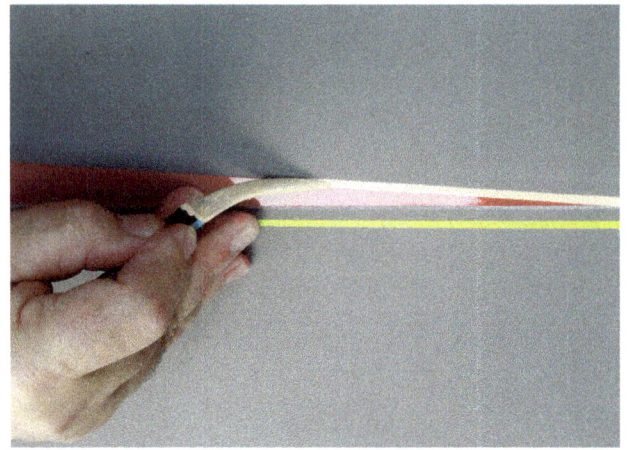

I stripe the deck lid next.

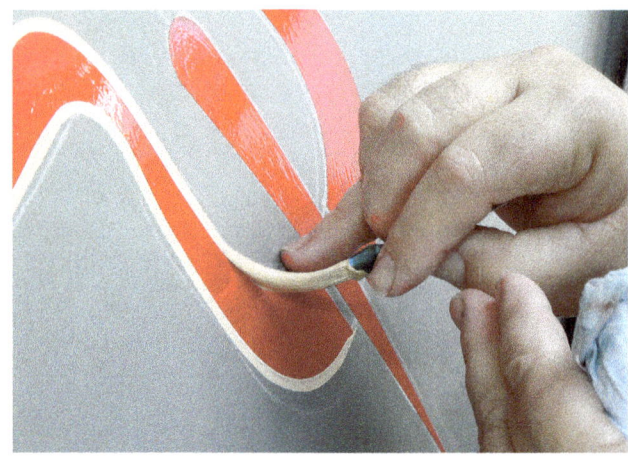

Now I move to the inside. You can see how using two hands can help.

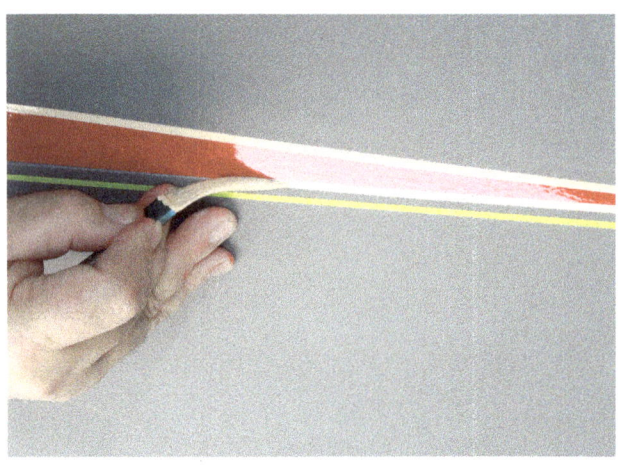

Bringing the bottom line together. Notice how I use the green tape as a guide.

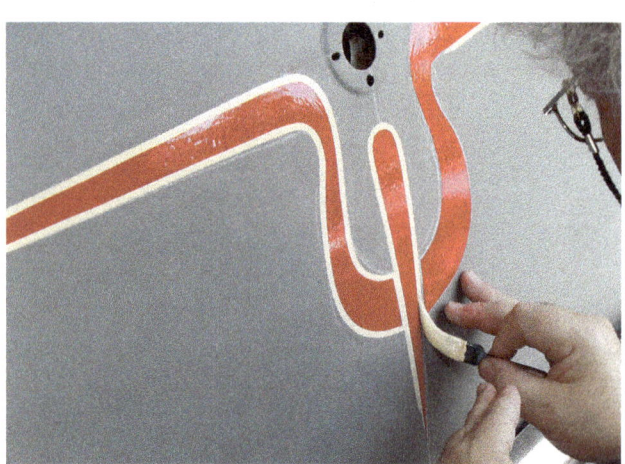

The center is next.

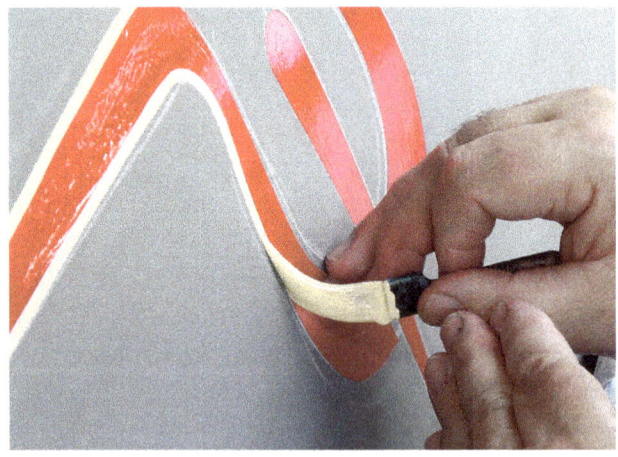

I stripe the outside first.

A close up of the striping on the right side.

A couple of lines are added to the design, similar to what I did on other parts of the car.

Now it's back to the cherry red for some additions.

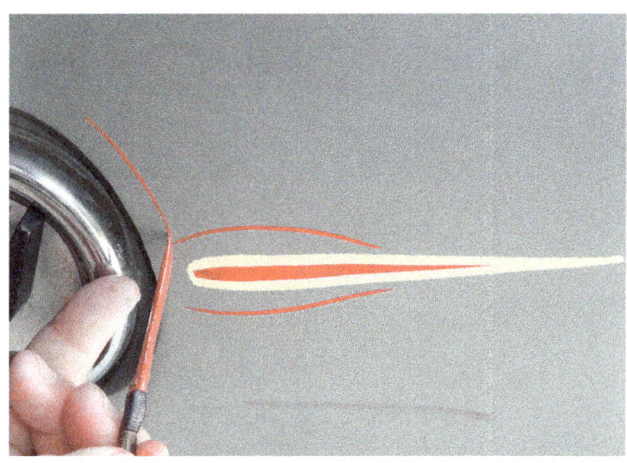

Using a Mack 000, I continue to embellish the basic design.

Progress shot of our nearly finished tailgate.

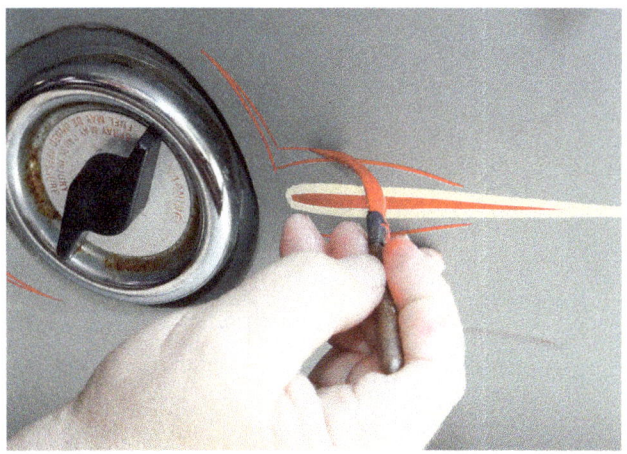

Just one more line.

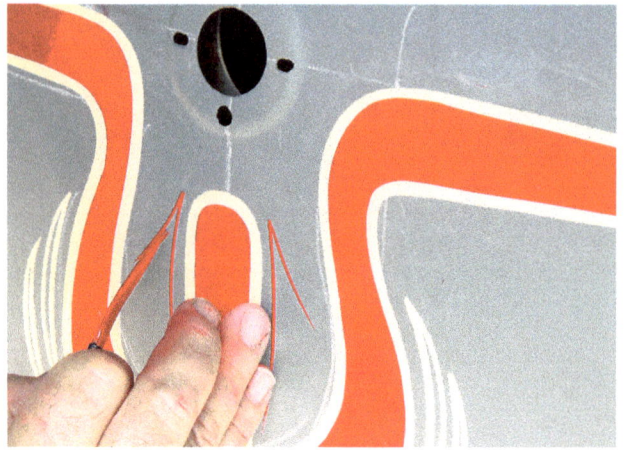

I add a couple of lines...

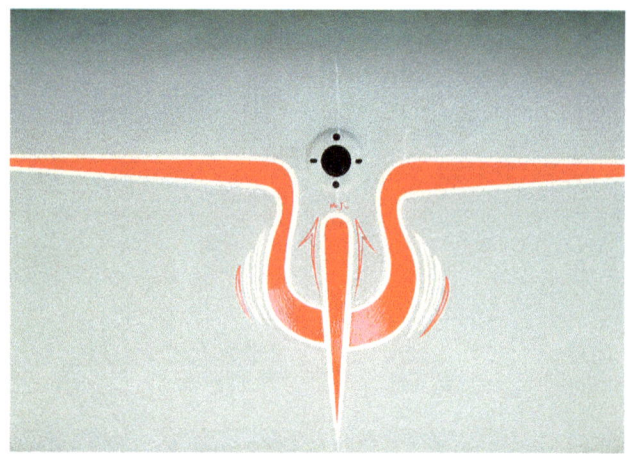

The finished tailgate.

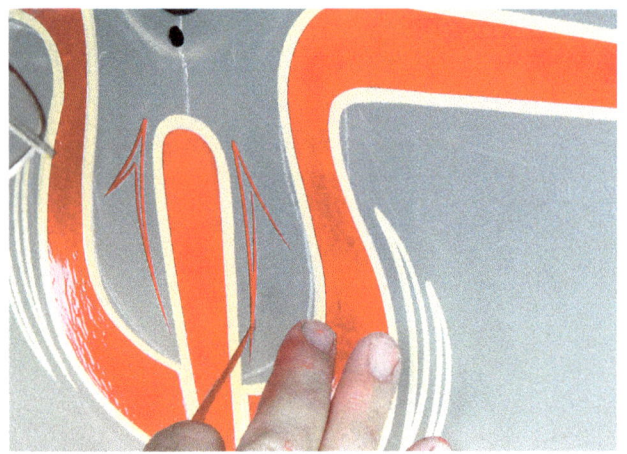

...in cherry red...

The side and antenna designs.

...to both the inside and the outside of the main design.

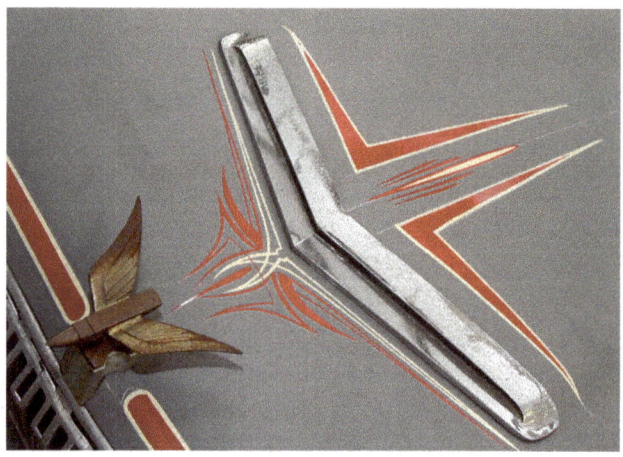

The hood completed.

Q&A: Mr. J

Tell us a little about yourself, and how you became a striper?

My cousin gave me a small car book, one of the 25 cent magazines, and he said, "you're an artist, you ought to do some pinstriping like they have in this magazine." I was 11 or 12 at the time. I tried it and I was hooked. I think that first magazine had a story from Von Dutch about striping, and that's how it started for me. In those days there was no one to teach you, of course.

What do you like to do when you don't have a customer looking over your shoulder?

Lately I've been doing small sculptures. I made one of Artie with the glasses on - and gave it to him. I make them out of plastic and epoxy, and then paint it afterwards.

What do you like to use for brushes?

Of course I use Xcaliber, and also a variety of Macks.

What do you like for paint?

I like Ronan, they seem to have a great product. It dries quick and covers well. Sometimes I have to use the urethanes, but I would rather use the Ronan.

When you're doing something like a panel, do you plan it out ahead of time or just work on the fly?

Most of the time I work on the fly, sometimes I draw part of the design out ahead of time with a stabilo, depends on how much time I have.

Are there absolutes in terms of design, in terms of placement and how many times a line can cross another line?

Not really. I like the KISS theory: Keep It Simple Stupid. Don't get confused, don't get too complex. Do one design and do it well. Stay with four or five lines, concentrate on that. It's like a musician who plays one song until they're really good at it, then they build on that song.

Who inspires you, where do you get your ideas?

Everybody, all my peers. I'm fortunate to be surrounded by guys as good - or way better - than I am. They let me hang around because I've fooled them into thinking I'm better than I am. Also the masters like Von Dutch, Larry Watson, Ed Roth, Dean Jeffries, and Andy Southard.

How do you pick colors?

It depends on what it is. If it's a hot rod, I might use complementary colors, or match the interior. If it's a truck, I tend to use colors the customer likes. But the stripes should always complement the paint job, not be more important than the paint. Like a string of pearls on a beautiful woman, the pearls aren't the whole show.

Final Words of wisdom?

If a person wants to stripe, they need to just try it. And practice. Don't get discouraged. If you copy a design - at least copy something good. Be sure you have a lot of friends, so you can stripe their cars for free - to start with. The money will come later.

Another man born to stripe, Mr. J's been striping cars and painting signs since high school.

Chapter Eleven

Zeke's Panel

Stripes of a Polish Persuasion

Whether it's his Polish DNA, or the fact that Zeke does a lot of his work on big eighteen wheeler rigs, his pinstripe work is in a class by itself. Where most pinstripe artists would zig, Zeke zags. Where most would use a straight line, Zeke produces curves, loops, more curves, and lines that get fatter before stopping in space, with a short cross line just before the end. The design seen here sits on a pedestal of sorts, the whole thing is wrapped in a border that can only be called unique, especially the corners. So before assuming that all pinstripers use the same basic designs, consider the work of Zeke Lemanski, a truly unique artist.

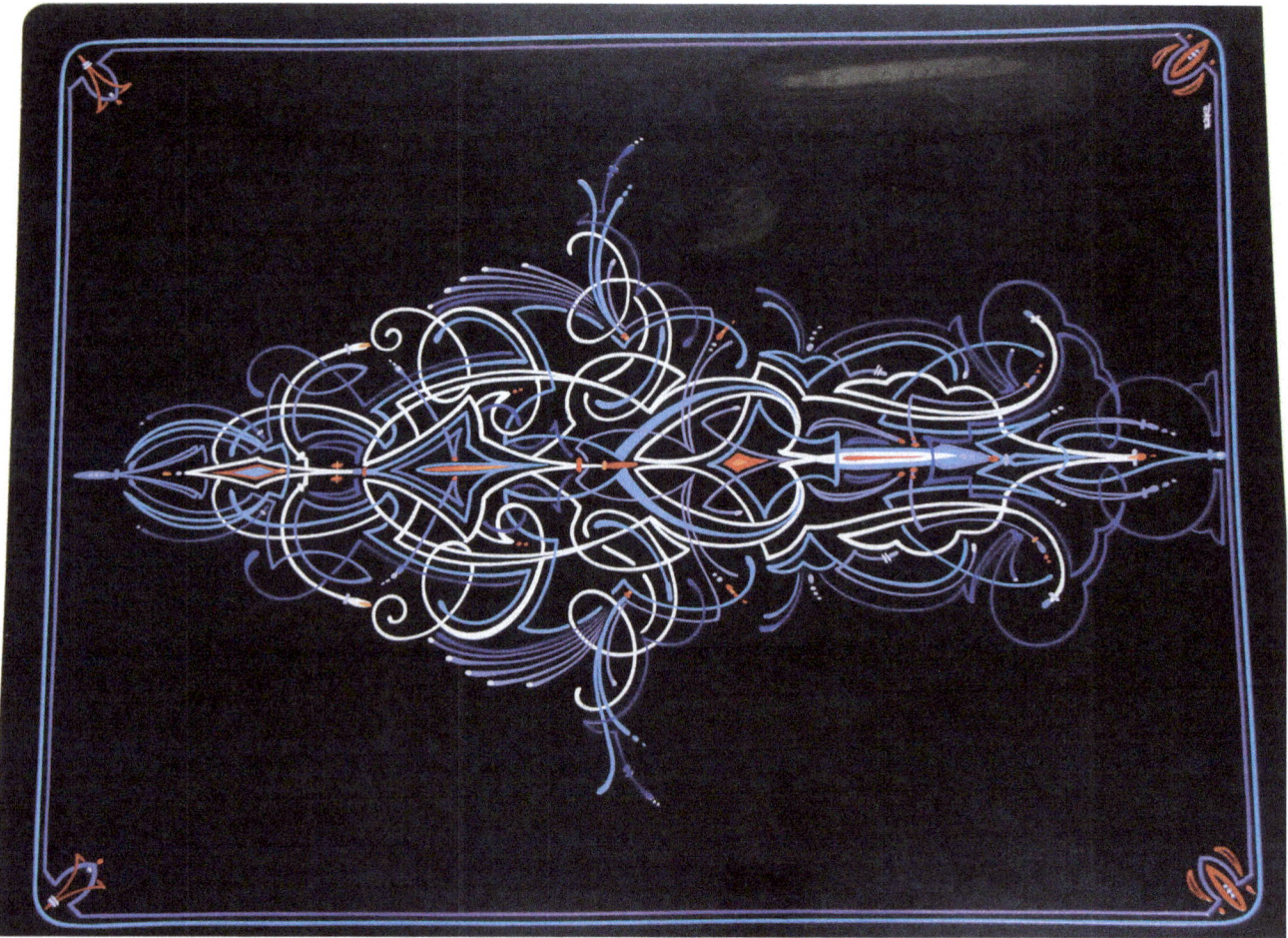

In a class by himself, Zeke creates panels with a certain old-world charm, filled with features that are truly unique.

Brushes: Mack Bobbo, Liner

Paint: Kustom Shop

Artist Comments:
I utilize the grid system that I design and manufacture to lay out the grids and scroll guides used for the background on this piece.

I start by laying out grid lines using a Stripe-a-line grid and a white marking pencil. The grid I'm using is #1 of the grid system I design and manufacture. Using this helps to ensure a well balanced design.

Using my curve and scroll grid #13, I add scrolls, curves and arches.

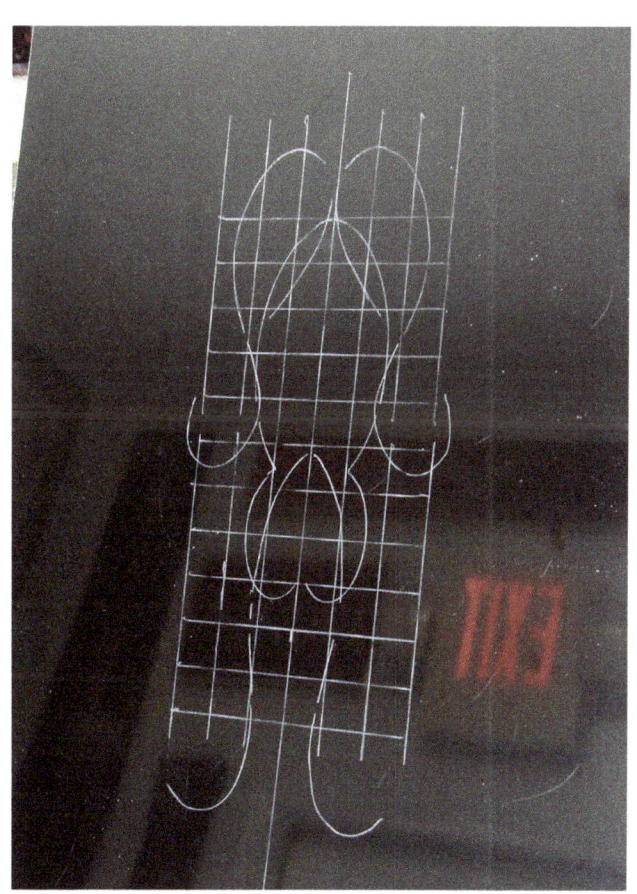

Using this basic background layout will help keep my design balanced, even when adding detail later.

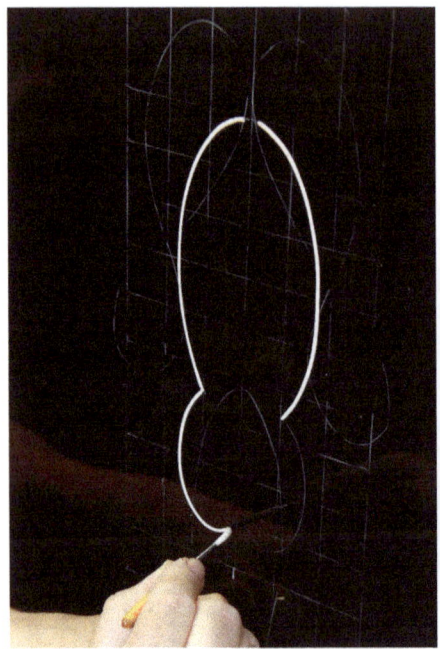

I'm using a Mack Bobbo, super quad #0 brush. The lines I drew with the aid of my grid now help guide me as I begin to paint the basic structure of the design.

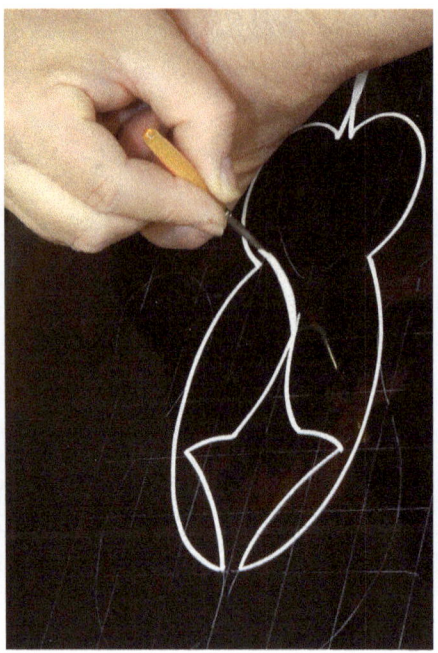

As I add more detail I'm using reference points off the grid.

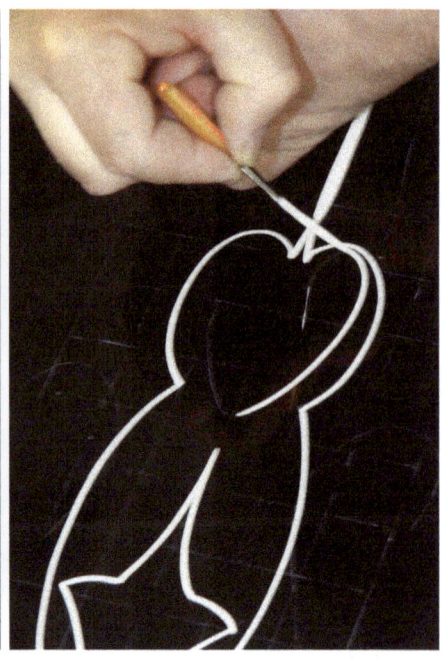

I continue adding lines and curves, trying to make an interesting and well balanced design.

Adding more detail to the center of the design will draw your eye to the middle of the layout.

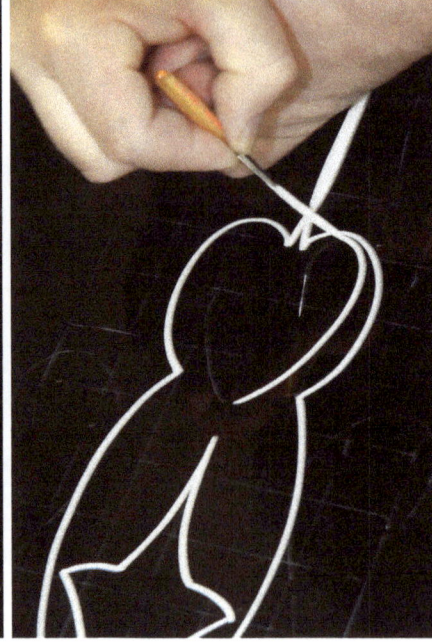

While turning or scrolling the Bobbo brush I use just the tip of the brush, and simply move my hand or wrist as the brush follows my movements.

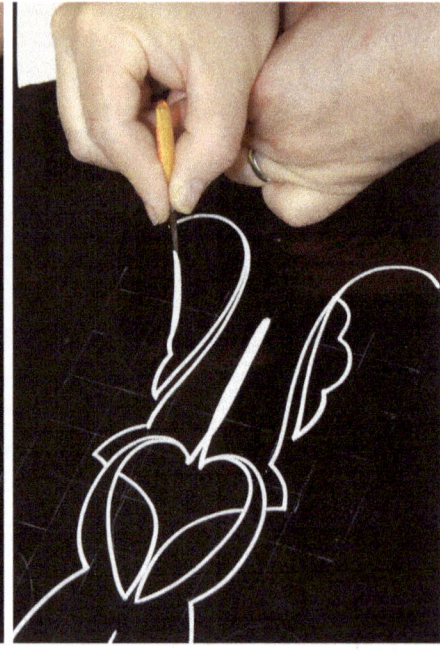

Pressure is the key to maintaining the width of your lines. Keeping the paint loose and at a constant, even mix will keep the lines clean.

Here I'm adding short scrolls and curves, changing the flow of the straight lines.

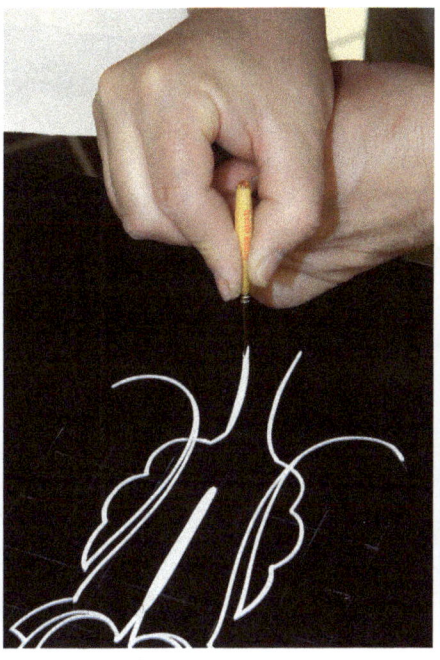

This small detail makes for a much more interesting layout, and is easy to do with the Bobbo brush.

I now move to the top of my panel and add some longer, tapered lines.

Pull the brush using just the tip, no need to twist the brush between your fingers. This little brush, surprisingly, can pull a fairly long line.

Adding a bit of detail to the end of a single line helps to give it a finished look.

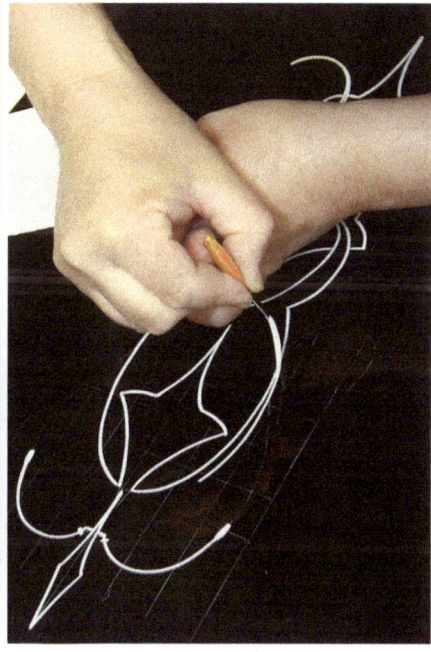

A second line here will add weight to the design and help to fill space.

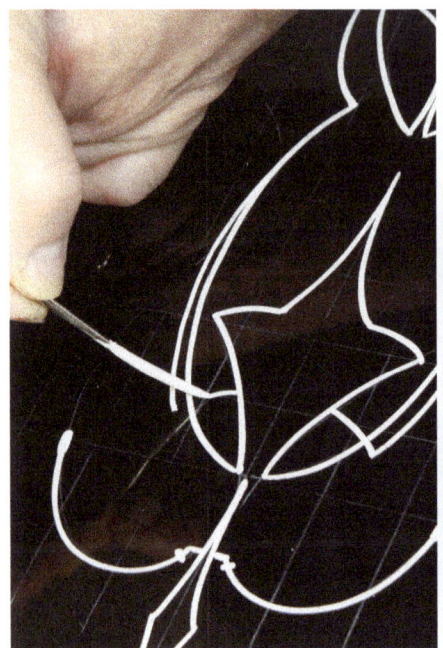

This brush enables me to finish ends of lines or add detail such as this connecting line.

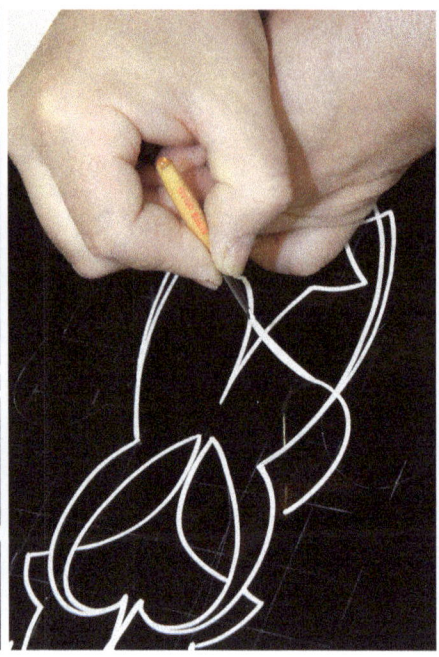

As I add more lines, I keep in mind that I need to leave open spaces for additional colors and lines.

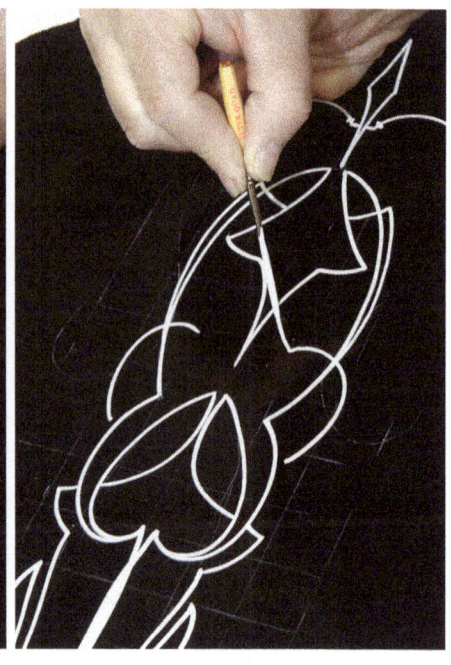

Adding lines and curls in opposite directions makes for a more interesting design.

Additional lines help fill open areas. I try to visualize the finished piece - as I think ahead to adding more color.

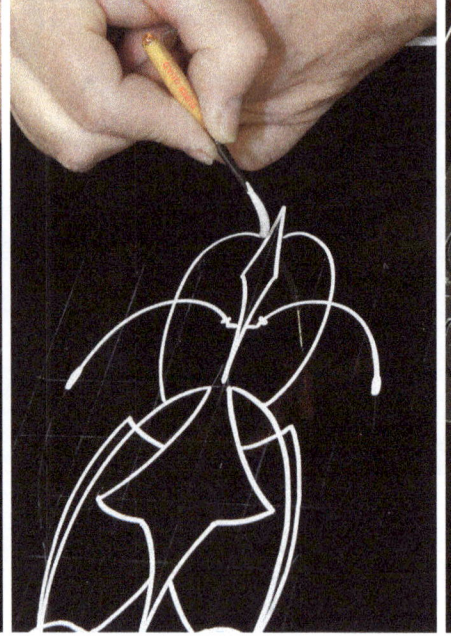

My intent here is to build a structure in white which will be my main contrasting color, and then the second and third colors will accent the main design.

With the white paint dry to the touch, I add additional curves and scrolls. Using my Stripe-a-line grid, these overlapping scrolls are quick and easy to add - as the grid is clear – allowing for perfect alignment.

With my guides sketched out, I begin to add my complex scrolls.

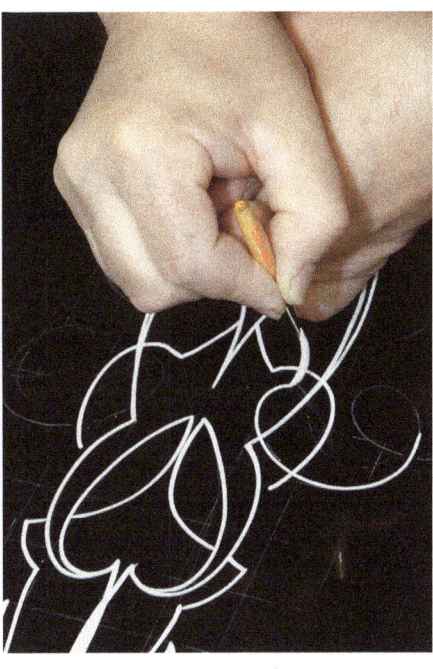

I'm tying in the scrolls with lines that I've previously left open.

Using my original scrolls as a reference, I add detail to the design.

I build this scroll in several moves. Having a defined guide will ensure a very precise, tight turn.

When doing the tight turns I find that slowing down helps to control the tip, as well as maintain good coverage with my paint.

This very tight turn requires me to slow down, which allows the tip to rotate into the curl.

Here again I've drawn complex loops on either side of my design and begin to follow the guides.

As I follow the guides I'm confident that I will be able to replicate them accurately on the opposite side.

Using a white marking pencil to mark my guide lines means that I will not wipe or smudge the lines when I go over them with paint.

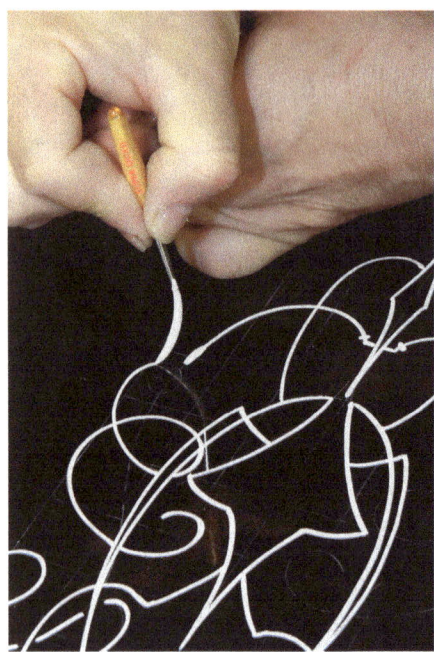

Another benefit to using white pencil instead of powder; it ensures that the paint will not creep or pull into the powder.

The paint from the brush flows easily over the white guides without leaving any texture or powder in the paint.

With my white striping finished, I begin adding my second color. From here on any additional colors I add will be darker than previous ones.

At this point I'm starting in the center of my design.

As I add the second color I keep in mind that I need to fill the negative, open spaces.

I try to vary my overlaps, making some appear as though they are weaving over - and under - my original design.

Now that the white paint is dry I can place my hand on the surface to maintain control while I pull between the lines and tight curves.

The Bobbo brush allows for clean starts and stops.

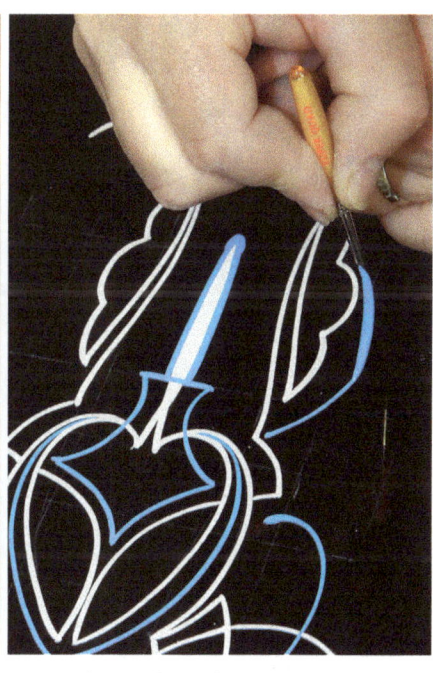

I use the grid guide again and visually try to keep the lines in balance as I add additional ones around the main design.

Zeke's Helmet

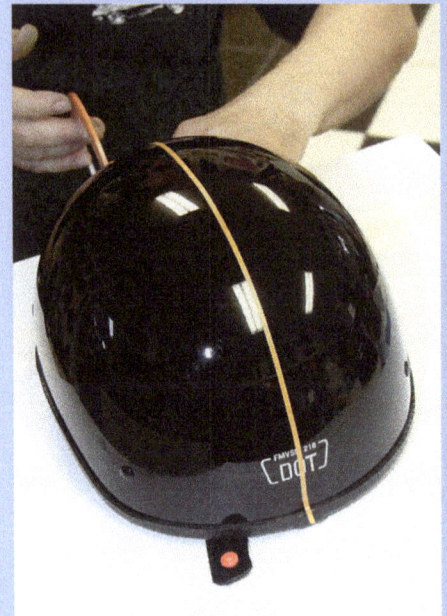

I find the center of the helmet and mark it using 1/8 inch tape. Then I use a white pencil to mark guides on either side of the tape.

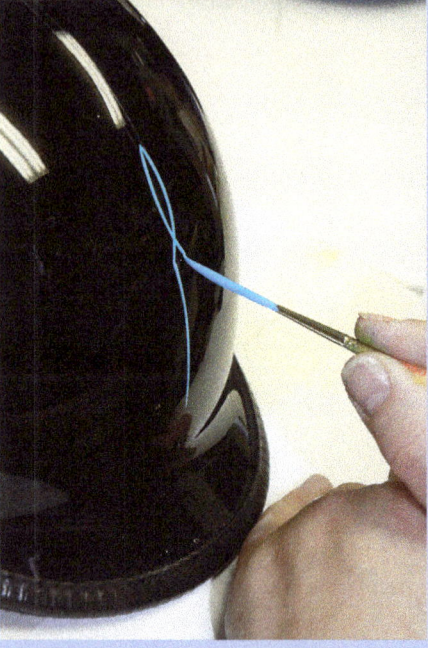

After removing the tape I begin to stripe the front of the helmet. Creating a center line will aid in creating a balanced design.

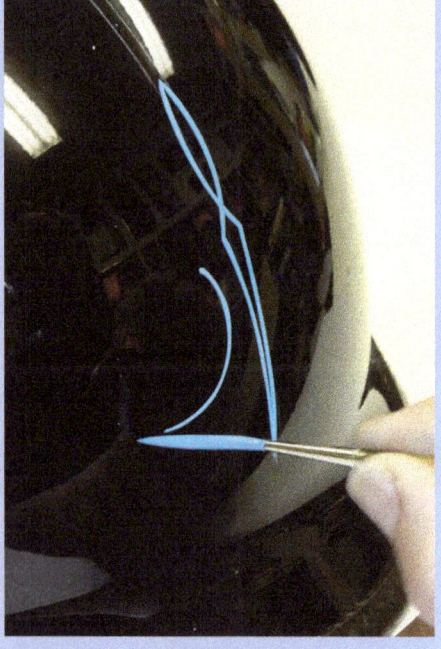

Here I'm adding a simple curve to the left, and right, as I continue to complete the front of the helmet.

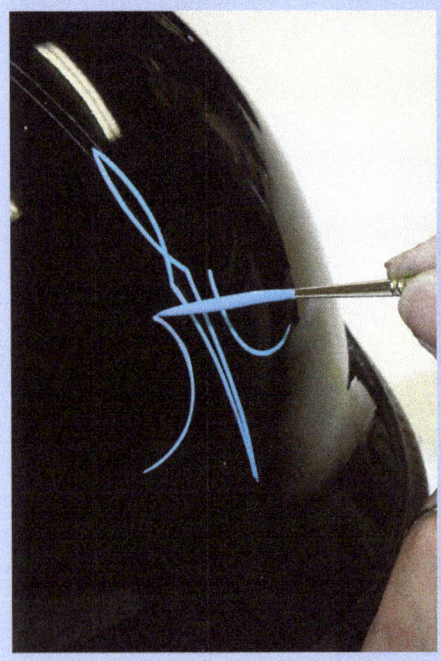

Combining the curves in the center of the design, without crossing over, leaves the center open and uncluttered.

Detailed arches and curves are no problem with my Bobbo. The lines appear to weave, making for an interesting one-color design.

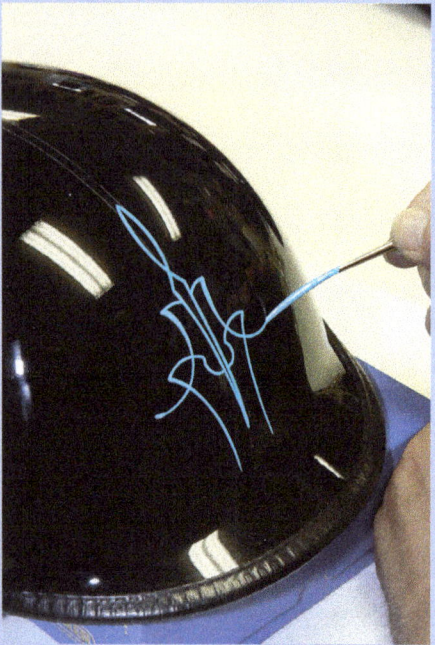

By adding a drop at the end of the single line, I provide a finishing touch that's simple and easy to do.

Zeke's Helmet

As I'm pulling an S-shaped line, I'm also looking at the center line to keep my shape balanced.

With a simple design it's important to keep the two sides balanced.

Adding a second line will give weight to the design.

I'm trying to make it interesting, while still keeping it simple.

Here I'm filling in the central area of the design.

Adding some downward stripes helps to finish the design.

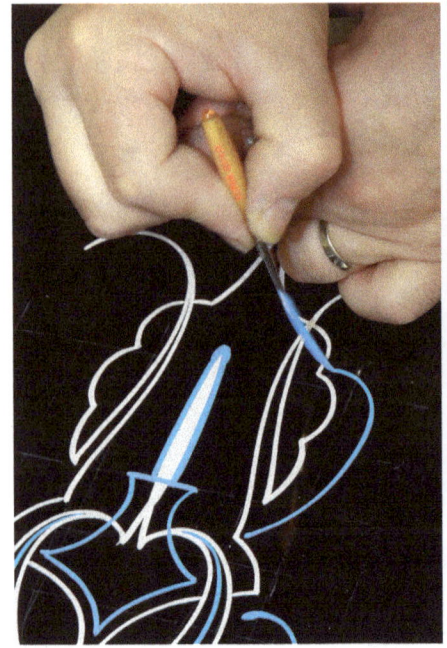 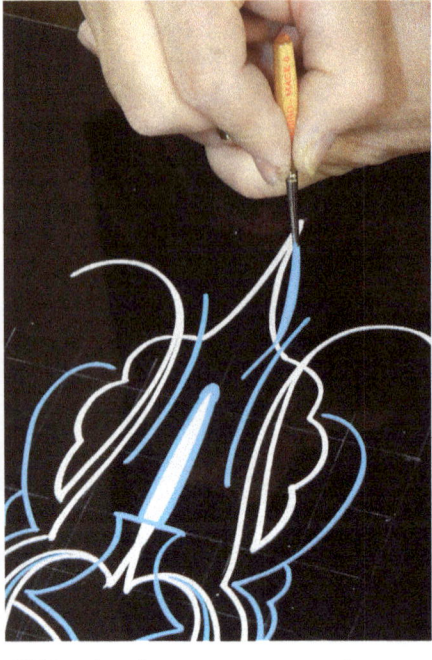 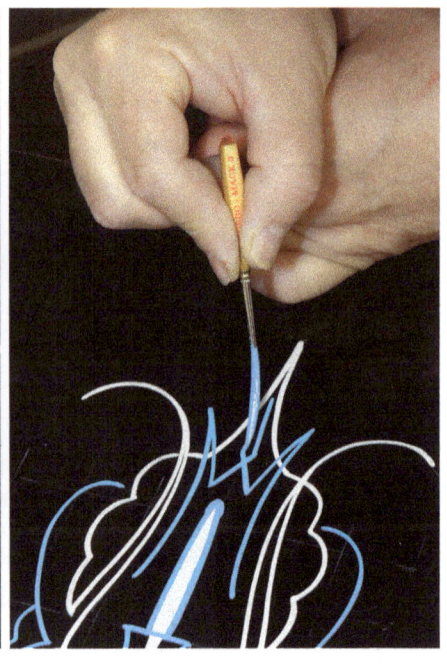

Using my second color I outline some of the bolder, filled teardrops. This helps to soften the edges of the white.

Filling in the open spaces and creating opposing curves and lines helps bring shape to the design.

Some of the smaller details - that really add a bit of complexity - are simpler to do with this great little brush.

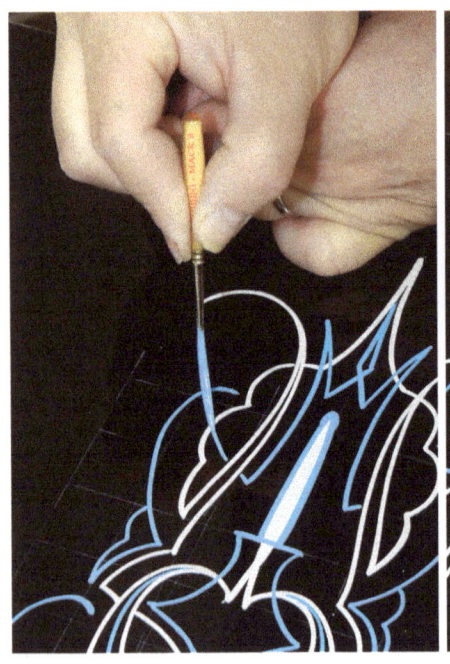  

The over and under line affect creates a weaved look - which makes for an interesting design.

As I add my second color, I remind myself to leave space for additional colors.

At this point I'm just using my original white design as a visual guide to accent with the second color.

As I'm adding and filling spaces I keep a visual image of the finished piece - to maintain just the right amount of balance with the blue.

Since the white is dry, the brush flows over it without skipping or dragging. This makes for nice clean lines.

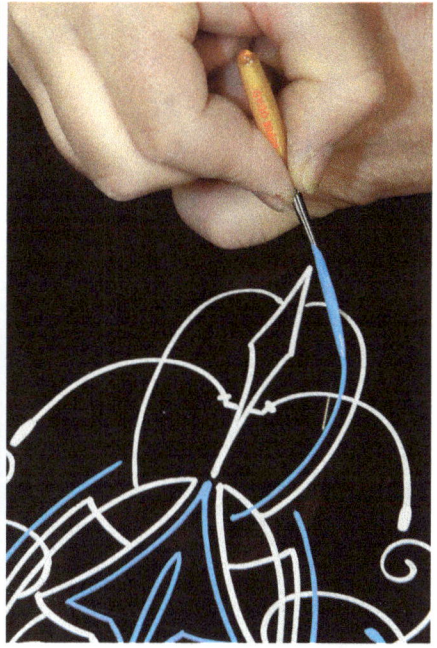

As I work to the top, or bottom, of the design I try to apply less of the second color. This will make the design look tapered and balanced.

Although most of the lines are of the same width, filling in at certain focal points adds depth to the design.

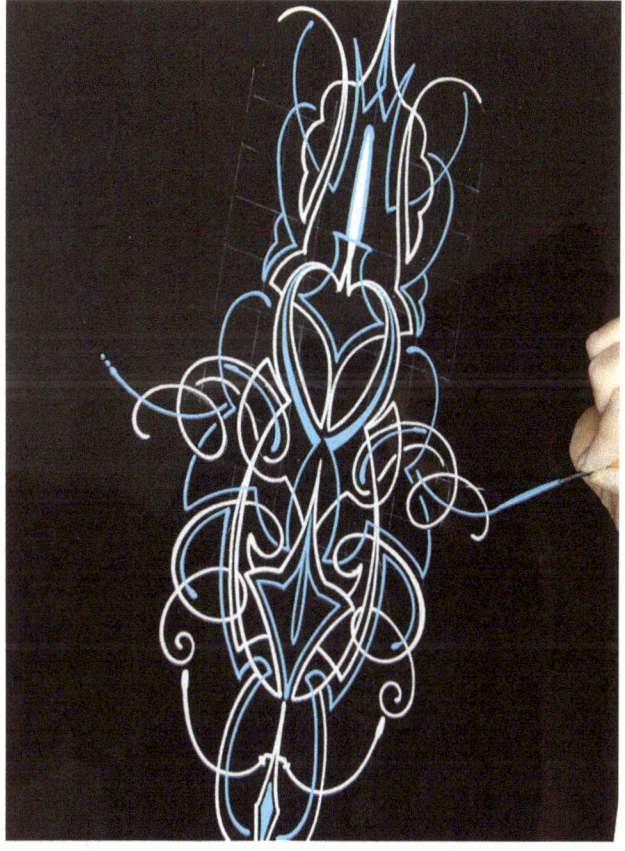

Striping a curve in the opposite direction of the main white scroll takes the design in a new direction and adds a bit of flare.

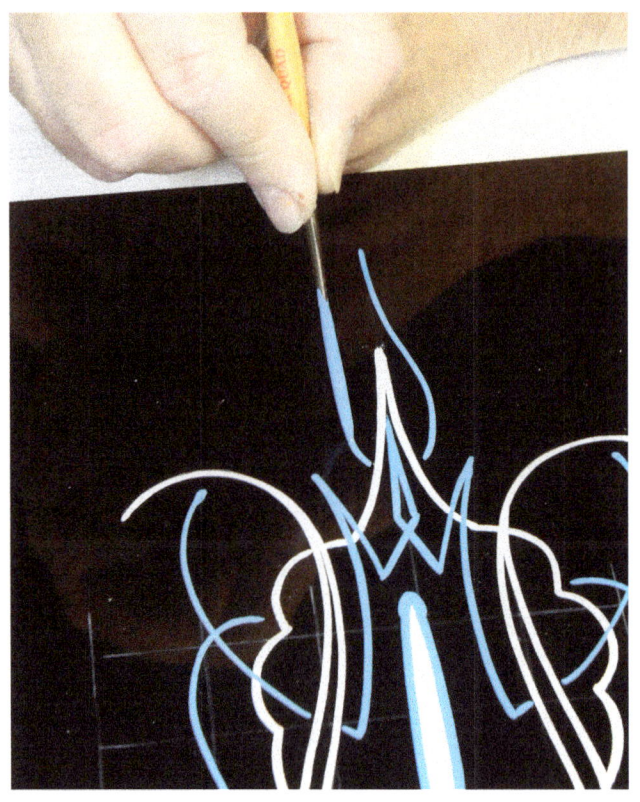

I pull additional blue lines at the top and bottom.

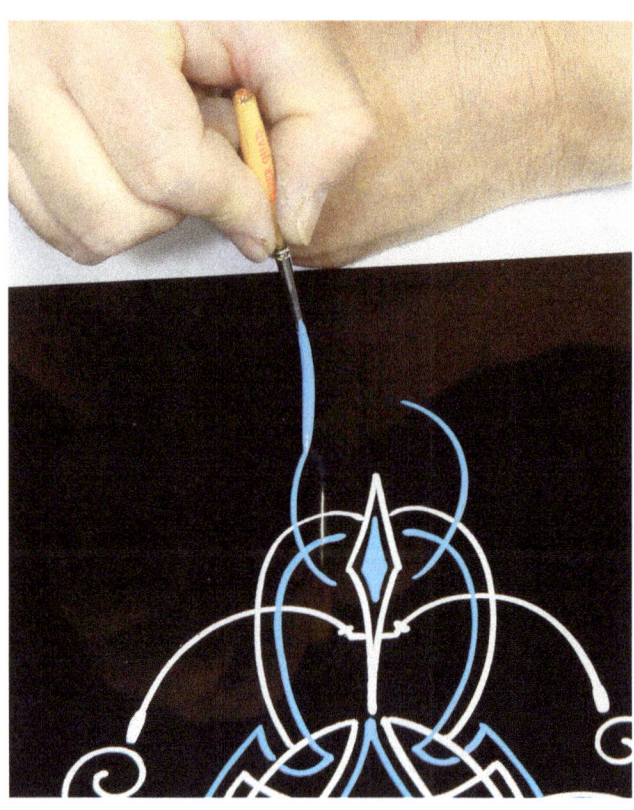

I add some finishing touches with the blue.

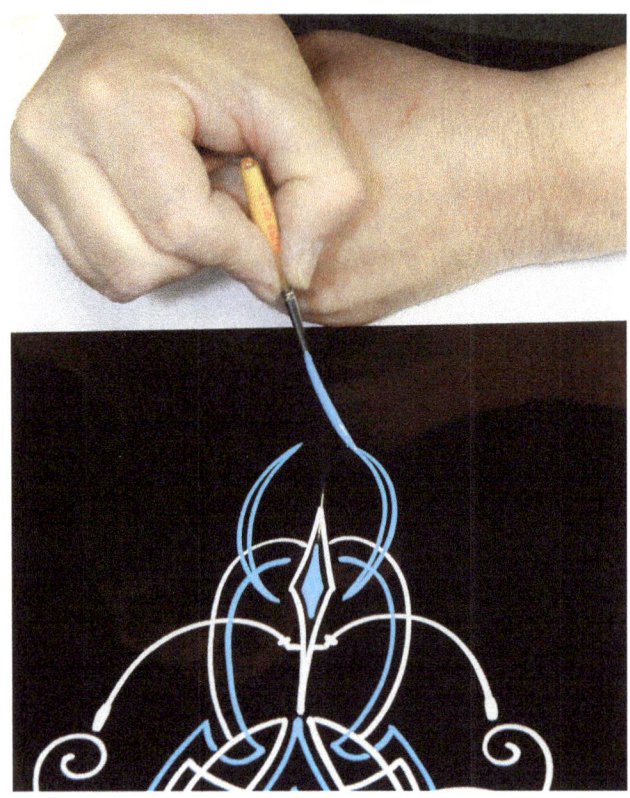

Doubling the bottom blue line will finish the last of the design.

Here I mix the third color - which will be a mix of light blue and purple.

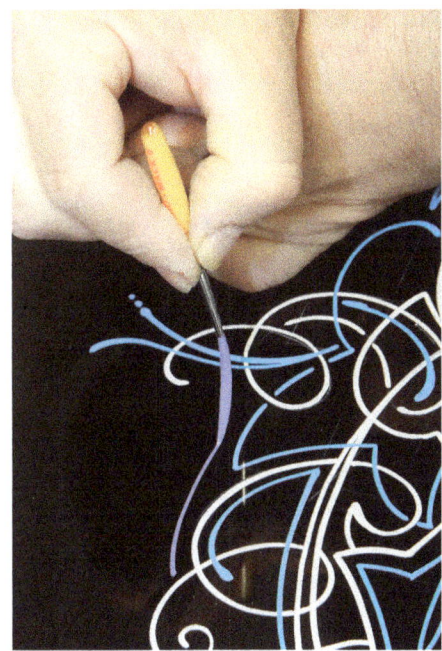  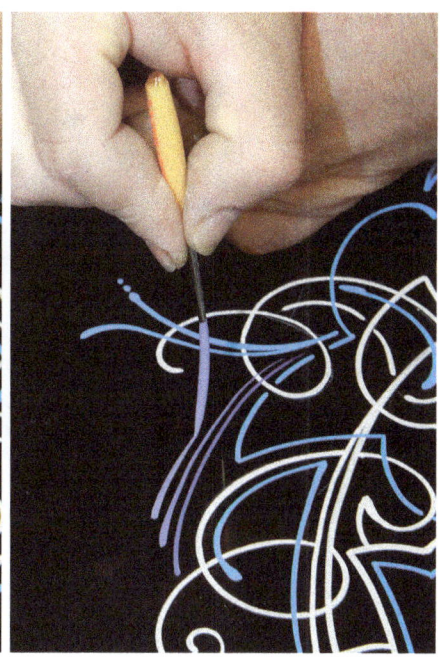

I'm starting to add some long tapered teardrops. In this case I use them as a filler. I repeat this left to right.

As I add the additional teardrops, I mix in a small amount of white paint to each. This creates a gradient fill effect.

By dropping the teardrops as I paint them, I create a tapered wing look.

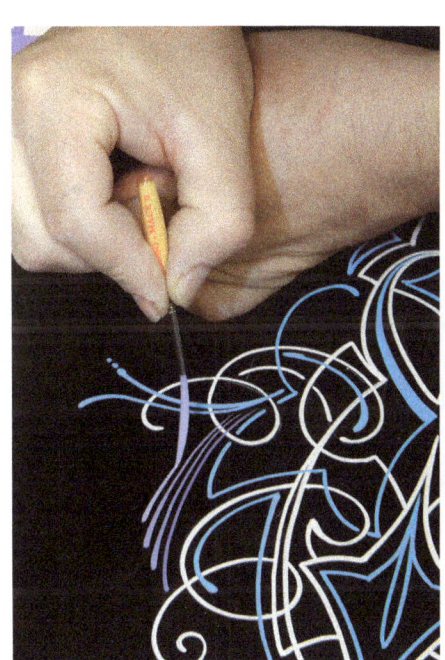  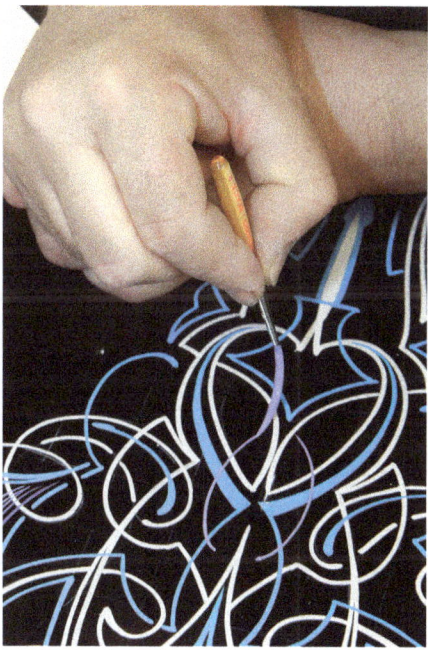

Tapering the teardrops and pulling them into a vanishing point creates an eye appealing effect.

Keeping uniform space between the lines helps maintain a clean, balanced look.

Using the same purple/blue mix, I add thin lines that contrast with the heavier lines.

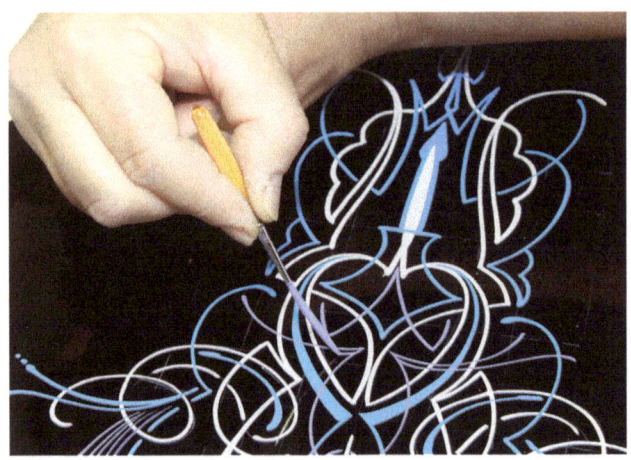

With a third color - and thin lines - I fill in some of the open space I've left for just this reason.

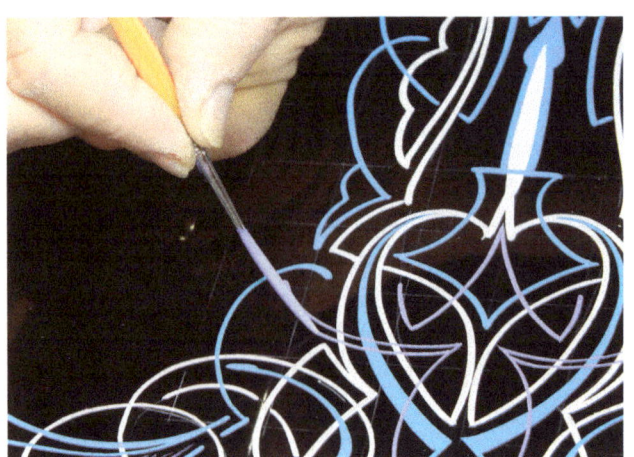

Doubling up on a line creates the appearance of a bold line, without making it a solid bold line.

Here again the blue has dried, allowing for smooth pulls over the existing two colors.

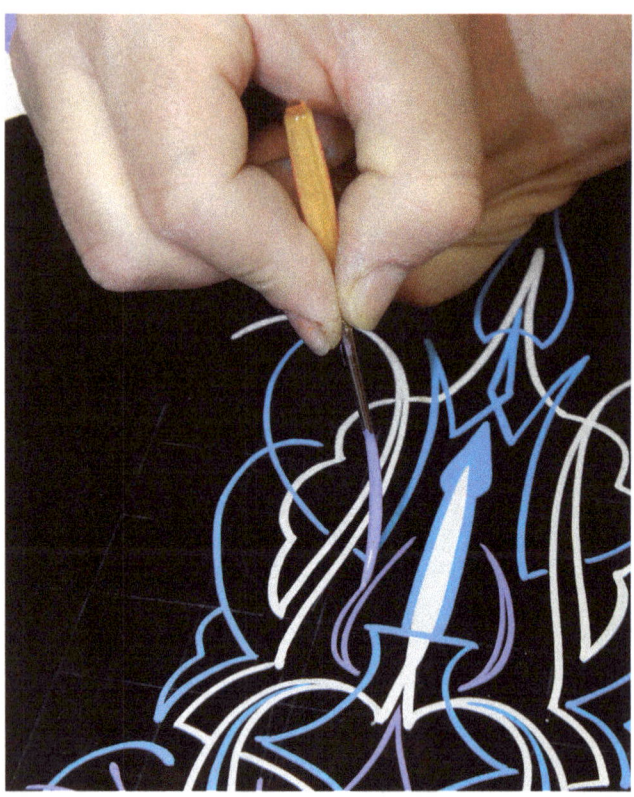

Looking at my design I pick and choose where my third color will provide the best accent.

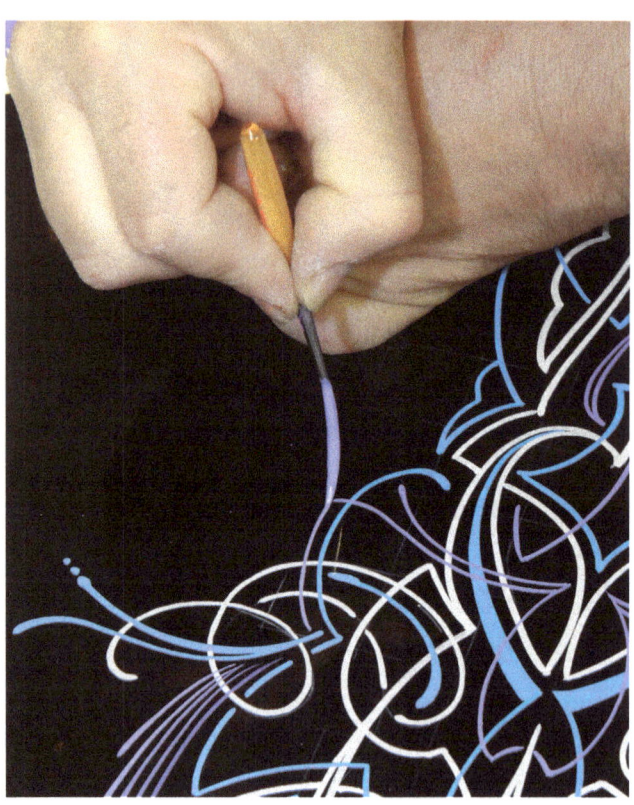

At this point you can get creative. Here I'm pulling fine lines where they will best complement the finished design.

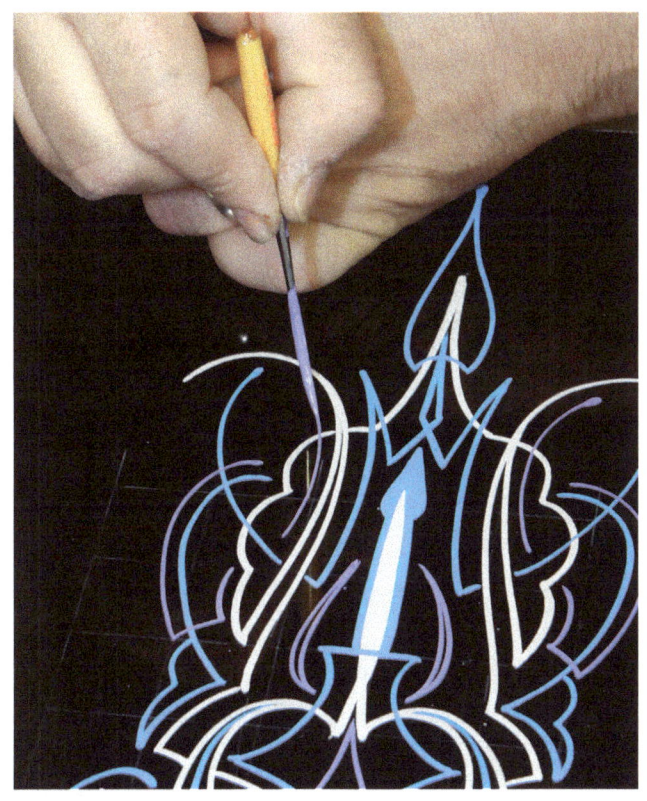

I've used the same brush for this entire panel. Here again pressure is the key in creating extremely fine lines.

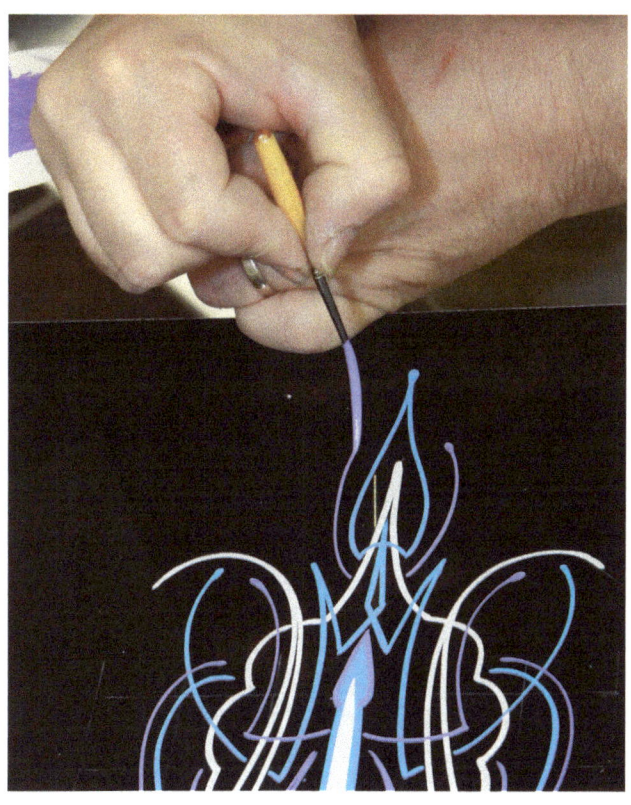

Keeping a symmetrical flow and color balance is what I've striving to achieve.

Since I use such small amounts of paint, I do all my mixing on a palette.

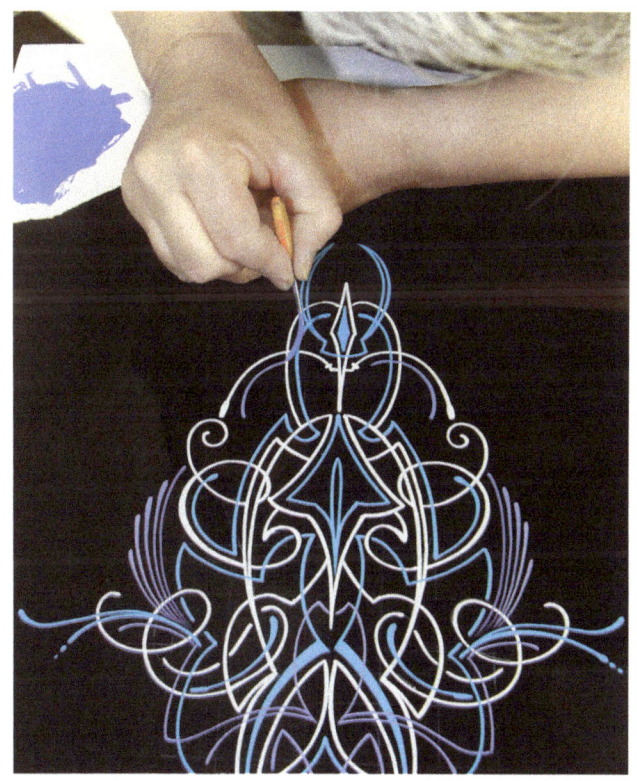

As I keep adding more lines, I'm trying to keep it balanced. Even though this may be complex - it has to flow together.

Space between the lines helps to keep the design open and defined.

I add a small tapered point to the base of the design.

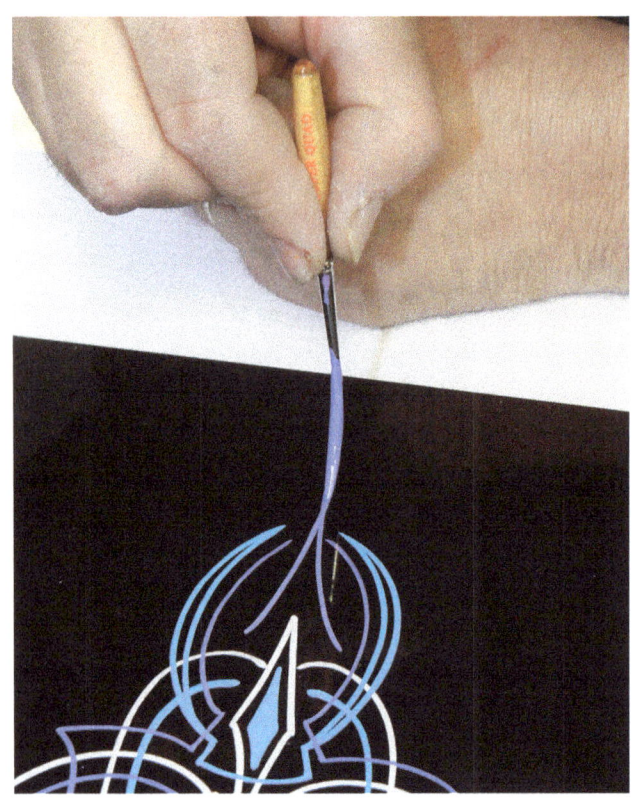

The over and under effect works well here.

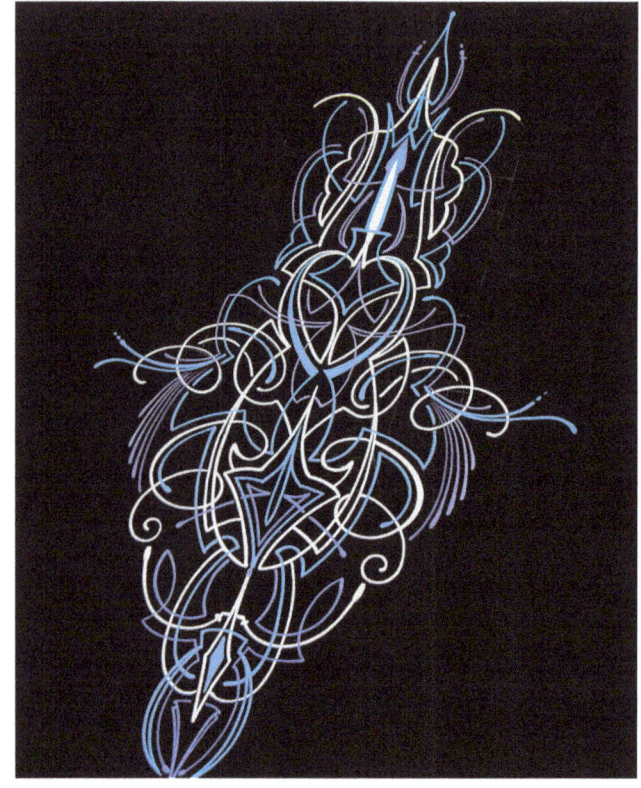

Three colors and almost done...this might be an appropriate stopping point.

I'm preparing to "grid out" the corners. Using my Stripe-a-line grid with corner cut-outs, I'm able to make the four corners identical.

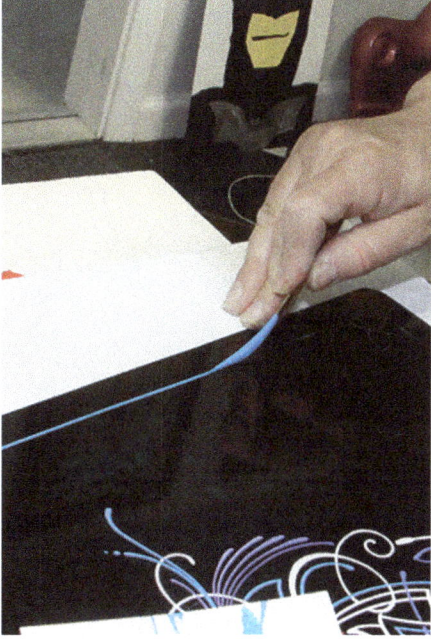

I'm using my long liner brush, which holds plenty of paint for pulling long body lines. I guide my hand along using the edge of the panel.

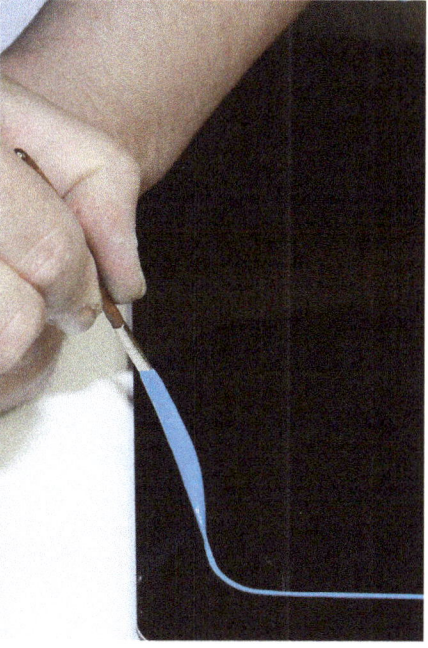

As I approach the corner I will slow down, then slowly turn and lift the brush to bring it up onto its tip.

This is what I consider eye catchers. Contrasting colors - in small amounts - placed on areas of the design that draw your attention.

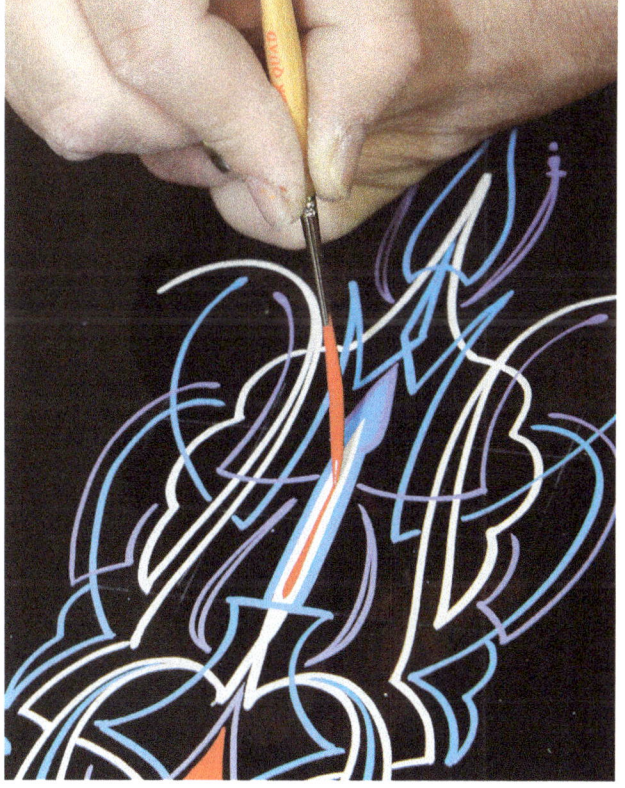

This is where a little does a lot. Well placed and balanced colors make your work pop a little more.

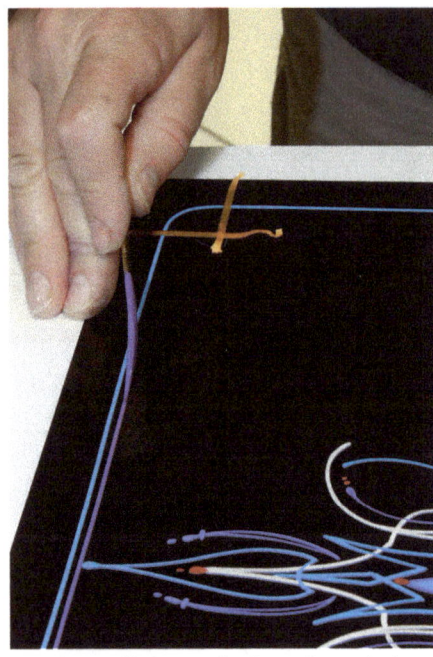

Taping off the end of my lines helps to keep the inside corner designs clean and symmetrical.

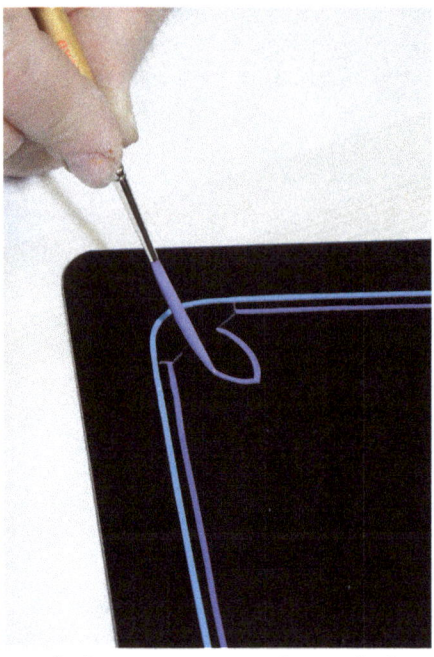

With the corners precisely marked, I begin to add more detail.

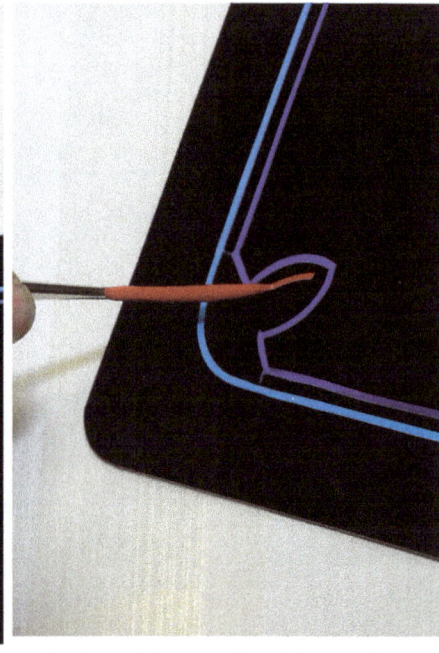

A little red here will add just the right accent.

Some additional red paint finishes the corners nicely.

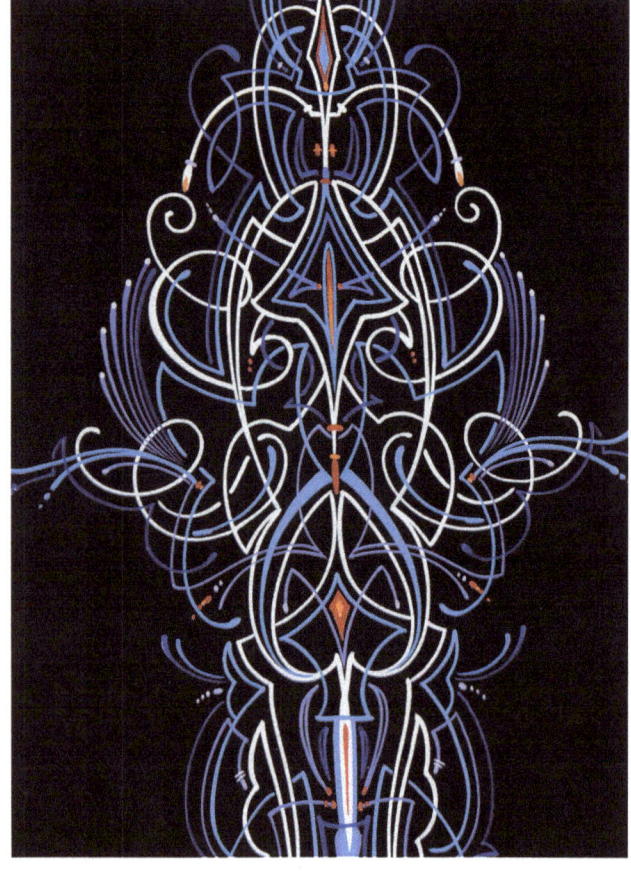

I've added dots, dashes and teardrops to finish lines and open areas. These are added where I felt more lines would be overwhelming. In this case the dots add a softer look to the design.

Q&A: Zeke

Zeke, tell us a little about yourself, and how you became a striper?

At age 13 I saw a local pinstriper doing a dune buggy at my cousin's gas station. I was so fascinated by how effortlessly he created swirls and designs that I was inspired to pursue pinstiping and lettering. He also lettered vehicles, it was all hand work, no vinyl. The creativity was phenomenal. To back up, I was always into the art field, doodling, drawing, and sketching. So getting into striping was a natural.

What do you like to use for brushes?

I use the standard Mack brush, the 10 series, and the Hot Licks are good, too. You need the right brush for the right job. For outlining flames I might use a Tom Kelly. Xcaliber is excellent for tight bends, they don't flop over at all. The Bobbo super quad is what I use for a lot of my work.

What do you like for paint?

I use One-Shot, also Kustom Shop, which dries within an hour. Also Ronan, and sometimes House of Kolor. You have to pick the paint that works the best for you. I always use a hardener for any of the paints, it makes them more durable.

Are there absolutes in terms of design, in terms of placement and how many times a line can cross another line?

When I do a design on a vehicle I make it flow with the body style or body lines of that vehicle. I try to balance the stripes so the design has some flow, so it doesn't fight or blow against the curve. I use under and overs, it gives it a 3-D effect and makes people stop and look.

Who inspires you, where do you get your ideas?

Trade publications, the internet, I like the pinstriping events, it's an opportunity to meet other artists, we all feed off each other.

How do you pick colors, and how did you learn to mix colors to match a certain color?

If the background is dark, I pick a light color as the foundation for my design - a color that won't clash with the main color. I try to stay in one family of color when I choose colors. For the second color, I try to judge the feel or mood of the vehicle. A blue or purple has a very different feel than blue and red. Sometimes the color of the stripes is determined by the interior colors.

Any final words of wisdom?

I don't know if they're words of wisdom, but I've developed a series of templates that I think make striping a lot easier. Templates have been used for generations. These allow me to not only draw curves, but to manipulate the curves in an endless variety of positions. I can use these in layering situations - to place one on top of the other - they are clear so you can come up with interesting options and combinations.

These are not designed to take over the design process, they just add to the possibilities. It's another tool.

Focused and intense, Zeke has some very specific ideas about the design of his panels and pinstriping.

Wolfgang Books On The Web
http://www.wolfpub.com

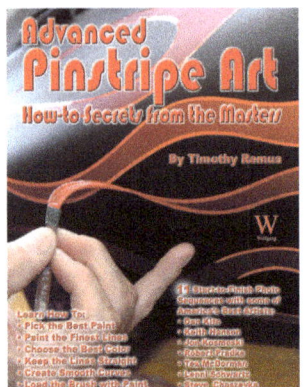

ADVANCED PINSTRIPE ART

Since the days of Von Dutch, hot rod and motorcycle enthusiasts have used pinstripes both as stand-alone art, and as a compliment to a flame or graphic paint job.

Timothy Remus uses over 500 color images to present the work of 11 well-known pinstripe artists. Each chapter presents one start-to-finish project and an interview with the artist. The photo sequences take the viewer from the initial sketch to the finished design. Text explains each step of the artwork; the interviews explain the artist's choice for paint and brushes. The artwork, often complimented with gold leaf or airbrush colors, is done on panels as well as various vehicles and components.

| Eleven Chapters | 144 Pages | $27.95 | Over 400 photos, 100% color |

ADVANCED AIRBRUSH ART

Like a video done with still photography, this book is made up entirely of photo sequences that illustrate each small step in the creation of an airbrushed masterpiece. Watch as well-known masters like Vince Goodeve, Chris Cruz, Steve Wizard and Nick Pastura start with a sketch and end with a NASCAR helmet or motorcycle tank covered with graphics, murals, pinups or all of the above.

Interviews explain each artist's preference for paint and equipment, and secrets learned over decades of painting. Projects include a chrome eagle surrounded by reality flames, a series of murals, and a variety of graphic designs.

This is a great book for anyone who takes their airbrushing seriously and wants to learn more.

| Ten Chapters | 144 Pages | $27.95 | Over 400 photos, 100% color |

TATTOO BIBLE BOOK ONE

Whether you are preparing for your first tattoo or your twenty-seventh, you need artwork and designs that are just-right. Tattoo Bible, authored by Superior Tattoo, provides well over 500 pieces of unique flash art - flash never before compiled into one single book.

While most tattoo books available today concentrate on one specific genre, this Tattoo Bible covers many different genres and the ideas are endless.

This is not just a book to add to your collection - this is your collection. You can combine different pieces of art from within the book, or just take them as is. This book is for you and your imagination to do with as you wish.

Published by ArtKulture, an imprint of Wolfgang Publications, with images that are both striking and very useful to both the tattoo shop, and the tattoo aficionado.

| Ten Chapters | 144 Pages | $27.95 | Over 400 photos, 100% color |

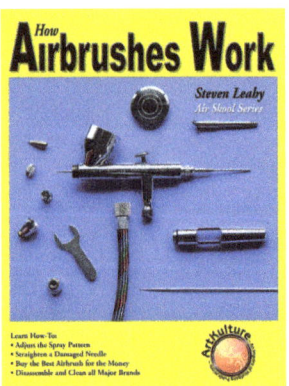

HOW AIRBRUSHES WORK

How Airbrushes Work is a comprehensive look at airbrush use, maintenance and repair. The book begins with a brief look at airbrush history, then moves to a discussion of the various airbrush types. Too many first-time airbrush users have trouble because they don't know how to clean and maintain the airbrush. This new book from Wolfgang Publications explains how to disassemble, clean and repair all the major brands. Even the best airbrush in the world isn't any good without a source of air. Steve discusses different compressor types and the advantages or disadvantages of each.

Two chapters explain airbrush painting basics - from types of paint to trigger control, and the three basic strokes all painters need to know. Steve closes the book with a gallery of airbrush art, and an airbrush buyer's guide to help readers choose wisely when they buy their first, or their fifth, airbrush.

| Nineteen Chapters | 144 Pages | $27.95 | Over 400 photos, 100% color |

Wolfgang Publication Titles

For a current list visit our website at www.wolfpub.com

ILLUSTRATED HISTORY
Triumph Motorcycles	$32.95

BIKER BASICS
Sheet Metal Fabrication	$27.95
How to FIX American V-Twin MC	$27.95

COMPOSITE GARAGE
Composite Materials Handbook #1	$27.95
Composite Materials Handbook #2	$27.95

HOP-UP EXPERT
How to Hop & Customize Your Bagger	$27.95
How to Hop & Customize Your Softail	$27.95

OLD SKOOL SKILLS
Barris: Grilles, Scoops, Fins and Frenching (Vol. 2)	$24.95
Barris: Flames Scallops, Paneling and Striping (Vol. 4)	$24.95

HOT ROD BASICS
How to Air Condition Your Hot Rod	$27.95
How to Chop Tops	$24.95

MOTORCYCLE RESTORATION SERIES
Triumph Restoration - Unit 650cc	$29.95
Triumph MC Restoration Pre-Unit	$29.95
Harley-Davidson Panhead Restoration	$34.95

AIR SKOOL SKILLS
How Airbrushes Work	$27.95
How to Airbrush Pin-Ups	$27.95
Air Brushing 101	$27.95
Airbrush Bible	$27.95

PAINT EXPERT
Advanced Custom Motorcycle Painting	$27.95
Advanced Airbrush Art	$27.95
Advanced Custom Painting Techniques	$27.95
Advanced Pinstripe Art	$27.95
Kustom Painting Secrets	$19.95
Custom Paint & Graphics	$27.95
Pro Airbrush Techniques	$27.95
Pro Pinstripe Techniques	$27.95

SHEET METAL
Advanced Sheet Metal Fabrication	$27.95
Ultimate Sheet Metal Fabrication	$24.95
Sheet Metal Bible	$29.95

CUSTOM BUILDER SERIES
Advanced Custom Motorcycle Wiring	$27.95
Advanced Custom Motorcycle Assembly & Fabrication	$27.95
Advanced Custom Motorcycle Chassis	$27.95
How to Build a Cheap Chopper	$27.95
How to Build a Chopper	$27.95

TATTOO U Series
Body Painting	$27.95
Tattoo- From Idea to Ink	$27.95
Tattoos Behind the Needle	$27.95
Advanced Tattoo Art	$27.95
Tattoo Bible Book One	$27.95
Tattoo Bible Book Two	$27.95

HOME SHOP
How to Paint Tractors & Trucks	$27.95

NOTEWORTHY
Guitar Building Basics	
Acoustic Assembly at Home	$27.95

Sources

Coast Airbrush
www.coastairbrush.com
715-635-5557
888 KOLOR IT
Coast Airbrush is the source for LA D'ORE Leaf products used in Chapter Seven.

Custom Cut Aluminum
800-322-8848
Source for aluminum panels.

East Coast Artie
475 Sandy Lane Suite G
Surfside Beach, SC 29575
artschilling@sc.rr.com
www.eastcoastartie.com

Grifhold
PO Box 10
Webster, NY 14580
800-344-6445
www.grifhold.com
Pounce wheels and other artist supplies.

Han-See Pounce box
www.hancymfg.com
Available at Dick Blick, Midwest Sign & Screen Supply, and a variety of Sign Supply companies.

House of Kolor
www.houseofkolor.com
www.TCPglobal.com/HokPaint

Howie Nisgor
Pinstriping by Howie
6 Arbor Hill Road
Poughkeepsie, NY
845-462-3217 (shop)

Jimmy Jackson
Jimmy Jackson Design
475 Sandy Lane Suite G
Surfside Beach, SC 29575
Jimmy did the "base paint" on Artie's case from Chapter Seven.

Kustom Shop, E-Z flow paint
www.tcbglobal.com/kustomshop

Mikey and Diana Frederick
Unique Signs
519 Center Ave
Mamaroneck, NY 10543
914-698-8150
usigns@optonline.net

Mack
www.mackbrush.com

Mr. J/Xcaliber
www.xcaliberart.com
39 Dundee Ave
Paterson, NJ 07503
201-935-7010

Nub
www.nubgrafix.com
(Be sure to read Nub's story on the home page)

One-Shot
www.1shot.com
Available at TCP Global, Eastwood and many sign and paint supply companies.

T.J. Ronan Paint Corp.
749 East 135th Street
Bronx, NY 10454
718-292-1100 or 800-247-6626
www.ronanpaints.com
Available at Paint.Smarter.com, Dick Blick and other sign supply houses.

Watkins AB
8930 Airport Highway
Holland OH 43528
419-868-5882
Bill painted the panels used throughout the book

Zenom "Zeke" Lemanski
362 Chickopee St
Chickopee, MA 01013
413-594-8886
zeke@signtechniques.net

www.ingramcontent.com/pod-product-compliance
Lightning Source LLC
Chambersburg PA
CBHW061212230426
43665CB00032B/2989